Fred M. Heath
Martha Kyrillidou
Consuella A. Askew
Editors

Libraries Act on Their LibQUAL+™ Findings: From Data to Action

Libraries Act on Their LibQUAL+™ Findings: From Data to Action has been co-published simultaneously as *Journal of Library Administration*, Volume 40, Numbers 3/4 2004.

Pre-publication REVIEWS, COMMENTARIES, EVALUATIONS . . .

"**A** VERY USEFUL TOOL FOR ALL TYPES OF LIBRARIES. After five years of experimentation in hundreds of different types of libraries, the promise of this tool is realized in this excellent compilation of uniformly high-quality chapters."

Carla J. Stoffle, MSLS
Dean of Libraries and Center for Creative Photography University of Arizona

D0094380

More pre-publication
REVIEWS, COMMENTARIES, EVALUATIONS . . .

" **A** VALUABLE ADDITION to the growing body of library literature on performance measures, metrics, and assessment. . . . Particularly suitable for college and university libraries, library consortia, and health sciences libraries. . . . Practitioners describe how LibQUAL+™ can be used to optimize resource decisions, modify staffing patterns, contribute to strategic planning efforts, and improve physical spaces and service strategies for new and redesigned library facilities."

Brinley Franklin, MLS, MBA
Director
University of Connecticut Libraries;
Chair
Association of Research Libraries
Statistics & Measurement Committee

The Haworth Information Press
An Imprint of The Haworth Press, Inc.

Libraries Act on Their LibQUAL+™ Findings: From Data to Action

Libraries Act on Their LibQUAL+™ Findings: From Data to Action has been co-published simultaneously as *Journal of Library Administration*, Volume 40, Numbers 3/4 2004.

The *Journal of Library Administration* Monographic "Separates"

Below is a list of "separates," which in serials librarianship means a special issue simultaneously published as a special journal issue or double-issue *and* as a "separate" hardbound monograph. (This is a format which we also call a "DocuSerial.")

"Separates" are published because specialized libraries or professionals may wish to purchase a specific thematic issue by itself in a format which can be separately cataloged and shelved, as opposed to purchasing the journal on an on-going basis. Faculty members may also more easily consider a "separate" for classroom adoption.

"Separates" are carefully classified separately with the major book jobbers so that the journal tie-in can be noted on new book order slips to avoid duplicate purchasing.

You may wish to visit Haworth's Website at . . .

http://www.HaworthPress.com

. . . to search our online catalog for complete tables of contents of these separates and related publications.

You may also call 1-800-HAWORTH (outside US/Canada: 607-722-5857), or Fax 1-800-895-0582 (outside US/Canada: 607-771-0012), or e-mail at:

docdelivery@haworthpress.com

Libraries Act on Their LibQUAL+™ Findings: From Data to Action, edited by Fred M. Heath, EdD, Martha Kyrillidou, MEd, MLS, and Consuella A. Askew, MLS (Vol. 40, No. 3/4, 2004). *Focuses on the value of LibQUAL+™ data to help librarians provide better services for users.*

The Changing Landscape for Electronic Resources: Content, Access, Delivery, and Legal Issues, edited by Yem S. Fong, MLS, and Suzanne M. Ward, MA (Vol. 40, No. 1/2, 2004). *Focuses on various aspects of electronic resources for libraries, including statewide resource-sharing initiatives, licensing issues, open source software, standards, and scholarly publishing.*

Improved Access to Information: Portals, Content Selection, and Digital Information, edited by Sul H. Lee (Vol. 39, No. 4, 2003). *Examines how improved electronic resources can allow libraries to provide an increasing amount of digital information to an ever-expanding patron base.*

Digital Images and Art Libraries in the Twenty-First Century, edited by Susan Wyngaard, MLS (Vol. 39, No. 2/3, 2003). *Provides an in-depth look at the technology that art librarians must understand in order to work effectively in today's digital environment.*

The Twenty-First Century Art Librarian, edited by Terrie L. Wilson, MLS (Vol. 39, No. 1, 2003). *"A MUST-READ addition to every art, architecture, museum, and visual resources library bookshelf." (Betty Jo Irvine, PhD, Fine Arts Librarian, Indiana University)*

The Strategic Stewardship of Cultural Resources: To Preserve and Protect, edited by Andrea T. Merrill, BA (Vol. 38, No. 1/2/3/4, 2003). *Leading library, museum, and archival professionals share their expertise on a wide variety of preservation and security issues.*

Distance Learning Library Services: The Tenth Off-Campus Library Services Conference, edited by Patrick B. Mahoney (Vol. 37, No. 1/2/3/4, 2002). *Explores the pitfalls of providing information services to distance students and suggests ways to avoid them.*

Electronic Resources and Collection Development, edited by Sul H. Lee (Vol. 36, No. 3, 2002). *Shows how electronic resources have impacted traditional collection development policies and practices.*

Information Literacy Programs: Successes and Challenges, edited by Patricia Durisin, MLIS (Vol. 36, No. 1/2, 2002). *Examines Web-based collaboration, teamwork with academic and administrative colleagues, evidence-based librarianship, and active learning strategies in library instruction programs.*

Evaluating the Twenty-First Century Library: The Association of Research Libraries New Measures Initiative, 1997-2001, edited by Donald L. DeWitt, PhD (Vol. 35, No. 4, 2001). *This collection of articles (thirteen of which previously appeared in ARL's bimonthly newsletter/ report on research issues and actions) examines the Association of Research Libraries' "new measures" initiative.*

Impact of Digital Technology on Library Collections and Resource Sharing, edited by Sul H. Lee (Vol. 35, No. 3, 2001). *Shows how digital resources have changed the traditional academic library.*

Libraries and Electronic Resources: New Partnerships, New Practices, New Perspectives,
edited by Pamela L. Higgins (Vol. 35, No. 1/2, 2001). *An essential guide to the Internet's impact on electronic resources management past, present, and future.*

Diversity Now: People, Collections, and Services in Academic Libraries, edited by Teresa Y. Neely, PhD, and Kuang-Hwei (Janet) Lee-Smeltzer, MS, MSLIS (Vol. 33, No. 1/2/3/4, 2001). *Examines multicultural trends in academic libraries' staff and users, types of collections, and services offered.*

Leadership in the Library and Information Science Professions: Theory and Practice, edited by Mark D. Winston, MLS, PhD (Vol. 32, No. 3/4, 2001). *Offers fresh ideas for developing and using leadership skills, including recruiting potential leaders, staff training and development, issues of gender and ethnic diversity, and budget strategies for success.*

Off-Campus Library Services, edited by Ann Marie Casey (Vol. 31, No. 3/4, 2001 and Vol. 32, No. 1/2, 2001). *This informative volume examines various aspects of off-campus, or distance learning. It explores training issues for library staff, Web site development, changing roles for librarians, the uses of conferencing software, library support for Web-based courses, library agreements and how to successfully negotiate them, and much more!*

Research Collections and Digital Information, edited by Sul H. Lee (Vol. 31, No. 2, 2000). *Offers new strategies for collecting, organizing, and accessing library materials in the digital age.*

Academic Research on the Internet: Options for Scholars & Libraries, edited by Helen Laurence, MLS, EdD, and William Miller, MLS, PhD (Vol. 30, No. 1/2/3/4, 2000). *"Emphasizes quality over quantity. . . . Presents the reader with the best research-oriented Web sites in the field. A state-of-the-art review of academic use of the Internet as well as a guide to the best Internet sites and services. . . . A useful addition for any academic library." (David A. Tyckoson, MLS, Head of Reference, California State University, Fresno)*

Management for Research Libraries Cooperation, edited by Sul H. Lee (Vol. 29, No. 3/4, 2000). *Delivers sound advice, models, and strategies for increasing sharing between institutions to maximize the amount of printed and electronic research material you can make available in your library while keeping costs under control.*

Integration in the Library Organization, edited by Christine E. Thompson, PhD (Vol. 29, No. 2, 1999). *Provides librarians with the necessary tools to help libraries balance and integrate public and technical services and to improve the capability of libraries to offer patrons quality services and large amounts of information.*

Library Training for Staff and Customers, edited by Sara Ramser Beck, MLS, MBA (Vol. 29, No. 1, 1999). *This comprehensive book is designed to assist library professionals involved in presenting or planning training for library staff members and customers. You will explore ideas for effective general reference training, training on automated systems, training in specialized subjects such as African American history and biography, and training for areas such as patents and trademarks, and business subjects.* Library Training for Staff and Customers *answers numerous training questions and is an excellent guide for planning staff development.*

Collection Development in the Electronic Environment: Shifting Priorities, edited by Sul H. Lee (Vol. 28, No. 4, 1999). *Through case studies and firsthand experiences, this volume discusses meeting the needs of scholars at universities, budgeting issues, user education, staffing in the electronic age, collaborating libraries and resources, and how vendors meet the needs of different customers.*

The Age Demographics of Academic Librarians: A Profession Apart, by Stanley J. Wilder (Vol. 28, No. 3, 1999). *The average age of librarians has been increasing dramatically since 1990. This unique book will provide insights on how this demographic issue can impact a library and what can be done to make the effects positive.*

Collection Development in a Digital Environment, edited by Sul H. Lee (Vol. 28, No. 1, 1999). *Explores ethical and technological dilemmas of collection development and gives several suggestions on how a library can successfully deal with these challenges and provide patrons with the information they need.*

Scholarship, Research Libraries, and Global Publishing, by Jutta Reed-Scott (Vol. 27, No. 3/4, 1999). *This book documents a research project in conjunction with the Association of Research Libraries (ARL) that explores the issue of foreign acquisition and how it affects collection in international studies, area studies, collection development, and practices of international research libraries.*

Managing Multicultural Diversity in the Library: Principles and Issues for Administrators, edited by Mark Winston (Vol. 27, No. 1/2, 1999). *Defines diversity, clarifies why it is important to address issues of diversity, and identifies goals related to diversity and how to go about achieving those goals.*

Information Technology Planning, edited by Lori A. Goetsch (Vol. 26, No. 3/4, 1999). *Offers innovative approaches and strategies useful in your library and provides some food for thought about information technology as we approach the millennium.*

The Economics of Information in the Networked Environment, edited by Meredith A. Butler, MLS, and Bruce R. Kingma, PhD (Vol. 26, No. 1/2, 1998). *"A book that should be read both by information professionals and by administrators, faculty and others who share a collective concern to provide the most information to the greatest number at the lowest cost in the networked environment." (Thomas J. Galvin, PhD, Professor of Information Science and Policy, University at Albany, State University of New York)*

OCLC 1967-1997: Thirty Years of Furthering Access to the World's Information, edited by K. Wayne Smith (Vol. 25, No. 2/3/4, 1998). *"A rich–and poignantly personal, at times–historical account of what is surely one of this century's most important developments in librarianship." (Deanna B. Marcum, PhD, President, Council on Library and Information Resources, Washington, DC)*

Management of Library and Archival Security: From the Outside Looking In, edited by Robert K. O'Neill, PhD (Vol. 25, No. 1, 1998). *"Provides useful advice and on-target insights for professionals caring for valuable documents and artifacts." (Menzi L. Behrnd-Klodt, JD, Attorney/Archivist, Klodt and Associates, Madison, WI)*

Economics of Digital Information: Collection, Storage, and Delivery, edited by Sul H. Lee (Vol. 24, No. 4, 1997). *Highlights key concepts and issues vital to a library's successful venture into the digital environment and helps you understand why the transition from the printed page to the digital packet has been problematic for both creators of proprietary materials and users of those materials.*

The Academic Library Director: Reflections on a Position in Transition, edited by Frank D'Andraia, MLS (Vol. 24, No. 3, 1997). *"A useful collection to have whether you are seeking a position as director or conducting a search for one." (College & Research Libraries News)*

Emerging Patterns of Collection Development in Expanding Resource Sharing, Electronic Information, and Network Environment, edited by Sul H. Lee (Vol. 24, No. 1/2, 1997). *"The issues it deals with are common to us all. We all need to make our funds go further and our resources work harder, and there are ideas here which we can all develop." (The Library Association Record)*

Interlibrary Loan/Document Delivery and Customer Satisfaction: Strategies for Redesigning Services, edited by Pat L. Weaver-Meyers, Wilbur A. Stolt, and Yem S. Fong (Vol. 23, No. 1/2, 1997). *"No interlibrary loan department supervisor at any mid-sized to large college or university library can afford not to read this book." (Gregg Sapp, MLS, MEd, Head of Access Services, University of Miami, Richter Library, Coral Gables, Florida)*

Access, Resource Sharing and Collection Development, edited by Sul H. Lee (Vol. 22, No. 4, 1996). *Features continuing investigation and discussion of important library issues, specifically the role of libraries in acquiring, storing, and disseminating information in different formats.*

Managing Change in Academic Libraries, edited by Joseph J. Branin (Vol. 22, No. 2/3, 1996). *"Touches on several aspects of academic library management, emphasizing the changes that are occurring at the present time. . . . Recommended this title for individuals or libraries interested in management aspects of academic libraries." (RQ American Library Association)*

Libraries and Student Assistants: Critical Links, edited by William K. Black, MLS (Vol. 21, No. 3/4, 1995). *"A handy reference work on many important aspects of managing student assistants. . . . Solid, useful information on basic management issues in this work and several chapters are useful for experienced managers." (The Journal of Academic Librarianship)*

The Future of Resource Sharing, edited by Shirley K. Baker and Mary E. Jackson, MLS (Vol. 21, No. 1/2, 1995). *"Recommended for library and information science schools because of its balanced presentation of the ILL/document delivery issues." (Library Acquisitions: Practice and Theory)*

Monographic "Separates" list continued at the back

Libraries Act on Their LibQUAL+™ Findings: From Data to Action

Fred M. Heath
Martha Kyrillidou
Consuella A. Askew
Editors

Libraries Act on Their LibQUAL+™ Findings: From Data to Action has been co-published simultaneously as *Journal of Library Administration*, Volume 40, Numbers 3/4 2004.

The Haworth Information Press®
An Imprint of The Haworth Press, Inc.

New York • London • Victoria (AU)
www.HaworthPress.com

Published by

The Haworth Information Press®, 10 Alice Street, Binghamton, NY 13904-1580 USA

The Haworth Information Press® is an imprint of The Haworth Press, Inc., 10 Alice Street, Binghamton, NY 13904-1580 USA.

Libraries Act on Their LibQUAL+™ Findings: From Data to Action has been co-published simultaneously as *Journal of Library Administration*™, Volume 40, Numbers 3/4 2004.

© 2004 by The Haworth Press, Inc. All rights reserved. No part of this work may be reproduced or utilized in any form or by any means, electronic or mechanical, including photocopying, microfilm and recording, or by any information storage and retrieval system, without permission in writing from the publisher. Printed in the United States of America.

The development, preparation, and publication of this work has been undertaken with great care. However, the publisher, employees, editors, and agents of The Haworth Press and all imprints of The Haworth Press, Inc., including The Haworth Medical Press® and Pharmaceutical Products Press®, are not responsible for any errors contained herein or for consequences that may ensue from use of materials or information contained in this work. Opinions expressed by the author(s) are not necessarily those of The Haworth Press, Inc. With regard to case studies, identities and circumstances of individuals discussed herein have been changed to protect confidentiality. Any resemblance to actual persons, living or dead, is entirely coincidental.

Cover design by Kerry E. Mack.

Library of Congress Cataloging-in-Publication Data

Libraries act on their LibQUAL+ findings : from data to action / Fred M. Heath, Martha Kyrillidou, Consuella A. Askew, editors.
     p. cm.
     "Co-published simultaneously as Journal of Library Administration, volume 40, numbers 3/4 2004."
     Includes bibliographical references and index.
     ISBN 0-7890-2601-5 (alk. paper) – ISBN 0-7890-2602-3 (soft cover : alk. paper)
     1. Library surveys–United States. 2. Academic libraries–Administration. 3. Libraries–Quality control. 4. Information services–Quality control. 5. LibQUAL+. I. Heath, Fred M., 1944- II. Kyrillidou, Martha. III. Askew, Consuella A. IV. Journal of library administration.
Z731.L5415 2004
025.1'977–dc22
                                                 2004011241

Indexing, Abstracting & Website/Internet Coverage

Journal of Library Administration

This section provides you with a list of major indexing & abstracting services. That is to say, each service began covering this periodical during the year noted in the right column. Most Websites which are listed below have indicated that they will either post, disseminate, compile, archive, cite or alert their own Website users with research-based content from this work. (This list is as current as the copyright date of this publication.)

Abstracting, Website/Indexing Coverage . . . . Year When Coverage Began

- *AATA Online: Abstracts of International Conservation Literature (formerly Art & Archeology Technical Abstracts)*
  <http://aata.getty.edu>. **2004**

- *Academic Abstracts/CD-ROM* **1993**

- *Academic Search: database of 2,000 selected academic serials, updated monthly: EBSCO Publishing* **1995**

- *Academic Search Elite (EBSCO)* **1993**

- *AGRICOLA Database (AGRICultural OnLine Access)*
  <http://www.natl.usda.gov/ag98> **1991**

- *AGRIS <http://www.fao.org/agris/>* **1991**

- *Business & Company ProFiles ASAP on CD-ROM*
  <http://www.galegroup.com> **1996**

- *Business ASAP* **1994**

- *Business ASAP–International <http://www.galegroup.com>* **1984**

- *Business International and Company ProFile ASAP*
  <http://www.galegroup.com> **1996**

- *Business Source Corporate: coverage of nearly 3,350 quality magazines and journals; designed to meet the diverse information needs of corporations; EBSCO Publishing*
  <http://www.epnet.com/corporate/bsourcecorp.asp> **1993**

- *Computer and Information Systems Abstracts*
  <http://www.csa.com>. **2004**

(continued)

(continued)

(continued)

Special Bibliographic Notes related to special journal issues (separates) and indexing/abstracting:

- indexing/abstracting services in this list will also cover material in any "separate" that is co-published simultaneously with Haworth's special thematic journal issue or DocuSerial. Indexing/abstracting usually covers material at the article/chapter level.
- monographic co-editions are intended for either non-subscribers or libraries which intend to purchase a second copy for their circulating collections.
- monographic co-editions are reported to all jobbers/wholesalers/approval plans. The source journal is listed as the "series" to assist the prevention of duplicate purchasing in the same manner utilized for books-in-series.
- to facilitate user/access services all indexing/abstracting services are encouraged to utilize the co-indexing entry note indicated at the bottom of the first page of each article/chapter/contribution.
- this is intended to assist a library user of any reference tool (whether print, electronic, online, or CD-ROM) to locate the monographic version if the library has purchased this version but not a subscription to the source journal.
- individual articles/chapters in any Haworth publication are also available through the Haworth Document Delivery Service (HDDS).

Libraries Act on Their LibQUAL+™ Findings: From Data to Action

CONTENTS

ALL HAWORTH INFORMATION PRESS
BOOKS AND JOURNALS ARE PRINTED
ON CERTIFIED ACID-FREE PAPER

ABOUT THE EDITORS

Fred M. Heath, EdD, is Vice Provost and Director, the University of Texas at Austin General Libraries. Previously he served as Dean and Director of the Texas A&M University Libraries and holder of the Sterling C. Evans Endowed Chair, a position that he held since 1993. During his tenure at Texas A&M libraries, the evaluation of the SERVQUAL instrument in a research library environment was initiated. With colleagues at ARL and Texas A&M University, Dr. Heath is currently a co-PI for the FIPSE-funded LibQUAL+™ project and the NSF/NSDL (National Science Foundation/National Science Digital Library) project. The latter effort will explore the application of the LibQUAL+™ protocol in the digital library environment. Dr. Heath is Past President of the ARL Board of Directors and has been a member of the Advisory Board of SPARC (Scholarly Publishing and Academic Resources Coalition), Chair of the Texas Council of State University Librarians, and Chair of the Big 12 Plus Library Consortium. He is a contributor to four monographs and is the author of numerous journal articles.

Martha Kyrillidou, MEd, MLS, is Director, ARL Statistics and Measurement Program. She has interdisciplinary experience in libraries and evaluation and measurement with specialization in the application of quantitative research methodologies in libraries. Ms. Kyrillidou supports the work of the ARL Statistics and Measurement Committee, which recently embarked upon a major initiative–the New Measures Initiative–to identify and disseminate information about tools that help libraries manage their operations more effectively and contain costs. One of these tools is LibQUAL+™, for which she is a Project Manager.

Consuella A. Askew, MLS, was the LibQUAL+™ Program Specialist at the time this volume was written. Prior to ARL, she was an Associate Librarian and the Distance Education Specialist at Founders Library, Howard University. Her professional background is a combination of experience in academic libraries and the college classroom. Ms. Askew has taught undergraduate courses in English and Education while working in the academic library setting. She is currently working on her doctorate in Higher Education Administration at Florida International University.

Preface

The traditional passive and implicit means of assuring academic quality within universities are in flux.[1] In this ongoing age of accountability, higher education institutions find themselves answerable to legislative funding bodies and accreditation agencies. The latter require that institutions provide them with more direct measures of student outcomes.[2] In response, academic departments and units, particularly academic libraries, find themselves seeking more aggressive and explicit means of describing the impact of their contributions to their institutional mission as each vies for their share of available resources. In addition to the issues of accountability and funding, the Internet and other emerging information and learning technologies have contributed to the need for academic libraries to explore new metrics beyond the traditional expenditure metrics to assess library service performance. Following the shift in emphasis in higher education over the past 10-15 years–from teaching to learning–libraries must also turn their assessment focus outward to their users to gain an adequate measure of their service performance. It has been noted more than once in the professional literature that the amount of inputs does not predict service quality.[3] Moreover, service quality is not based solely on the perception of the librarians who provide these services, but rather it is highly dependent on the perception of the users.

In response to this shifting paradigm of assessment, the Association of Research Libraries in partnership with Texas A&M University libraries developed the LibQUAL+™ survey instrument. First piloted in the spring of 2000, this Web-based instrument measuring users' perceptions of library service quality has been developed and refined over four

[Haworth co-indexing entry note]: "Preface." Askew, Consuella A. Co-published simultaneously in *Journal of Library Administration* (The Haworth Information Press, an imprint of The Haworth Press, Inc.) Vol. 40, No. 3/4, 2004, pp. xxi-xxii; and: *Libraries Act on Their LibQUAL+™ Findings: From Data to Action* (ed: Fred M. Heath, Martha Kyrillidou, and Consuella A. Askew) The Haworth Information Press, an imprint of The Haworth Press, Inc., 2004, pp. xvii-xviii. Single or multiple copies of this article are available for a fee from The Haworth Document Delivery Service [1-800-HAWORTH, 9:00 a.m. - 5:00 p.m. (EST). E-mail address: docdelivery@haworthpress.com].

© 2004 by The Haworth Press, Inc. All rights reserved.

iterations. As of June 2003, this Web survey has been completed by almost a quarter million respondents representing four countries, three languages, and seven different library types. Such participation in the LibQUAL+™ program indicates that libraries of all types–academic, public, state, etc.–and on a global scale are recognizing the need to explore innovative ways to describe their contributions to their institutions and to their public. The LibQUAL+™ survey is just one of the tools they are using to do so.

The 15 articles in this volume are representative of the 164 libraries that participated in the spring 2002 iteration of the LibQUAL+™ survey. The following articles provide examples of how these libraries have used their LibQUAL+™ data to identify opportunities for improving their library services and programs; to initiate further data exploration; and to inform needed change. Examples of how some libraries have used their qualitative data to supplement the quantitative findings are also provided. The articles have been arranged to present varying perspectives from differing library contexts–beginning with library consortia, to library type, and then by individual library.

These articles constitute a mere fraction of the literature produced by LibQUAL+™ participants. Additional papers, reports, and presentations produced by survey participants can be found on the Publications page of the LibQUAL+™ Web site:[4]
<http://www.libqual.org/Publications/index.cfm>.

Consuella A. Askew

REFERENCES

1. David D. Dill, "Academic Accountability and University Adaptation: The Architecture of an Academic Learning Organization," *Higher Education*, 38 (1999): 127-154.

2. Dees Stallings, "Measuring Success in the Virtual University," *The Journal of Academic Librarianship*, 28, no. 1 (2002): 47-53.

3. See, for example, Colleen Cook, Fred Heath, and Bruce Thompson, "Zones of Tolerance" in Perceptions of Library Service Quality: A LibQUAL+™ Study. *portal: Libraries and the Academy*, 3 no. 1 (2003): 113-123; Fred Heath et al., "ARL Index and Other Validity Correlates of LibQUAL+™," *portal: Libraries and the Academy*, 2, no. 1 (2002): 27-42; Danuta A. Nitecki, "Changing the Concept and Measure of Service Quality in Academic Libraries," *Journal of Academic Librarianship*, 22, no. 3 (1996): 181-190.

4. For more information about the LibQUAL+™ survey, visit the Web site at: <http://www.libqual.org>.

The Starving Research Library User: Relationships Between Library Institutional Characteristics and Spring 2002 LibQUAL+™ Scores

Martha Kyrillidou
Fred M. Heath

SUMMARY. The relationship between library institutional characteristics such as volumes held, volumes added gross, current serials, total staff and expenditures, and the scores on the four LibQUAL+™ service quality dimensions (*Affect of Service*, *Access to Collections*, *Information Control*, and *Library as Place*) are analyzed across a group of 130+ libraries that participated in spring 2002 for the members of the Association of Research Libraries and the participating libraries that are not members. Service quality indices, especially as measured by the service affect dimension, appear to have a slightly inverse relation to collection investments reflecting the higher expectations and harder-to-meet demands of the research library user. Relationships between in-

---

Martha Kyrillidou is Director, ARL Statistics and Measurement Program, Association of Research Libraries, Washington, DC (E-mail: martha@arl.org).

Fred M. Heath is Vice Provost and Director of General Libraries, University of Texas, Austin, TX (E-mail: fheath@austin.utexas.edu).

[Haworth co-indexing entry note]: "The Starving Research Library User: Relationships Between Library Institutional Characteristics and Spring 2002 LibQUAL+™ Scores." Kyrillidou, Martha, and Fred M. Heath. Co-published simultaneously in *Journal of Library Administration* (The Haworth Information Press, an imprint of The Haworth Press, Inc.) Vol. 40, No. 3/4, 2004, pp. 1-11; and: *Libraries Act on Their LibQUAL+™ Findings: From Data to Action* (ed: Fred M. Heath, Martha Kyrillidou, and Consuella A. Askew) The Haworth Information Press, an imprint of The Haworth Press, Inc., 2004, pp. 1-11. Single or multiple copies of this article are available for a fee from The Haworth Document Delivery Service [1-800-HAWORTH, 9:00 a.m. - 5:00 p.m. (EST). E-mail address: docdelivery@haworthpress.com].

http://www.haworthpress.com/web/JLA
© 2004 by The Haworth Press, Inc. All rights reserved.
Digital Object Identifier: 10.1300/J111v40n03_01

stitutional characteristics and service quality indices are also explored for OhioLINK and AAHSL, the two consortia groups that participated in 2002. *[Article copies available for a fee from The Haworth Document Delivery Service: 1-800-HAWORTH. E-mail address: <docdelivery@haworthpress.com> Website: <http://www.HaworthPress.com> © 2004 by The Haworth Press, Inc. All rights reserved.]*

KEYWORDS. LibQUAL+™, ARL Membership Criteria Index, collection indices, library expenditures, service quality indicators, OhioLINK, AAHSL, regression analysis, correlations

INTRODUCTION

Born as one of the ARL New Measures Initiative projects and with strong roots in the assessment practices established at Texas A&M during the 90s, LibQUAL+™ has been extensively documented in the literature as a viable, well-researched and robust assessment mechanism for measuring perceived library service quality from a user's perspective.[1] LibQUAL+™ has been grounded in the research library environment through the application of extensive qualitative and quantitative methods. Its application was expanded into additional contexts in higher education as mandated by the Fund for the Improvement of Post-Secondary Education (FIPSE) grant received to support the project over the three-year period ending in August 2003.

The number of participating libraries in the LibQUAL+™ almost quadrupled in spring 2002 from 43 to 164 including two major groups of libraries. One group represented a state-wide library consortium, OhioLINK, and a second group represented libraries from the Association of Academic Health Sciences Libraries (AAHSL). The OhioLINK participation brought for the first time in the project 57 institutions (including a sizeable group of 15 community college libraries) representing the diversity of higher education at a state-wide level, since OhioLINK represents all postsecondary educational institutions in the state of Ohio. AAHSL was represented with a group of 35 health science libraries. In 2002, there were also two special research libraries participating: the New York Public Library and the Smithsonian Institution libraries.[2] Table 1 presents a brief summary of the institutional data reported by the spring 2002 participating libraries including data on general library characteristics as well as LibQUAL+™ scores (total plus

TABLE 1. Descriptive Statistics of Institutional Data, Spring 2002 LibQUAL+™

	Mean	Std. Deviation	N
Volumes Held	1,695,390	3,757,234	154
Volumes Added Gross	38,419	51,077	148
Current Serials	12,644	15,711	150
Total Expenditures	8,461,004	9,809,924	150
Total Staff (Proff + Support)	99	113	151
ARL Membership Criteria Index Score 2000-01	−4.29	3.15	139
LibQUAL+™ Total Score Minimum	6.51	0.23	162
LibQUAL+™ Total Score Desired	7.89	0.12	162
LibQUAL+™ Total Score Perceived	6.95	0.33	162
Affect of Service Minimum	6.56	0.27	162
Affect of Service Desired	7.92	0.14	162
Affect of Service Perceived	7.13	0.38	162
Library as Place Minimum	6.04	0.34	162
Library as Place Desired	7.43	0.22	162
Library as Place Perceived	6.61	0.51	162
Personal Control Minimum	6.75	0.21	162
Personal Control Desired	8.14	0.15	162
Personal Control Perceived	7.07	0.29	162
Access to Information Minimum	6.57	0.21	162
Access to Information Desired	7.92	0.16	162
Access to Information Perceived	6.80	0.31	162

scores for each one of the four dimensions: Affect of Service, Access to Information, Library as Place, and Personal Control).

ARL AND NON-ARL LIBRARIES

There was a total of 164 libraries participating: 69 ARL and 95 non-ARL. Data on ARL health science libraries and branch libraries that participated independently from the main campus are included in the ARL cohort. The main criterion in determining the ARL group was whether these libraries provided data that were included in the ARL statistics–either as independent entities or as part of a larger institutional reporting effort. As a result some libraries identified as ARL libraries in this study are simply small components of a larger ARL library setting.

Data on library characteristics–such as volumes held, volumes added gross, current serials, total expenditures, and total staff (professional plus support staff)–were also collected. As a result we were able to calculate the ARL Membership Criteria Index Scores[3] for 139 libraries participating in spring 2002, 66 of them ARL and 73 non-ARL libraries (see Table 2). Volumes held, volumes added gross, current serials, total expenditures and total staff (professional plus support staff) have higher values for ARL libraries as expected. On average, ARL libraries that participated in the spring 2002 LibQUAL+™ group had 5.3 times more serials and 3.8 times more volumes than non-ARL libraries. In particular, non-ARL libraries reported on average a little more than half a million volumes held, more than 15,800 volumes added gross, 4,290 serial subscriptions, about three million in expenditures and 38 staff members. ARL libraries reported on average more than two million volumes, more than 48,000 volumes added, 18,426 serial subscriptions, and expenditures of about ten million dollars with 177 staff members. Therefore, a sizable difference exists in the ARL membership criteria index scores for these two groups of libraries with ARL libraries having an average index score of -2.43 and non-ARL libraries -5.96, a difference that is not random but rather systematic as expressed with low probabilities of occurrence that define statistically significant differences.

THE RELATIONSHIP BETWEEN ARL INDEX SCORES AND LibQUAL+™ SCORES

The relationship between the ARL Index scores and LibQUAL+™ scores was explored in a small group of 35 ARL libraries using the spring 2001 data.[4] The spring 2002 data allow us to explore this relation in a larger group of libraries and re-evaluate the direction and the strength of the relationship if one takes into account a more diverse set of institutions. Table 3 presents the correlations of the LibQUAL+™ Perceived Scores with the ARL Membership Criteria Index Scores. Although in spring 2001 most of these relations were near zero, the spring 2002 data show a moderate negative relation of the ARL membership criteria index scores with the LibQUAL+™ scores across all four dimensions and the total score. Even the additional element of Information Access (the '+' in LibQUAL+™) has a low negative correlation with the ARL Membership Criteria Index. These findings serve as another indicator that libraries are facing increasing challenges in meeting users' perceptions of quality of service that go beyond the abundant availability of local resources. Such challenges are more acute in a traditionally rich information setting, the research library setting. In the

TABLE 2. ARL and Non-ARL Differences on Variables Comprising the ARL Membership Criteria Index, Spring 2002 LibQUAL+™

	Non-ARL Mean	Std. Deviation	ARL Mean	Std. Deviation	F
Volumes Held	536,175	581,233	2,602,104	2,151,107	62.34**
Volumes Added Gross	15,849	29,073	61,487	48,316	46.53**
Current Serials	4,290	4,986	22,871	18,426	68.72**
Total Expenditures	3,039,908	2,902,634	14,653,608	10,257,869	86.02**
Total Staff (Proff + Support)	38	37	177	129	77.77**
ARL Membership Index Score	−5.96	2	−2.43	3	63.15**
Libraries Reporting	73		66		

**$p < .001$

TABLE 3. Pearson Correlations of LibQUAL+™ Perceived Scores with ARL Membership Criteria Index Scores–Spring 2002

	ARL Index	Total LibQUAL+™	Affect	Place	Control	Access
ARL Index	1.000					
Total LibQUAL+™	−0.390**	1.000				
Affect	−0.390**	0.913**	1.000			
Place	−0.401**	0.816**	0.560**	1.000		
Control	−0.329**	0.940**	0.817**	0.728**	1.000	
Access	−0.197*	0.887**	0.777**	0.654**	0.848**	1.000
N	139	162	162	162	162	162

**$p < .001$
*$p < .05$

'rich' research library setting users are highly skilled, have specialized and diverse information needs that are not easily met by the mere availability of resources, rich as they may be. Library users in comprehensive research library settings are clearly more demanding and harder to please. It might be a paradox of the information-rich society that creates starving research library users, or simply an assurance that despite all the information that is available to us, there is a lot more information still lacking and needed, especially by users located in intensive research library settings.

The amount of resources available, of course, is only a part of the overall concept of service quality and may have little to do with the provision of dedicated service to users. With increased availability of electronic resources today, smaller institutions are better able to meet and exceed users' expectations of library service quality. The presence of OhioLINK institutions in spring 2002 with the wide availability of electronic resources clearly places a number of smaller institutions in a better position to meet and often exceed users' expectations even though those resources are not physically present on the local campuses. Also, the results from health science libraries in the cohort–smaller than the large comprehensive research libraries–suggest an ability to achieve improved perceptions of library service quality in highly specialized environments.

Further, because it is often associated with a specific building or location, the issue is raised of whether the diagnostic possibilities of these scores are more identifiable in smaller institutional settings where "the library as place" is easier to define. The more diffuse the library, whether in a comprehensive research library setting or within a complex social and collaborative setting, the more likely that additional measurement tools and research methodologies will be needed to identify the specific diagnostic and remedial actions that individuals in complex organizations might need to develop.

The four LibQUAL+™ subscale scores were also used to predict the ARL Membership Criteria Index scores for the 139 institutions participating in 2002 in a multiple regression analysis replicating analysis performed in the 2001 data.[5] The R^2 from this analysis was .28 as compared to .06 from the 2001 data, a slightly larger effect size indicating that knowledge of the four LibQUAL+™ subscale means explains 28 percent of the variability in the Index scores of these 139 libraries. This result reflects the slightly higher correlations of the LibQUAL+™ subscale scores with the Index.

Even more interesting are the beta weights and structure coefficients from this analysis presented in Table 4.[6] With 139 libraries participating this year we know a lot more about the relation between library investments as represented by the ARL index and indices of library service quality. As reported in Table 4, the LibQUAL+™ subscale score most associated with the ARL Membership Criteria Index scores was *Access to Collections* ($\beta = .525$) only when we account for the other scales. The structure coefficient for *Access to Collections* is the smallest of the four subscales and has a negative relation to the ARL membership criteria

TABLE 4. ARL Membership Criteria Index Score Predicted by the Four LibQUAL+™ Perceived Subscale Scores (n = 139 Institutions)

LibQUAL+™ scale	r_s	β
Affect (AAvgPer1)	−0.743	−.500
Place (AAvgPer2)	−0.764	−.406
Control (AAvgPer3)	−0.627	−.055
Access (AAvgPer4)	−0.375	.525

R-squared = .28, df = 4/134, p < .001

index scores (r_s = −.375) indicating that the other three LibQUAL+™ dimensions are also measuring aspects of the *Access to Collections* dimension which are absorbed, or accounted for, when we examine the beta weights. *Affect of Service* is the dimension that clearly has the strongest negative relation with the ARL membership criteria Index (r_s = −.743, β = .50) which represents a library investment in collections index. *Library as Place* also has negative relation with collections indices, a slightly stronger relation though in the absence of controlling for all four dimensions of library service quality, as indicated by a slightly higher structure coefficient compared to its beta weight (r_s = −.764, β = −.406). Moreover, the *Information Control* dimension is clearly important in predicting collection indices in a bivariate relation as indicated by a strong negative structure coefficient (r_s = −.627, β = −.05) but in the presence of all four LibQUAL+™ dimensions it seems to be absorbed in the other three as indicated by the almost zero value of the beta weight.

In summary, the LibQUAL+™ subscale that measures *Affect of Service* has a moderate negative relationship with index scores whereas the *Access to Information* dimension has a moderate positive relationship. The relationships between collection indices and service quality scores seem to be changing as we are including different and diverse sets of institutions in LibQUAL+™. Library service quality as measured by the qualities of empathy, reliability and warmth of library staff may be easier to achieve in smaller places. Large, complex and relatively affluent-in-resources libraries face a challenge of catering to the needs of increasingly diverse and demanding users.

THE RELATIONSHIP BETWEEN EXPENDITURES AND LibQUAL+™ SCORES FOR OhioLINK, AAHSL AND OTHER LIBRARIES

The bivariate relationship between LibQUAL+™ scores and expenditures was also examined across three groups of libraries, the OhioLINK participants, AAHSL and a third group that included all libraries that were not part of OhioLINK or AAHSL, with a series of Pearson-r correlation coefficients summarized in Table 5. The relationships between expenditures and the four dimensions of library services are low and close to zero for both OhioLINK and AAHSL libraries. A slightly positive and moderate relationship exists between expenditures

TABLE 5. Pearson Correlations of LibQUAL+™ Scores with Expenditures for OhioLINK, AAHSL and Other Libraries–Spring 2002

Group		Expenditures	Total LibQUAL+™	Affect	Place	Control	Access
OhioLINK	Expenditures	1.00					
	Total LibQUAL+™	−0.16	1.00				
	Affect	−0.16	0.88**	1.00			
	Place	−0.23	0.80**	0.45**	1.00		
	Control	−0.14	0.93**	0.71**	0.81**	1.00	
	Access	0.03	0.90**	0.78**	0.67**	0.79**	1.00
	N	50	57	57	57	57	57
AAHSL	Total Expenditures	1.00					
	Total LibQUAL+™	0.04	1.00				
	Affect	−0.17	0.89**	1.00			
	Place	0.14	0.77**	0.46**	1.00		
	Control	0.07	0.91**	0.83**	0.54**	1.00	
	Access	0.19	0.89**	0.77**	0.59**	0.86**	1.00
	N	33	35	35	35	35	35
Other	Total Expenditures	1.00					
	Total LibQUAL+™	0.03	1.00				
	Affect	0.03	0.93**	1.00			
	Place	−0.17	0.81**	0.61**	1.00		
	Control	0.08	0.95**	0.87**	0.69**	1.00	
	Access	0.34*	0.87**	0.79**	0.59**	0.86**	1.00
	N	66	70	70	70	70	70

**p < .001
*p < .05

and the *Access to Collections* dimension for those libraries that are not affiliated with the two participating consortia. The question of how resources and expenditures related to LibQUAL+™ scores was also explored at the AAHSL meeting in San Francisco in November 2002. A series of graphics, coined as the 'red hot chili peppers,' are presented in a PowerPoint presentation exploring in a graphical manner, some of the bivariate relations of resource metrics such as the ARL membership criteria index and the LibQUAL+™ scores for OhioLINK, AAHSL and other libraries that have been discussed in this article:[7] <http://www.libqual.org/documents/admin/SFNov2002_MK2.ppt>.

In conclusion, LibQUAL+™ data offer one of the richest sources of information about libraries ever collected. To meet some of the demands of the analysis, institutional participants are provided with their own institutional data-files as well as summary notebooks of the information for their library and are encouraged to further analyze and report the results back to the community. The LibQUAL+™ project team also hosted meetings for both the OhioLINK and the AAHSL groups where participants were given the opportunity to review the results and interpret the findings. ARL is providing additional training opportunities to LibQUAL+™ participants to enhance their skills in both qualitative and quantitative data analysis. One of these opportunities is the annual ARL Annual Service Quality Evaluation Academy, where participants learn basic concepts in measurement and data analysis, enhance relevant software skills such as using Atlas.ti to analyze the content of the interviews or open-ended survey questions, and SPSS for quantitative data analysis.[8]

The relationships between institutional characteristics and LibQUAL+™ scores need to be explored continually every year as different groups and types of libraries implement the LibQUAL+™ total market survey. The context of these relationships is likely to evolve as new evidence is gathered year after year and as these different groups of libraries participate in LibQUAL+™. Our collective understanding of the relationship between service quality as measured by LibQUAL+™ and library investments is not only changing in front of our eyes, but it is transforming the way we view and define library success. To the extent that library success, whether defined with collection indices or service quality indices, relates to actual improvements in the outcomes achieved by our users, though, is still a large question that begs for an empirically substantiated answer.

NOTES

1. Colleen C. Cook, *A Mixed Methods Approach to the Identification and Measurement of Academic Library Service Quality Constructs: LibQUAL+™.* Doctoral dissertation, Texas A&M University, 2001; Cook, Colleen and Heath, Fred "The Association of Research Libraries LibQUAL+™ Project: An Update," *ARL Newsletter: A Bimonthly Report on Research Library Issues and Actions from ARL, CNI and SPARC,* 211 (August 2000): 12-14; _____. "Users' Perceptions of Library Service Quality: A LibQUAL+™ Qualitative Interview Study," *Library Trends* 49, no. 4 (2001): 548-584; Colleen Cook, Fred Heath, Martha Kyrillidou, and Duane Webster, "The Forging of Consensus: A Methodological Approach to Service Quality Assessment in Research Libraries–The LibQUAL+™ Experience." In Joan Stein, Martha Kyrillidou and Denise Davis (Eds.), *Proceedings of the 4th Northumbria International Conference on Performance Measurement in Libraries and Information Services* (Washington, DC: Association of Research Libraries, 2002): 93-104; Colleen Cook, Fred Heath, and Bruce Thompson, "Users' Hierarchical Perspectives on Library Service Quality: A LibQUAL+™ Study," *College and Research Libraries* 62 (2001): 147-153; _____. "Score Norms for Improving Library Service Quality: A LibQUAL+™ Study," *portal: Libraries and the Academy* 2, no. 1 (January 2002): 13-26; Colleen Cook and Bruce Thompson, "Scaling for the LibQUAL+™ Instrument: A Comparison of Desired, Perceived and Minimum Expectation Responses versus Perceived Only." In Joan Stein, Martha Kyrillidou and Denise Davis (Eds.), *Proceedings of the 4th Northumbria International Conference on Performance Measurement in Libraries and Information Services:* (Washington, DC: Association of Research Libraries, 2002): 211-214; Colleen Cook, Fred Heath, Bruce Thompson, and R. L. Thompson, "The Search for New Measures: The ARL LibQUAL+™ Study–A Preliminary Report," *portal: Libraries and the Academy* 1 (2001): 103-112; Colleen Cook, Fred Heath, R. L. Thompson, and Bruce Thompson, "Score Reliability in Web- or Internet-based Surveys: Unnumbered Graphic Rating Scales versus Likert-type Scales," *Educational and Psychological Measurement* 61 (2001): 697-706; Colleen Cook and Bruce Thompson, "Higher-order Factor Analytic Perspectives on Users' Perceptions of Library Service Quality," *Library Information Science Research* 22 (2000): 393-404; _____. "Reliability and Validity of SERVQUAL Scores Used to Evaluate Perceptions of Library Service Quality," *Journal of Academic Librarianship* 26, 248-258; _____. "Psychometric Properties of Scores from the Web-based LibQUAL+™ Study of Perceptions of Library Service Quality," *Library Trends* 49, no. 4 (2001): 585-604; Fred Heath, Colleen Cook, Martha Kyrillidou, and Bruce Thompson, "ARL Index and Other Validity Correlates of LibQUAL+™ Scores," *portal: Libraries and the Academy* 2, no. 1 (January 2002): 27-42; Bruce Thompson, "Representativeness versus Response Rate: It Ain't the Response Rate!" Paper presented at the Association of Research Libraries (ARL) Measuring Service Quality Symposium on the New Culture of Assessment: Measuring Service Quality, Washington DC (October 2000); Bruce Thompson, Colleen Cook, and Fred Heath, "The LibQUAL+™ Gap Measurement Model: The Bad, the Ugly and the Good of Gap Measurement," *Performance Measurement and Metrics* 1 (2000): 165-178; _____. "How Many Dimensions Does It Take to Measure Users' Perceptions of Libraries? A LibQUAL+™ Study," *portal: Libraries and the Academy* 1 (2001): 129-138; Bruce Thompson, Colleen Cook, and R. L. Thompson, "Reliability and Structure of LibQUAL+™ Scores," *portal: Libraries and the Academy* 2, no. 1:

3-12. An updated bibliography is also available at: <http://www.libqual.org/Publications/index.cfm>.

2. These two libraries are not included in most of the analysis presented in this article because of their uniqueness.

3. Martha Kyrillidou, "Research Library Trends: ARL Statistics," *Journal of Academic Librarianship* 26, no. 6 (November 2000): 427-436, available at <http://www.arl.org/stats/arlstat/jal99.html>. Also see ARL Membership Criteria Index <http://www.arl.org/stats/factor.html>.

4. Fred Heath, Colleen Cook, Martha Kyrillidou, and Bruce Thompson, "ARL Index and Other Validity Correlates of LibQUAL+™ Scores," *portal: Libraries and the Academy* 2, no. 1 (January 2002): 27-42.

5. Ibid, 36-37.

6. Bruce Thompson and G. M. Borrello, "The Importance of Structure Coefficients in Regression Research," *Educational and Psychological Measurement* 45 (1985): 203-209.

7. Martha Kyrillidou, "AAHSL Spring 2002 LibQUAL+™ Results," PowerPoint presentation presented at the AAHSL meeting on Nov 12, 2002, San Francisco, CA: <http://www.libqual.org/documents/admin/SFNov2002_MK2.ppt>.

8. For more information on the Service Quality Evaluation Academy, see: <http://www.arl.org/stats/libqual/academy04.html>.

CONSORTIA

Defending and Expanding Library Turf–
The Need for Scalable Consumer Research

Tom Sanville

SUMMARY. The LibQUAL+™ survey is a necessary and complementary tool in our arsenal that enables us to measure our effectiveness
and determine where improvements must be made. The power of
LibQUAL+™ is that it transcends a local campus survey. When executed across the consortium, it allows us to compare the results with our
activity measurements and apply the results relative to both our local and
statewide programs and funding. As a broad-base measure of user satisfaction, it is an important and necessary tool. Most importantly, it provides highly credible perspectives from our undergraduate students and
graduate students–perspectives that we can look at by campus, by consortium, or groups in between. *[Article copies available for a fee from The
Haworth Document Delivery Service: 1-800-HAWORTH. E-mail address:
<docdelivery@haworthpress.com> Website: <http://www.HaworthPress.com>
© 2004 by The Haworth Press, Inc. All rights reserved.]*

Tom Sanville is Executive Director, OhioLINK, Columbus, OH (E-mail: tom@
ohiolink.edu).

[Haworth co-indexing entry note]: "Defending and Expanding Library Turf–The Need for Scalable Consumer Research." Sanville, Tom. Co-published simultaneously in *Journal of Library Administration* (The
Haworth Information Press, an imprint of The Haworth Press, Inc.) Vol. 40, No. 3/4, 2004, pp. 13-17; and: *Libraries Act on Their LibQUAL+™ Findings: From Data to Action* (ed: Fred M. Heath, Martha Kyrillidou, and
Consuella A. Askew) The Haworth Information Press, an imprint of The Haworth Press, Inc., 2004,
pp. 13-17. Single or multiple copies of this article are available for a fee from The Haworth Document Delivery
Service [1-800-HAWORTH, 9:00 a.m. - 5:00 p.m. (EST). E-mail address: docdelivery@haworthpress.com].

http://www.haworthpress.com/web/JLA
© 2004 by The Haworth Press, Inc. All rights reserved.
Digital Object Identifier: 10.1300/J111v40n03_02

KEYWORDS. LibQUAL+™, consortia, benchmarking, user satisfaction, library service quality

There never has been a better and more necessary time than now for the creation, development, and ongoing use of the LibQUAL+™ survey. It is increasingly important to make the case for library funding by demonstrating that we are not only essential but also effective. With very tight and now diminishing higher education budgets, even essential services are not immune from the budget ax.

Globally, libraries are using consortia to improve their buying power as well as obtain additional funding. The creation of the International Coalition of Library Consortia (http://www.library.yale.edu/consortia) is evidence that this approach is widespread and growing. What is missing is the ability to measure and evaluate across a consortium the impact of the group's initiatives. Consortia struggle with the collection of compatible, consortium-wide usage statistics. To this point there has been no ready-ability to collect consistent multi-institutional consumer survey data. The LibQUAL+™ survey is a breakthrough capability to support consortium agendas and objectives with solid consortium-wide research.

In the case of the OhioLINK community, we fully recognize it's not just an issue for each library. In Ohio, our fortunes are interlocked. The perceptions of our individual effectiveness are inter-related with use of the OhioLINK program as a communal tool to advance information access. Our ability to get the most funding from the 83 individual administrations and from the Ohio Board of Regents for our central budget is dependent on our collective demonstration of a higher level of effectiveness than possible as individuals.

Several forces make the need for more measurement of library effectiveness paramount. These forces are at work in a continually evolving world and are interrelated. The evolution and relative importance of each, ebbs and flows over time. What are these forces?

Fundamental Change in Information Delivery–We all know about the electronic information explosion. The critical lesson is that the delivery of information is no longer our unique turf. With the ease of electronic information creation and delivery and the possibility of financial gain, there is new competition for the library "space." Take your pick of those who are trying, from Questia to course management software vendors to vendors serving libraries who repackage content, to the faculty themselves (e.g., Proquest Company's XanEdu). Notions of a fundamentally different approach to information delivery than the library are now on the table. As higher education budgets tighten, administrators even see the possibility of off-loading the traditional cost of the library directly to the students and faculty.

Who Manages Information–The increasing use of technology in all facets of higher education results in a convergence of information, instruction, and research. Not only does a library find it feasible and practical to expand its operations into the traditional realm of instruction and research, but vice versa. A prime example is distance learning and how information resources support it. Another example is the so-called institutional repository (http://www.arl.org/sparc/IR/ir.html). What should be the roles of the library, the IT department, and the academic units in a repository's development and operation? Diverse campus units are converging on each other's territory, relying on the increasing power of ubiquitous technology.

Fundamental Changes in the Economy–Even if not fundamental, certainly we are now experiencing more than a momentary economic problem at the state and national level. Most states are having extraordinarily difficult times and in many cases higher education and public libraries' funding is or will be under attack. No doubt our economic fortunes will ebb and flow and will continue to be cyclical, but these problems may be much more than short-term manifestations of quickly correctable problems. They may recur more frequently and take longer to bounce back. The impact of the aging of baby-boomers is coming home to roost; all states are facing run-away medical costs, and in some states there are fundamental structural tax flaws as the economy has shifted from goods to services.

Higher education is seen as a discretionary expense relative to other state needs. Cutting higher education support is seen as having a low political downside even though studies show the long-term correlation between education levels and income. Within higher education the library budget is also likely to be seen as more discretionary than other areas. It's a place where corners can be cut and the consequences hard to see let alone measure in the short term. In this swirling environment it is critical that the library knows what it is doing, why it is doing it, and knows whether what it is doing is or is not effective. The LibQUAL+™ survey is an important new tool in this process.

From the very beginning of the OhioLINK program we have tried to measure a broad array of activity measures, such as books requested

and ILL's filled, database searches, and electronic document and image downloads. From the beginning, we have embedded these into
our annual reports and budget requests. We have used these measures
relentlessly to demonstrate the effectiveness and popularity of the cooperative investment in the program. The 2001 and 2002 OhioLINK
Snapshots are good examples of how we have utilized activity measures
effectively (see http://www.ohiolink.edu/about/).

What we need more of are output and user satisfaction measures. The
Snapshots for 2001 and 2002 also include user-supplied testimonials of
how access to OhioLINK-provided resources improves instruction and
research. If a picture is worth a thousand words then the graphs, tables,
and few testimonials included in our Snapshots can be quite effective.

The LibQUAL+™ survey is a necessary and complementary tool in
our arsenal that enables us to measure our effectiveness and determine
where improvements must be made. The power of LibQUAL+™ is that
it transcends a local campus survey. When executed across the consortium it allows us to compare the results with our activity measures and
apply the results relative to both our local and statewide programs and
funding. As a broad-base measure of user satisfaction it is an important
and necessary tool. Most importantly, it provides highly credible perspectives from our undergraduate students and graduate students that
we can look at by campus, by consortium, or groups in-between.

Jeff Gatten's *OhioLINK LibQUAL+™ 2002 Final Report* describes
the OhioLINK community's experience in executing and collecting
20,000 user responses from 58 campuses. My purpose is not to cover
Jeff's analysis or review the results but to put their use in perspective.
We have already cited key findings in our last budget request for central
funds. It has provided additional validation of the impact the program is
having. The survey has already been valuable in adding emphasis to the
necessity of looking for ways to make our Web sites easier to use. With
information and presentation materials provided by Jeff Gatten to
OhioLINK libraries, each has been able to create effective local presentations for campus administrations. We have yet to fully tap results of
the spring 2002 survey. We have more ways yet to analyze the results.

An additional dimension of the LibQUAL+™ survey cannot be ex-
ploited until the survey is executed again. We will have the results of 45
surveys from spring 2003. We can begin analyzing longitudinal data.
How does our performance change over time? Are we doing better or
worse? Between the 2002 and 2003 LibQUAL+™ surveys, a major

change occurred in our services. We are anxious to see if the latest survey results confirm what we have seen in our activity measurements.

There is no doubt that we see the LibQUAL+™ instrument as an ongoing evaluation tool. Assuming its continuing availability, the most likely scenario is to try to execute the survey in lockstep across the consortium every several years. This will maximize the ways in which we can analyze the data. It is the most frequent repetition our users can be asked to do. It is also the most likely timetable for economic affordability.

A final word about the limitations of LibQUAL+™ or, frankly, any consumer research instrument. Complex questions cannot necessarily be addressed with a single research instrument. But, there is a strong tendency to want one tool to do more than it possibly can be designed to do effectively. Further, the moment results are seen from a survey it always causes "researcher's regret." Invariably, the results are never as clear as hoped for and immediately raise additional questions. Why couldn't we have asked the question differently or asked more questions? LibQUAL+™ is designed to do what it does very effectively. But like any survey it raises as many questions as it may answer. As with any survey, the results cannot be viewed outside of other information and other perspectives. Within the array of available and needed research, LibQUAL+™ is vitally important. Texas A&M and ARL are to be commended for the development of LibQUAL+™. It is a tool that the library community should support and nurture.

The OhioLINK LibQUAL+™ 2002 Experience:
A Consortium Looks at Service Quality

Jeff Gatten

SUMMARY. Are Ohio's college students and faculty satisfied with service at their campus libraries? In an effort to find out, fifty-seven OhioLINK libraries participated in the Association of Research Libraries' LibQUAL+™ 2002 survey. OhioLINK is a consortium of seventy-eight Ohio universities, colleges, community colleges, and the State Library of Ohio. When compared to the aggregate national data and aggregate ARL data, OhioLINK's service quality as measured by perceived performance above minimum expectations equals or exceeds peer group comparisons, especially on the key dimensions of "access to information" and "personal control." Examination of the data, both with national peer groups and OhioLINK-internal peer comparisons, reveals evidence of a positive OhioLINK impact on academic libraries in Ohio. The unique environment provided to academic libraries in Ohio through the OhioLINK program suggests that other consortia libraries may find peer comparisons within a consortium to be more beneficial than similar comparisons with the national LibQUAL+™ data. *[Article copies available for a fee from The Haworth Document Delivery Service: 1-800-HAWORTH. E-mail address: <docdelivery@haworthpress.com> Website: <http://www.HaworthPress.com> © 2004 by The Haworth Press, Inc. All rights reserved.]*

Jeff Gatten is Assistant Dean, Collection Management, and OhioLINK LibQUAL+™ Coordinator, Kent State University, Kent, OH (E-mail: jgatten@kent.edu).

[Haworth co-indexing entry note]: "The OhioLINK LibQUAL+™ 2002 Experience: A Consortium Looks at Service Quality." Gatten, Jeff. Co-published simultaneously in *Journal of Library Administration* (The Haworth Information Press, an imprint of The Haworth Press, Inc.) Vol. 40, No. 3/4. 2004, pp. 19-48; and: *Libraries Act on Their LibQUAL+™ Findings: From Data to Action* (ed: Fred M. Heath, Martha Kyrillidou, and Consuella A. Askew) The Haworth Information Press, an imprint of The Haworth Press, Inc., 2004, pp. 19-48. Single or multiple copies of this article are available for a fee from The Haworth Document Delivery Service [1-800-HAWORTH, 9:00 a.m. - 5:00 p.m. (EST). E-mail address: docdelivery@haworthpress.com].

http://www.haworthpress.com/web/JLA
© 2004 by The Haworth Press, Inc. All rights reserved.
Digital Object Identifier: 10.1300/J111v40n03_03

KEYWORDS. LibQUAL+™, consortia, library service quality, peer comparison, OhioLINK

INTRODUCTION

Are Ohio's college students and faculty satisfied with service at their campus libraries? In an effort to find out, 57 OhioLINK libraries participated in the Association of Research Libraries' (ARL) LibQUAL+™ 2002 survey.[1] ARL and Texas A&M University Libraries created the LibQUAL+™ survey instrument, adapted from the widely tested and accepted SERVQUAL survey, a total market survey assessing service quality used by for-profit companies. In 2002, LibQUAL+™ utilized a Web-based survey instrument consisting of 25 core items to ask library users to evaluate their library services along four dimensions: access to information, affect of service, personal control, and the library as "place."

OhioLINK is a consortium of 78 Ohio universities, colleges, community colleges, and the State Library. Its goal is to expand access to the latest research and scholarly thinking across a broad range of academic disciplines. It supports and improves the Ohio higher education community's ability to produce 21st century quality graduates and scholarly research. More than 600,000 students, faculty, and staff have access to OhioLINK's integrated local and central catalogs, an online borrowing system, 90+ research databases including full-text resources, a multi-publisher e-journal collection, a digital media collection, and document delivery services.[2]

The OhioLINK community chose to participate in the LibQUAL+™ survey for several reasons. First, the community recently identified assessment as a priority for the next few years. Second, using LibQUAL+™ provides a common tool that will allow individual libraries to compare themselves to other OhioLINK affiliated libraries, as well as with other peer libraries across the country. Third, the LibQUAL+™ survey has already been tested with other libraries and the instrument has been revised based on the resulting data. This assures the libraries a quality library evaluation tool that is supported by a national organization. Finally, it was agreed that the evaluation tool could include five questions exclusive to the OhioLINK community. These questions would be created to evaluate statewide consortium practices not addressed in the standard LibQUAL+™ survey instrument.[3]

OhioLINK PARTICIPATION

In October 2001, the OhioLINK Library Advisory Council's (LAC) Assessment Task Force met to begin developing the five questions that OhioLINK could add to the LibQUAL+™ survey. The OhioLINK Committee Chairs worked with their respective committees to answer the question: What does your committee believe are the top five OhioLINK services on which our library users (e.g., students, faculty, staff) should be surveyed? The goal was to draft five questions that would provide useful information about the quality of OhioLINK services.

At the Assessment Task Force (ATF) meeting, recommendations from the OhioLINK committees were used to identify common themes for drafting the five questions. The questions needed to be suitable for, and conform to, the LibQUAL+™ survey item format. The ATF also reviewed the 25 core items that appeared on the Spring 2002 LibQUAL+™ survey to avoid duplicating topics. Four members of the ATF conducted one-on-one testing of the five questions with library users at their sites. Based on the results of the testing, the questions were revised and posted to the Assessment Task Force listserv for comment. Final wording of the five OhioLINK local questions was reviewed at the November 16, 2001 Library Advisory Council meeting. The ATF submitted the final version of each question to the Council which was in turn submitted to ARL.

The ATF also made recommendations to the ARL/Texas A&M University (TAMU) LibQUAL+™ team regarding the demographic variables. These recommendations were a result of ATF internal discussions and a conference call held with some of the OhioLINK community college representatives of the ATF and the ARL/TAMU LibQUAL+™ team. It was understood that ARL would not necessarily be able to implement all of these recommendations (see Appendix A).

OhioLINK LibQUAL+™ DATA

During the spring 2002 implementation, the survey was completed by 20,401 library users from OhioLINK's fifty-seven sites (7,558 from universities, 8,992 from independent colleges, and 3,851 from two-year colleges). Of these, 19,554 were valid surveys used for the final data analysis (Appendix B and C). The 19,554 valid responses represent 27.8% of the total national data (see Table 1). For a complete description of how

TABLE 1. Total Number of Respondents Used for Each Analysis

	PUBLIC	PRIVATE	CC	BRANCH	TOTAL
All Users (except Library Staff)	5,038	9,363	3,439	1,248	19,088
Undergraduate	1,938	6,768	2,392	972	12,070
Graduate	1,351	755	0	53	2,159
Faculty	1,464	1,373	615	164	3,616
Total (Undergraduate, Graduate, Faculty)	4,753	8,896	3,007	1,189	17,845

valid responses were determined, see "2002 Data Screening" on page 5 of the *LibQUAL+™ Spring 2002 Survey Results–OhioLINK* notebook.[4]

The 2002 LibQUAL+™ survey instrument contained 25 core items designed to measure four dimensions of library service quality: (a) ACCESS to information, (b) AFFECT of service, (c) Personal CONTROL, and (d) library as PLACE. In addition, there were three general satisfaction questions pertaining to how one is treated, the level of support provided, and the overall quality of library services. The OhioLINK LibQUAL+™ instrument also included five additional questions designed specifically to assess OhioLINK services.

For each of the 25 questions plus the five OhioLINK-related questions, users were asked to indicate their minimum level of acceptable service, the desired level of service, and their perceived level of service provided. The minimum and desired scores for each question create a "zone of tolerance" with the perceived score being an indicator of performance relative to the zone. The differences of the perceived score from the minimum score (P-M) creates a gap score that indicates how far above or below the users' minimum expectations a library is performing on a given item (i.e., service adequacy).[5]

OhioLINK LibQUAL+™ DATA RESULTS

The following four charts (Charts 1-4) illustrate the P-M gap scores for each of the four dimensions, comparing all of OhioLINK (OL-all) and the OhioLINK 4-year schools (OL-4yr) results with the entire national results (Natl-all), the national results for 4-year schools (Natl-4yr), and the results for participating ARL members (ARL).

The two dimensions most impacted by OhioLINK services are "Access to Information" (Chart 1) and "Personal Control" (Chart 4). The

CHART 1. Access to Information

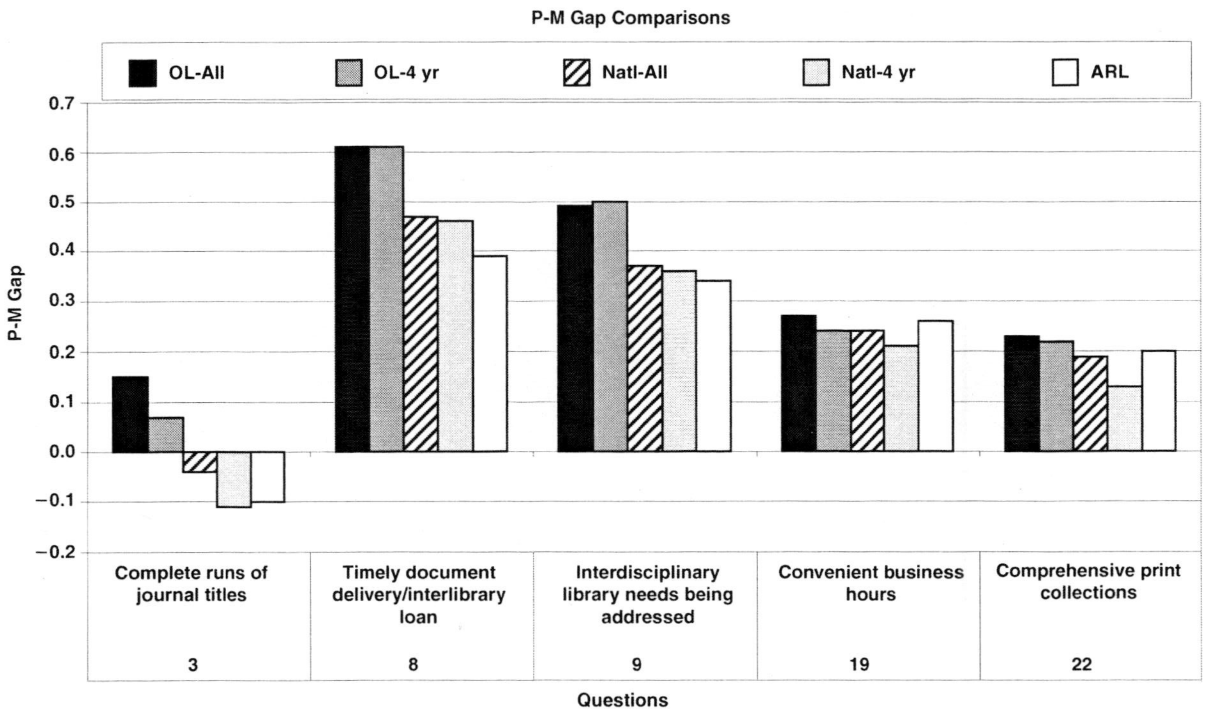

P-M Gap Comparisons
OL-All
OL-4 yr
Natl-All
Natl-4 yr
ARL
P-M Gap
0.7
0.6
0.5
0.4
0.3
0.2
0.1
0.0
−0.1
−0.2
Complete runs of journal titles
3
Timely document delivery/interlibrary loan
8
Interdisciplinary library needs being addressed
9
Convenient business hours
19
Comprehensive print collections
22
Questions

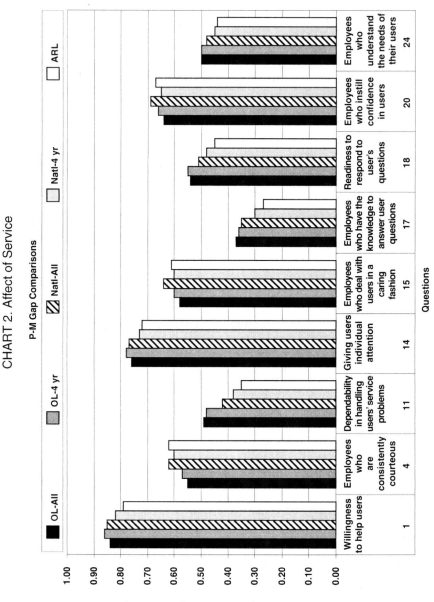

CHART 2. Affect of Service

P-M Gap Comparisons

Legend: ■ OL-All ▨ OL-4 yr ▨ Natl-All ▨ Natl-4 yr ☐ ARL

Questions:
- 1 — Willingness to help users
- 4 — Employees who are consistently courteous
- 11 — Dependability in handling users' service problems
- 14 — Giving users individual attention
- 15 — Employees who deal with users in a caring fashion
- 17 — Employees who have the knowledge to answer user questions
- 18 — Readiness to respond to user's questions
- 20 — Employees who instill confidence in users
- 24 — Employees who understand the needs of their users

Y-axis: P-M Gap (0.00 to 1.00)
X-axis: Questions

CHART 3. Library as Place

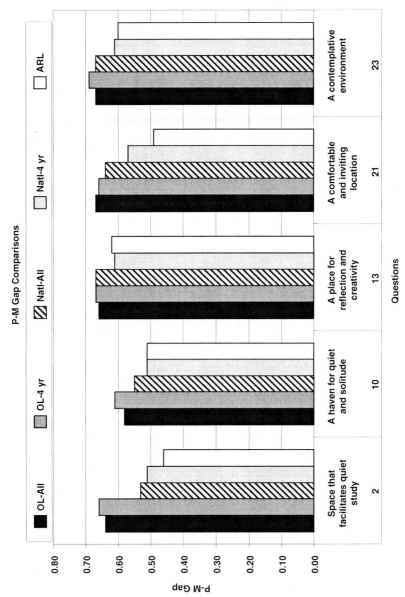

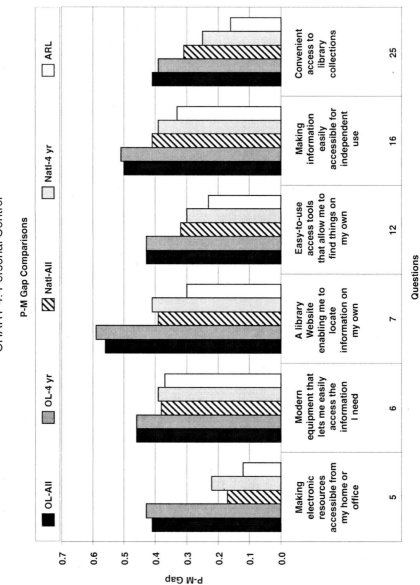

CHART 4. Personal Control

P-M Gap Comparisons

Legend: OL-All, OL-4 yr, Natl-All, Natl-4 yr, ARL

Question #	Question
5	Making electronic resources accessible from my home or office
6	Modern equipment that lets me easily access the information I need
7	A library Website enabling me to locate information on my own
12	Easy-to-use access tools that allow me to find things on my own
16	Making information easily accessible for independent use
25	Convenient access to library collections

Y-axis: P-M Gap (0.0 to 0.7)

X-axis: Questions

OhioLINK P-M gap scores on these two dimensions are higher than the national and ARL peer groups, meaning that OhioLINK as a group performs further above expectations than the comparative peer groups.

OhioLINK PEER GROUPS

Participating OhioLINK institutions were assigned to one of four groups (Appendix D) for purposes of analysis: (a) Public [public universities], (b) community college [two-year schools], (c) Private [private colleges], and (d) branch [branch campuses of universities].

Chart 5 illustrates the zones of tolerance for each of the OhioLINK peer groups across the four dimensions.

Chart 5 shows little difference between the community colleges and the branch campuses in terms of the minimum, desired, and perceived scores that make up the zones of tolerance. Independent sample t-tests ($p < .05$) for all twenty-five items using these two groups revealed few statistically significant differences. In the few instances where differences were detected, the mean differences were quite small. The results suggest no significant differences between the community colleges and the branch campuses in terms of service quality.

Chart 5 also shows that the private colleges are doing better than the public universities in terms of performing above minimum expectations. Interestingly, the perceived scores are similar, suggesting that the minimum expectations of service are lower at the private colleges, but perceptions of actual service quality are at the level of the public universities.

The following two charts (Charts 6 and 7) show the zones of tolerance for the specific questions that make up the two OhioLINK relevant dimensions: (a) access to information, and (b) personal control. Note on the "access" chart that the public universities have a negative P-M gap score for "complete runs of journal titles" although the perceived service level is quite similar to the private colleges. This means that expectations are higher for the public universities for this item. Both charts reflect the lower minimum expectations for the private colleges.

Chart 8 shows the zones of tolerance for the five OhioLINK-specific questions.

Chart 8 reveals that OhioLINK as a consortium does relatively well on meeting the expectations of users in terms of "convenience of borrowing books from other colleges." Perplexing are the negative P-M gap scores for both public universities and private colleges on the item

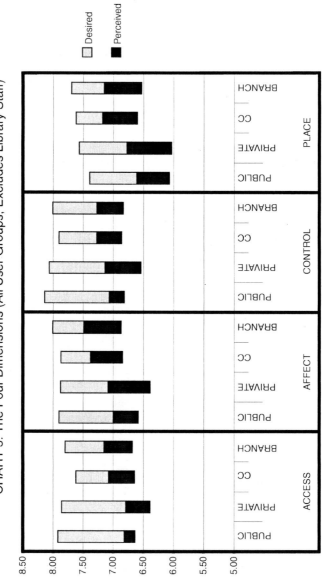

CHART 5. The Four Dimensions (All User Groups, Excludes Library Staff)

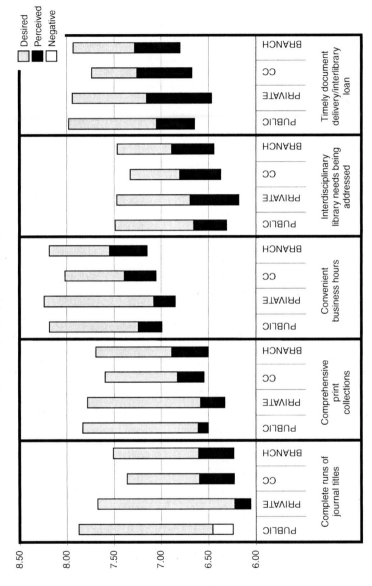

CHART 6. Zones of Tolerance = ACCESS

Legend:
- Desired
- Perceived
- Negative

Categories (left to right):
Complete runs of journal titles | Comprehensive print collections | Convenient business hours | Interdisciplinary library needs being addressed | Timely document delivery/interlibrary loan

Sub-categories: PUBLIC, PRIVATE, CC, BRANCH

Axis: 6.00, 6.50, 7.00, 7.50, 8.00, 8.50

CHART 7. Zones of Tolerance = CONTROL

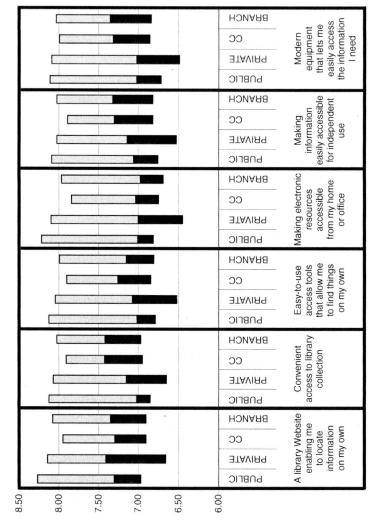

30

CHART 8. OhioLINK Questions

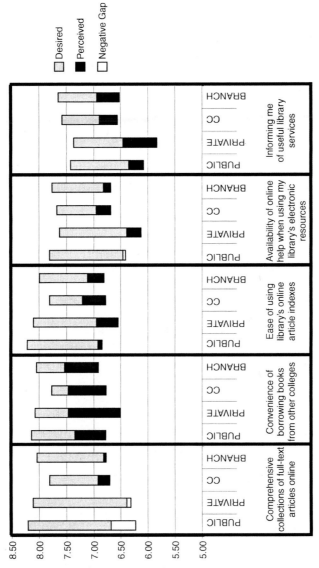

OhioLINK

31

regarding "comprehensive collections of full-text articles online" as well as the negative P-M gap score for the public universities on the "availability of online help when using my library's electronic resources." One might have expected similar scores across the OhioLINK peer groups for questions designed to measure OhioLINK services since these services are provided across all types of libraries.

Finally, the three general satisfaction questions at the end of the survey reveal greater satisfaction in the OhioLINK consortium compared to the national and ARL peer groups. Chart 9 shows the zones of tolerance for these three questions.

OhioLINK DEMOGRAPHIC GROUPS

Charts 10 through 15 illustrate the four dimensions and the five OhioLINK questions for each of three demographic groups: (a) undergraduate, (b) graduate, and (c) faculty.

Charts 10 and 11 show "undergraduate" student responses and reflect overall trends already seen in the data results. Private colleges tend to score lower minimum expectations and then reflect higher P-M gap scores. One interesting variation from the total aggregate OhioLINK results is that the undergraduate population at the private colleges indicate a perceived level of service slightly lower than minimum expectations in regards to "comprehensive collections of full-text articles online."

Charts 12 and 13 show "graduate" student responses. It is worth noting the low, and sometimes negative, P-M gap scores on the four dimensions. Results for the five OhioLINK questions show two-thirds of the zones of tolerance with negative P-M gap scores, demonstrating that graduate students are the most critical library users in that they do not perceive service levels to be meeting minimum expectations in most cases.

Charts 14 and 15 show "faculty" responses and reflect on the four dimensions that faculty at OhioLINK institutions generally have good feelings about their libraries, but slightly less so at the public universities. Interestingly, faculty scored lower P-M gap scores on the two OhioLINK-relevant dimensions of "access to information" and "personal control." For the five OhioLINK questions, faculty uniformly perceive service quality to be lower than minimum expectations on the "comprehensive collections of full-text articles online" question. Faculty at public universities scored the lowest P-M gap scores on all five questions, with negative P-M gap scores on three of the five items.

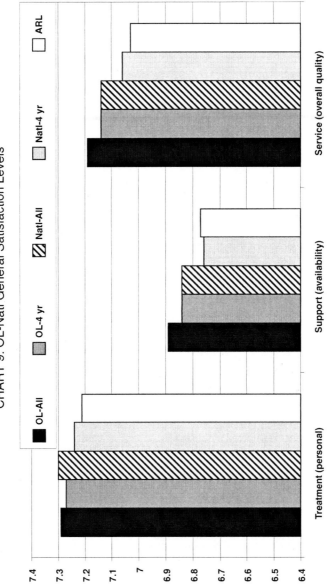

CHART 9. OL-Natl General Satisfaction Levels

Legend: OL-All, OL-4 yr, Natl-All, Natl-4 yr, ARL

Categories: Treatment (personal), Support (availability), Service (overall quality)

Y-axis: 6.4, 6.5, 6.6, 6.7, 6.8, 6.9, 7, 7.1, 7.2, 7.3, 7.4

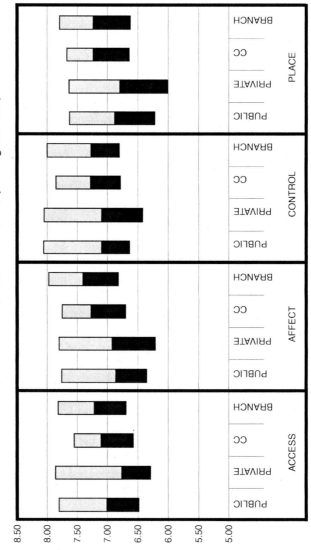

CHART 10. The Four Dimensions (Undergraduates)

34

CHART 11. Five OhioLINK Questions (Undergraduates)

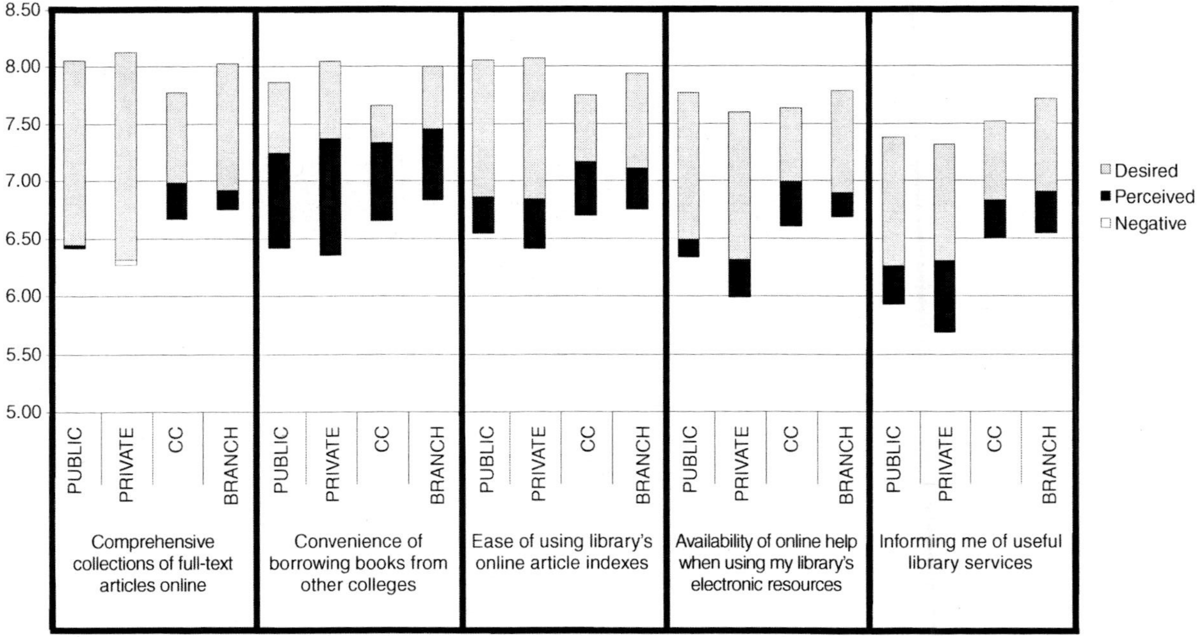

Legend: Desired, Perceived, Negative

Categories (left to right): Comprehensive collections of full-text articles online; Convenience of borrowing books from other colleges; Ease of using library's online article indexes; Availability of online help when using my library's electronic resources; Informing me of useful library services

Each category grouped by: PUBLIC, PRIVATE, CC, BRANCH

Y-axis scale: 5.00, 5.50, 6.00, 6.50, 7.00, 7.50, 8.00, 8.50

35

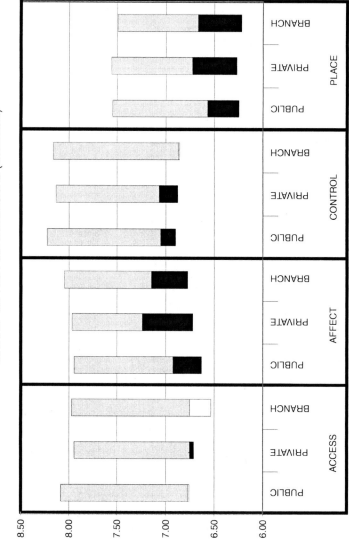

CHART 12. The Four Dimensions (Graduate)

36

CHART 13. Five OhioLINK Questions (Graduate)

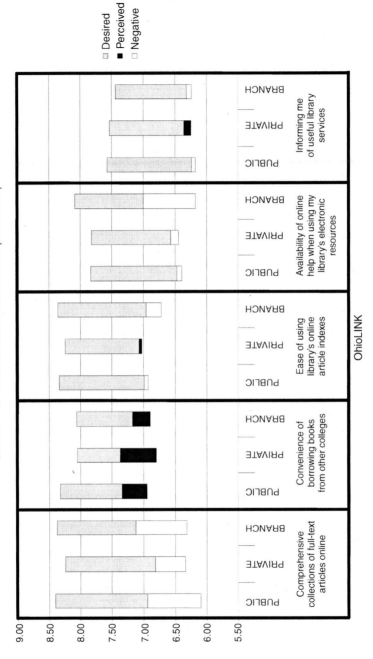

Legend:
- ☐ Desired
- ■ Perceived
- ☐ Negative

OhioLINK

Categories (left to right):
- Comprehensive collections of full-text articles online (PUBLIC, PRIVATE, BRANCH)
- Convenience of borrowing books from other colleges (PUBLIC, PRIVATE, BRANCH)
- Ease of using library's online article indexes (PUBLIC, PRIVATE, BRANCH)
- Availability of online help when using my library's electronic resources (PUBLIC, PRIVATE, BRANCH)
- Informing me of useful library services (PUBLIC, PRIVATE, BRANCH)

Scale: 9.00, 8.50, 8.00, 7.50, 7.00, 6.50, 6.00, 5.50

CHART 14. The Four Dimensions (Faculty)

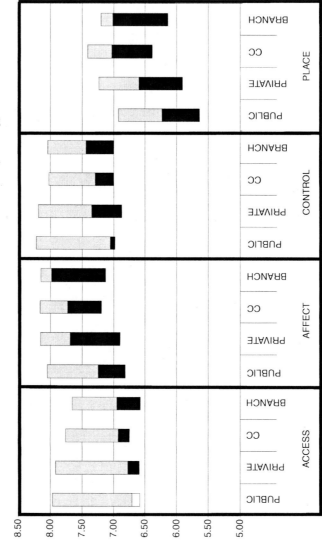

Desired
Perceived
Negative

38

CHART 15. Five OhioLINK Questions (Faculty)

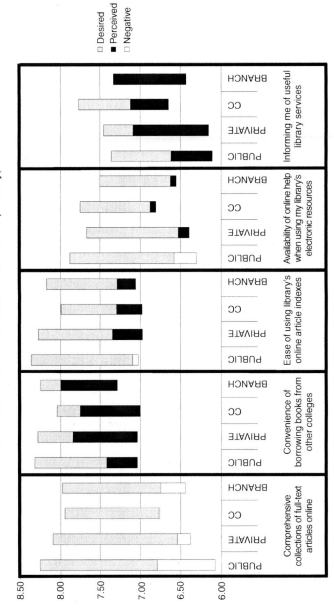

Legend: □ Desired ■ Perceived □ Negative

Categories: Comprehensive collections of full-text articles online; Convenience of borrowing books from other colleges; Ease of using library's online article indexes; Availability of online help when using my library's electronic resources; Informing me of useful library services

Groups: PUBLIC, PRIVATE, CC, BRANCH

Axis values: 6.00, 6.50, 7.00, 7.50, 8.00, 8.50

CONCLUSIONS

Several observations can be made from the OhioLINK LibQUAL+™ data:

- OhioLINK as a consortium has consistently higher P-M gap scores, especially on the relevant dimensions of "access to information" and "personal control." This seems to indicate that OhioLINK does make a positive difference in levels of satisfaction with library services.
- Minimum expectations at Ohio's private colleges are generally lower than other types of OhioLINK institutions. However, the perceived level of performance is typically equal to or above the level for Ohio's public universities. This may be evidence of an OhioLINK positive impact on the private colleges.
- Perceptions are below minimum expectations that Ohio's public universities will have "complete runs of journal titles." This may be a function of size since Ohio's public universities tend to have larger collections than the private colleges and therefore expectations may be adjusted based on the size of the collection (i.e., larger collections increase expectations). Perceived levels are similar between public universities and private colleges on this particular item.
- Minimum expectations on "access to information" items are generally higher for community colleges and branch campuses. This may be due to a higher expectation of convenience among the users of these libraries.
- Graduate students are the most critical demographic group on their perceptions of service quality in relation to minimum expectations, especially on access and collection content issues as reflected in the "access to information" dimension and the five OhioLINK questions. These results are not surprising given that this group of users likely places the most demands on academic library collections.
- Among the five OhioLINK questions, there seems to be a disconnect, especially among faculty, between perceptions of "comprehensive collections of full-text articles online" (lower perceptions) and "informing me of useful library services" (higher perceptions). Users believe they are relatively well informed regarding the availability of library services, but are relatively unsatisfied with the amount of full-text articles available to them. This is surprising given the large amount of electronic full-text articles available to institutions due to OhioLINK. Is this an education issue? Is

this a content issue? Is this an access issue? Or, is the demand for full-text insatiable?

RECOMMENDATIONS

The LibQUAL+™ survey results provide useful benchmark information for OhioLINK as a consortium to measure service quality and make comparisons on a national level as well as among OhioLINK member institutions. When compared to the aggregate national data and aggregate ARL data, OhioLINK's service quality as measured by perceived performance above minimum expectations equals or exceeds peer groups' comparisons, especially on the key dimensions of "access to information" and "personal control." Examination of the data, both with national peer groups and OhioLINK-internal peer comparisons, reveals evidence of a positive OhioLINK impact on academic libraries in Ohio.

Because of the unique environment provided academic libraries in Ohio through the OhioLINK program, member institutions may find individual peer comparisons with other OhioLINK institutions to be more beneficial than comparisons with the national LibQUAL+™ data. As reported elsewhere in the professional literature regarding the LibQUAL+™ survey, results serve more as signposts for further exploration rather than as definitive answers to service issues. A consortium may want to engage its members in the LibQUAL+™ survey if it is believed that the instrument can measure services impacted as a result of participating in the consortium. The OhioLINK community will continue its analysis of the aggregate OhioLINK data, especially in regards to demographic analysis by user group (e.g., undergraduate, graduate, faculty) and some of the behavioral variables such as frequency of library use.

NOTES

1. *Association of Research Libraries, "OhioLINK Joins LibQUAL+™ R&D,"* press release released on the Web 26 November 2001. Retrieved September 27, 2002, from the World Wide Web: http://www.arl.org/libqual/geninfo/ohiolinkpr.html.

2. Ibid.

3. Ibid.

4. Duane Webster and Fred Heath, *LibQUAL+™ Spring 2002 Survey Results–OhioLINK*. (Washington, DC: Association of Research Libraries, 2002).

5. Colleen Cook, Fred Heath, and Bruce Thompson, "'Zones of Tolerance' in Perceptions of Library Service Quality: A LibQUAL+™ Study." *portal: Libraries and the Academy* 3, no. 1 (2003): 113-123.

APPENDIX A

<u>Demographic Variables: Recommendations of the OhioLINK LAC Assessment Task Force</u>

DISCIPLINES:

We are recommending a slightly expanded list of disciplines that would be used for ALL LibQUAL+™ instruments. We have attempted to follow NCES categories to allow for any mapping of data to past or future discipline categories.

1. Agriculture/Environmental Studies
2. Applied Technologies and Trades
3. Architecture
4. Business
5. Communications/Journalism
6. Computer Science
7. Education
8. Engineering
9. Health Sciences
10. Humanities/Philosophy/Languages
11. Law
12. Performing and Fine Arts
13. Personal Improvement/Leisure
14. Science/Math
15. Social Sciences/History/Psychology
16. General Studies
17. Other
18. Undecided

RANK/INTENT:

For COMMUNITY COLLEGE STUDENT surveys ONLY, we recommend changing the "RANK" question to "INTENT." We recommend the following response options for INTENT. These same options are apparently used on other community college survey instruments.

a. no definite purpose in mind
b. to take a few courses for self-improvement
c. to take a few job-related courses
d. to take courses necessary for transferring to another 2-year college
e. to take courses necessary for transferring to a 4-year college or university
f. to complete a vocational/technical program
g. to obtain or maintain a certification
h. to obtain an Associate's degree
i. other

RANK:

For COMMUNITY COLLEGE FACULTY surveys only, we recommend changing the response options to: (a) Part-time and (b) Full-time.

APPENDIX B

Chronology

Summer 2001: OhioLINK and ARL sign a "Memorandum of Understanding."

September 24, 2001: The OhioLINK Library Advisory Council (LAC), a committee of academic library directors, meets in Columbus for an introduction and orientation to LibQUAL+™.

October 16, 2001: The OhioLINK LAC Assessment Task Force meets to begin developing five OhioLINK-related questions for the LibQUAL+™ 2002 survey.

October 30, 2001: An OhioLINK-only LibQUAL+™ listserv, separate and independent of the national LibQUAL+™ listserv, is created to communicate unique consortium information among OhioLINK participating institutions.

November 13, 2001: A conference call is held among community college representatives from the OhioLINK LAC Assessment Task Force, ARL staff, and Texas A&M University staff. The purpose of the conversation is to discuss the development of LibQUAL+™ demographic variables appropriate to a community college audience (Appendix A).

November 26, 2001: ARL asks for three volunteer OhioLINK sites to test the Spring 2002 LibQUAL+™ instrument. Ideally, one site would be a public university, one a 4-year private college, and one a community college and the institutions would have differing platforms from which to test (i.e., Linux, Windows, and Macs).

November 30, 2001: All-day LibQUAL+™ training session is held in Columbus for participating OhioLINK institutions. Colleen Cook and Bruce Thompson from Texas A&M present the program. ARL creates and hosts the Website used for registration.

December 17, 2001: Using the OhioLINK LibQUAL+™ listserv, participating libraries are reminded to be working on: (a) getting human subjects research clearance from their institutions research office by mid-January, (b) exploring how student, staff, and faculty e-mail addresses will be obtained, (c) deciding whether to offer local incentives, and (d) supplying ARL with a campus demographic profile and institutional logo.

February 4, 2002: OhioLINK participating libraries are reminded by the OhioLINK LibQUAL+™ Coordinator to: (a) get the e-mail addresses for the samples (e.g., undergrads, faculty), (b) draft e-mail letter of invitation for participation that will be sent to individuals in the samples, and (c) draft at least a 1st and 2nd follow-up e-mail letter. Samples of these letters can be found in the LibQUAL+™ 2002 "Policies and Procedures Manual."

March 4, 2002-May 10, 2002: LibQUAL+™ survey available for completion by individuals at participating institutions.

April 30, 2002: E-mail is posted to the national LibQUAL+™ listserv announcing LibQUAL+™ meetings at ALA in June. OhioLINK LibQUAL+™ Coordinator reminds participating institutions that there is no need to attend the "LibQUAL+™ Spring 2002 Participants Meeting" at ALA where institutions from outside of Ohio will be presented with their results (in fact, at this point it is not clear that Ohio's results will even be prepared by the time of ALA). Sometime in the summer there will be a meeting in Columbus for OhioLINK participants to receive their LibQUAL+™ results.

May 16, 2002: The latest plans regarding LibQUAL+™ results are released. This information supersedes previous communication on this topic: (a) if a representative from an OhioLINK institution attends the "The LibQUAL+™ Spring 2002 Participants Meeting" at the ALA Annual Conference, then they will receive their institution's results, the national aggregate data, and the OhioLINK aggregate data; or (b) if one does not attend the ALA Annual Conference, then one's institutional results, the national aggregate data, and the

APPENDIX B (continued)

OhioLINK aggregate data will be mailed to the institution. There is no fixed date when this mailing will occur. Participating OhioLINK institutions are asked not to contact ARL with questions about the results they receive in the mail. ARL was not prepared to handle a great influx of telephone or e-mail questions (one reason they prefer to distribute the results at meetings). OhioLINK libraries are asked to save questions for an end of summer meeting in Columbus. In the meantime, the OhioLINK LibQUAL+™ Coordinator offers to field questions to the extent possible and collect questions to be addressed at the meeting in Columbus.

August 29, 2002: OhioLINK hosts LibQUAL+™ results meeting in Columbus, Ohio, for participating institutions.

September 4, 2002: As a follow-up to the meeting in Columbus, the OhioLINK LibQUAL+™ Coordinator prepares an Excel file that allows one to add in local data results and then have peer group comparision charts updated automatically. This provides a good start for having illustrative peer-group information to share with administrators. The Excel file is e-mailed to all participating OhioLINK institutions.

APPENDIX C

Valid Responses by Demographics

	Undergraduate	Graduate	Faculty	Library Staff	Staff	Total
Antioch College	100		32	1	8	141
Ashland University	530	130	88	17	74	839
Belmont Technical College	162		23	8	27	220
Bowling Green State University	155	174	128	4	46	507
Bowling Green State University– Firelands College	109	1	10	1	8	129
Capital University	248	6	73	11	10	348
Case Western Reserve University	298	110	97	2	5	512
Cedarville University	606	4	87	18	34	749
Cincinnati Bible College and Seminary	65	46	30	4	22	167
Cincinnati State Technical and Community College	2		12	8		22
Clark State Community College Library	244		26	6	35	311
Cleveland State University	201	182	131	1	15	530
College of Mount St. Joseph	162	18	40	4	27	251
College of Wooster	522	4	56		1	583
Columbus State Community College	5		100	6	53	164

	Undergraduate	Graduate	Faculty	Library Staff	Staff	Total
Cuyahoga Comm. College (Metro, Eastern, & Western)	281	-	36	14	36	367
Denison University	304	2	70	11	45	432
Edison State Community College	112		19	5	8	144
Ohio Northern University	293	5	90		1	389
Kent State University–Kent Campus	228	71	207	4	7	517
Kent State University–Stark Campus	78	3	46	5	10	142
Lakeland Community College	158		39		1	198
Lorain County Community College	350		69	10	73	502
Malone College	246	23	43	6	15	333
Marietta College	144	15	35		4	198
Mount Carmel College of Nursing	38	1	17			56
Mount Union College	137		23	8	5	173
Muskingum College	342	12	42	5	28	429
Ohio Dominican College	280	14	42	10	38	384
Ohio State University	110	131	161	98	58	558
Ohio State University–Mansfield	105	9	18	4	3	139
Ohio State University and Central Ohio Technical College	156	20	29	4	16	225
Ohio University–Athens Campus	188	158	98	-	5	449
Ohio University–Eastern Campus	30	2	10	3	3	48
Ohio University–Lancaster	105	10	14			129
Ohio University–Southern Campus	118	4	8		11	141
Ohio University–Zanesville/Muskingum Area Tech. Coll.	182	4	14		2	202
Ohio Wesleyan University	220	2	71		14	307
Otterbein College	209	31	39	10	25	314
Owens Community College	651		136	4	65	856
Shawnee State University	89	1	31		1	122
Sinclair Community College	97		71	5	67	240
Terra Community College	211		25	1	29	266
University of Akron	121	92	114	8	2	337
University of Akron–Wayne College	89		15	6	6	116

APPENDIX C (continued)

	Undergraduate	Graduate	Faculty	Library Staff	Staff	Total
University of Cincinnati	164	288	183	75	74	784
University of Dayton	128	67	91		3	289
University of Findlay	68	15	44	8	21	156
University of Rio Grande/ Rio Grande Community College	18		26	8	19	71
University of Toledo	134	112	67	14	15	342
Ursuline College	103	40	37	12	5	197
Washington State Community College	101		33		19	153
Wittenberg University	457	1	72	7	5	542
Wright State University	200	99	270	1	13	583
Xavier University	486	206	76	6	63	837
Youngstown State University	348	43	74	16	49	530
TOTAL	12,070	2,159	3,616	466	1,243	19,554

APPENDIX D

Valid Responses by OhioLINK Internal Peer Groups

OhioLINK	Public	Comm. College	Private	Branch Campus
Antioch College			141	
Ashland University			839	
Belmont Technical College		220		
Bowling Green State University	507			
Bowling Green State University–Firelands College				129
Capital University			348	
Case Western Reserve University			512	
Cedarville University			749	
Cincinnati Bible College and Seminary			167	
Cincinnati State Technical and Community College		22		
Clark State Community College Library		311		
Cleveland State University	530			
College of Mount St. Joseph			251	
College of Wooster			583	

	Public	Comm. College	Private	Branch Campus
Columbus State Community College		164		
Cuyahoga Comm. College (Metro, Eastern, & Western)		367		
Denison University			432	
Edison State Community College		144		
Ohio Northern University			389	
Kent State University–Kent Campus	517			
Kent State University–Stark Campus				142
Lakeland Community College		198		
Lorain County Community College		502		
Malone College			333	
Marietta College			198	
Mount Carmel College of Nursing			56	
Mount Union College			173	
Muskingum College			429	
Oberlin College			884	
Ohio Dominican College			384	
Ohio State University	558			
Ohio State University–Mansfield				139
Ohio State University and Central Ohio Technical College				225
Ohio University–Athens Campus	449			
Ohio University–Eastern Campus				48
Ohio University–Lancaster				129
Ohio University–Southern Campus				141
Ohio University–Zanesville/Muskingum Area Tech. Coll.				202
Ohio Wesleyan University			307	
Otterbein College			314	
Owens Community College		856		
Shawnee State University	122			
Sinclair Community College		240		
Terra Community College		266		
University of Akron	337			
University of Akron–Wayne College				116
University of Cincinnati	784			
University of Dayton			289	
University of Findlay			156	
University of Rio Grande/Rio Grande Community College		71		
University of Toledo	342			
Ursuline College			197	
Washington State Community College		153		

APPENDIX D (continued)

	Public	Comm. College	Private	Branch Campus
Wittenberg University			542	
Wright State University	583			
Xavier University			837	
Youngstown State University	530			
TOTAL	5,259	3,514	9,510	1,271

HEALTH SCIENCES LIBRARIES

Exploring Outcomes Assessment: The AAHSL LibQUAL+™ Experience

Tamera Lee

SUMMARY. The Association of Academic Health Sciences Libraries (AAHSL) participated as one of two consortia in the 2002 pilot of LibQUAL+™; the other was the Ohio Library and Information Network (OhioLINK), a consortium of Ohio's college and university libraries and the State Library of Ohio. This report focuses on the AAHSL/ARL partnership, the AAHSL aggregate experience and results, and collaborative outcomes. Whereas AAHSL will continue LibQUAL+™ participation in 2003 with another cohort of participating libraries, a foundation for qualitative assessment within AAHSL has been grounded. Specifically, this report outlines the qualitative efforts of the AAHSL Task Force on Service Quality Assessment, for

Tamera Lee is Director of Libraries, Medical College of Georgia, Augusta, GA, and Chair of the Task Force on Quality Assessment, Association of Academic Health Sciences Libraries (E-mail: tlee@mail.mcg.edu).

[Haworth co-indexing entry note]: "Exploring Outcomes Assessment: The AAHSL LibQUAL+™ Experience." Lee, Tamera. Co-published simultaneously in *Journal of Library Administration* (The Haworth Information Press, an imprint of The Haworth Press, Inc.) Vol. 40, No. 3/4, 2004, pp. 49-58; and: *Libraries Act on Their LibQUAL+™ Findings: From Data to Action* (ed: Fred M. Heath, Martha Kyrillidou, and Consuella A. Askew) The Haworth Information Press, an imprint of The Haworth Press, Inc., 2004, pp. 49-58. Single or multiple copies of this article are available for a fee from The Haworth Document Delivery Service [1-800-HAWORTH, 9:00 a.m. - 5:00 p.m. (EST). E-mail address: docdelivery@haworthpress.com].

http://www.haworthpress.com/web/JLA
© 2004 by The Haworth Press, Inc. All rights reserved.
Digital Object Identifier: 10.1300/J111v40n03_04

49

which a team of nine members served, including Jane Blumenthal (Georgetown University), Diana Cunningham (New York Medical College), Rick Forsman (University of Colorado), Tamera Lee (Medical College of Georgia), Logan Ludwig (Loyola University-Chicago), James Shedlock (Northwestern University), Julie Sollenberger (University of Rochester), Susan Starr (University of California, San Diego) and Laurie Thompson (State University of New York Upstate). *[Article copies available for a fee from The Haworth Document Delivery Service: 1-800-HAWORTH. E-mail address: <docdelivery@haworthpress.com> Website: <http://www.HaworthPress.com> © 2004 by The Haworth Press, Inc. All rights reserved.]*

KEYWORDS. Qualitative assessment, benchmarking, consortia, LibQUAL+™, Association of Academic Health Sciences Libraries (AAHSL)

BACKGROUND

The Association of Academic Health Sciences Libraries (AAHSL) comprises the libraries serving the accredited U.S. and Canadian medical schools belonging to or affiliated with the Association of American Medical Colleges (AAMC). It includes other related libraries and organizations that lead in resolving information and knowledge management problems in the health care environment. AAHSL enhances the success of its members in advancing health through their recognized leadership in managing and utilizing the intellectual resources within and beyond the institution. Founded in 1977, AAHSL is a member of the Council of Academic Societies of the AAMC.

With a long history of compiling and analyzing comparative statistics to serve as useful benchmarks for member libraries,[1] AAHSL recognizes the increasing importance of outcome-measurements to be used as performance indicators. As part of its efforts to explore and implement new methods for measuring user satisfaction and other outcome-assessments, AAHSL partnered with ARL to develop a Memorandum of Understanding for the participation of a cross section of 36 AAHSL libraries in the spring 2002 pilot. These libraries represented multiple types of health sciences institutions, including ARL universities, branch campuses, free standing/independent institutions, private colleges and state university system components. The AAHSL project was funded generously by the National Library of Medicine, with shared costs by AAHSL and participating libraries to support deliverables.

The Task Force on Quality Assessment was created in July 2001 to lead AAHSL's involvement in a service quality assessment process and evaluate LibQUAL+™ as a qualitative measurement tool for academic health sciences libraries. All of the task force members participated in the survey and represented an effective cross section of membership. Specific task force goals include testing the usefulness of the instrument for benchmarking, testing the feasibility of customizing the instrument for the health sciences, determining the value of cross data analysis with AAHSL statistics, and gaining experience with an aggregate outcomes measurement process.

THE PROCESS

With an objective of ensuring a smooth study process for AAHSL participants, an action plan and a timeline were developed. In the summer of 2001, the Task Force coordinated the cohort registration and established a listserv to facilitate efficient communication for a myriad of issues and questions. In liaison with the ARL project management team, the Task Force drafted a procedural manual to serve as a guide and created a survey administration tip sheet for participants.

The Task Force clarified the importance of a clean set of collective data for AAHSL and defined demographics for respondents. This proved challenging. Although all are health sciences organizations with similar missions, the libraries vary widely in how they are administered and organized and how they identify user groups. Whereas some health sciences libraries of larger institutions wanted to be included as part of the AAHSL data set, the Task Force and ARL decided University-wide participation took precedence. To be a dual participant in the overall ARL study and in the AAHSL aggregate would incur additional costs; no institutions chose to do this.

Another Task Force challenge was to develop five unique AAHSL questions in collaboration with participants and in consultation with the National Library of Medicine. The main goal was to add service performance issues for the health sciences, especially priorities not included or covered sufficiently by the LibQUAL+™ survey. In keeping with LibQUAL+™ protocol, the items were phrased "When it comes to ...":

- providing health information when and where I need it
- employees teaching me how to access or manage information

- an environment that facilitates group study and problem solving
- access to information resources that support patient care
- having comprehensive electronic resources.

Of course, the new questions employed the LibQUAL+™ scale of 1 (low) to 9 (high) for minimum, desired and perceived service performance.

Although not viewed as a hurdle by many of the previous ARL participants, *human subjects clearance* was a significant issue for the AAHSL cohort. Given the growing concern about patient care, rights and safety, health sciences review boards are required by law and all are necessarily meticulous and thorough in their review. Following local review, the LibQUAL+™ protocol was permitted as a survey tool at all institutions.

THE RESPONDENTS

Given the relative smaller size of health sciences populations, the Task Force recommended that the AAHSL participants survey their entire user populations. Only those users who completed the survey in its entirety and with measurable consistency were included. From the LibQUAL+™ AAHSL Survey Results,[2] Figure 1 identifies AAHSL's 13,976 respondents by user group.

Figure 2 is modified to show the respondents for disciplines reflecting 5% or greater representation. Neither of these revealed any unexpected response variables.

Figure 3 charts average scores for the AAHSL aggregate general satisfaction ratings. Average scores for all user groups reflect a high level of overall satisfaction across three broad dimensions of library service. Given the clinical and research environment's premium on timeliness, ARL reliability results indicate higher AAHSL user expectations and levels of satisfaction compared to the ARL environment. As shown by Colleen Cook in the AAHSL results workshop,[3] health sciences library users have the highest performance expectations of all cohort groups for the 2002 survey. Important to note, however, is the fact that responses from the general academic campus reflect a higher response rate from undergraduate students, whose expectations and needs differ from the user profile of AAHSL institutions, consisting primarily of graduate level and above. A two-year comparison of the AAHSL and ARL aggregate survey results should be the focus of another study.

FIGURE 1. AAHSL–Respondents by User Group

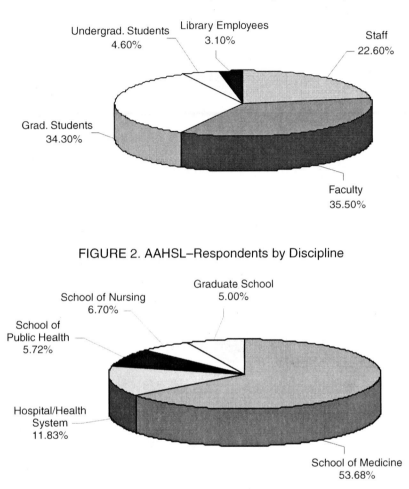

FIGURE 2. AAHSL–Respondents by Discipline

THE RESULTS

While analysis continues at local, regional and national levels, some findings were readily discernable from the ARL deliverables. Regarding frequency of library use, most respondents reported using the Library weekly, both on the premises (35.93%) and electronically (34.84%). Daily electronic use was reported by 31.83% and monthly use on premises was reported by 31.42%. This reported usage corresponded well with the high desire for comprehensive electronic re-

FIGURE 3. AAHSL–General Satisfaction

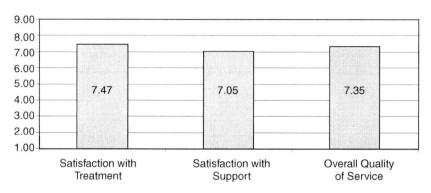

sources by students and faculty. The similarly reported building usage confirms that the library as place remains central to user expectations.

Service dimension gaps that fell below the level users expect and outside the LibQUAL+™ "zone of tolerance" varied by user group. For the aggregate of user groups, a satisfaction gap occurred for electronic resources accessible from home or office. For graduate students, convenient business hours recorded a similar deficit. Faculty were the least satisfied with complete runs of journal titles, electronic resources accessible from home or office, and comprehensive electronic resources. No dimension gaps were revealed for undergraduate students or for staff.

Generally, the factor identified as most desired by the AAHSL aggregate community overall is comprehensive electronic resources (8.44), followed closely by making electronic resources accessible from home or office (8.35). Service qualities most favored by specific user groups varied somewhat, although having comprehensive electronic resources was clearly most desired by faculty and students. Staff showed strongest desire for the LibQUAL+™ *service affect* dimension, including employees who are courteous consistently (8.55), willingness to help users (8.52), employees who have the knowledge to answer users' questions (8.46), and readiness to respond to users' questions (8.46).

Listserv discussion indicated that a significant percentage of the respondents provided optional comments. Informal communication hints that for many participants the comments are regarded as the most useful survey component. User comments added meaningful value to the quantitative data and provided significant educational and public relations opportunities for engaging user communities. Three strong themes emerged for the aggregate comments, including (1) need for more journals, especially online, (2) frustration with remote access problems, and (3) positive perceptions about staff. Despite the many critical remarks, participants felt gratified that the users appreciated library staff efforts.

Another useful view of the data was provided by Bruce Thompson through T-scores and norms tables.[4] As discussed by Cook, Heath, and Thompson, T-scores allow the examination of individual score norms for faculty and students and institutional scores in relation to scores of peer institutions.[5] While norms do not make value statements, institutional norms for perceived and gap scores enable the interpretation of LibQUAL+™ scores compared to other institutions. Further study of the norm tables is needed to enable qualitative benchmarking for AAHSL.

An interesting and noteworthy aspect of the AAHSL institutional norms is that one of the smaller health sciences libraries stands out as providing the most effective match of service expectations and perceptions. The overall norm-table for institutions of all types revealed this particular institution to have the only positive average service superiority score, indicating overall perceptions are *higher* than desired. This revelation triggered one of the AAHSL questions for exploration, i.e., "Do smaller health sciences libraries have higher levels of service satisfaction?" That library will participate in the broader constituency as a four-year private institution in the 2003 cohort. Perhaps the question can be answered in the next round of analysis.

THE FIVE AAHSL QUESTIONS

While further exploration and analysis are needed, the "comprehensive electronic resources" query was added by the task force to provide balance to the ARL query of "comprehensive print resources." Whereas summative data for the other four AAHSL queries showed needs for slight improvements for all user groups, "comprehensive electronic resources" reflected the highest desired enhancement by all user groups, and represented a significant gap in minimal expectations for faculty. The ARL research team advised the task force to reconsider this question as an unreasonable service demand, suggesting that comprehensive print resources may be more achievable. For the 2003 LibQUAL+™ cohort iteration, this question was revised to provide more focus, "Electronic resources matching my information needs."

RECOMMENDATIONS

As a result of the pilot, the Task Force developed a series of recommendations for participating libraries as follows:

- Present and publish results locally as part of overall assessment and as new listening measure.
- Benchmark results for regional and national publication.

Many of the participating institutions shared presentations with respective senior administrations, academic senates, student government associations, physical facilities planners and library staff. Some made immediate changes and others will repeat the survey in 2003 for a better view. A few incorporated LibQUAL+™ data into their annual performance metrics and other review processes. Others utilized LibQUAL+™ data to complement other assessment measures and create additional ones, such as focus groups. Examples, including a correlative test to consider the integration of qualitative and quantitative measures conducted by Lee, Dennison, and Joubert, are available at http://www. libqual.org/Publications/index.cfm.[6] Basically this test found no correlation between service-affect-gap score and annual expenditures. Presentations and poster sessions were produced for the Midwest and Southern Chapters of the Medical Library Association. A professional forum presentation was provided at the University of Georgia. Additional presentations and publications are expected in the future.

The Task Force recommended for itself and/or the AAHSL Annual Statistics Editorial Board the following:

- Compare selective LibQUAL+™ data with selective AAHSL Statistics to address specific questions and determine if correlations exist, e.g., How do the perceptions of the Service Affect dimension compare for libraries of different size and resource expenditures?

The Task Force recommended the following for AAHSL:

- Identify expertise or hire a consultant for SPSS to conduct comparative analysis amongst participating libraries and across types of libraries.
- Participate in the 2003 survey administration for a cross section of different (new and repeat) participating libraries to optimize assessment and maximize deliverables.

- Consider if and how a qualitative data component may be used in conjunction with the annual quantitative statistics for member libraries.
- Continue to support LibQUAL+™ assessment and development, other qualitative measurement activities and future initiatives in outcomes assessment.

AAHSL expects to send an application package nominating three people to participate in the ARL Service Quality Evaluation Academy held May 12-16, 2003 in San Antonio, Texas.[7] In addition to advancing assessment skills of the nominees, a major goal is to complete a project addressing the analysis of specific questions pertaining to the AAHSL aggregate. Further analysis is expected following the 2003 cohort results.

BENEFITS

The AAHSL/ARL partnership effected numerous qualitative benefits aside from the data results. For ARL, it assisted in furthering the applicability of LibQUAL+™ as a qualitative assessment tool across different types of institutions. The special cohort assisted ARL with promotion, training, and increased participation. For AAHSL, the partnership created a heightened awareness of the viability of outcomes assessment and a cost efficient protocol for listening to users. The additional five questions allowed AAHSL to include constructs for issues perceived as unique or more significant to health sciences libraries. It prompted further interest in testing the instrument's feasibility for a new cohort of hospital libraries. And perhaps most importantly, with a strong service orientation already in place, implementing a national survey contributed to the advancement of a culture of assessment and placed the academic community at the center of that assessment.

NOTES

1. Association of Academic Health Sciences Libraries. *Annual Statistics of Academic Medical Libraries in the United States and Canada.* Seattle: The Association. 24th ed: 2002. The *Annual Statistics of Medical School Libraries in the United States and Canada* is a publication of the Association of Academic Health Sciences Libraries. Published since 1978, the *Annual Statistics* provides comparative data on significant

characteristics of collections, expenditures, personnel and services in medical school libraries in the United States and Canada.

2. Duane, Webster and Fred Heath, *LibQUAL+™ Spring 2002 Survey Results– AAHSL.* (Washington, DC: Association of Research Libraries, 2002).

3. See <http://www.libqual.org/Publications/index.cfm> for full presentation slides.

4. For the 2002 LibQUAL+™ survey norms online, see <http://www.libqual.org/Manage/Results/Norms_2002/index.cfm>.

5. Colleen Cook, Fred Heath, and Bruce Thompson, "Score Norms for Improving Library Service Quality: A LibQUAL+™ Study," *portal: Libraries and the Academy,* 2 (2002): 13-26.

6. Doug Joubert, Lyn Dennison, and Tamera P. Lee, "*Considering the Integration of Quantitative and Qualitative,*" presented at the AAHSL meeting on Nov 12, 2002, San Francisco, CA.

7. The Service Quality Evaluation Academy is an intensive five-day program that focuses on both qualitative and quantitative methods for collecting and analyzing library service quality data. The program emphasizes basic concepts and skills in measurement and data analysis that will be applicable to service quality evaluations. For more information, see <http://www.libqual.org/Events/index.cfm>.

LibQUAL+™ in a Problem-Based Learning (PBL) Medical School: The Case Study of the Medical Library and Peyton T. Anderson Learning Resources Center (LRC) at Mercer University School of Medicine in Macon, Georgia

Jan H. LaBeause

SUMMARY. This case study looks at the LibQUAL+™ 2002 survey results for the Medical Library and Peyton T. Anderson Learning Resources Center (LRC) at Mercer University School of Medicine in Macon, Georgia. Mercer has a problem-based learning (PBL) curriculum with a strong community-based component and a small student body. The effect PBL has on the library and LRC was felt to be a major contributing factor in the library's survey results. Several of Mercer's scores were higher compared to other libraries: a higher average for

---

Jan H. LaBeause is Director of the Medical Library and Peyton T. Anderson Learning Resources Center, Mercer University School of Medicine, Macon, GA (E-mail: labeause_j@mercer.edu).

[Haworth co-indexing entry note]: "LibQUAL+™ in a Problem-Based Learning (PBL) Medical School: The Case Study of the Medical Library and Peyton T. Anderson Learning Resources Center (LRC) at Mercer University School of Medicine in Macon, Georgia." LaBeause, Jan H. Co-published simultaneously in *Journal of Library Administration* (The Haworth Information Press, an imprint of The Haworth Press, Inc.) Vol. 40, No. 3/4, 2004, pp. 59-72; and: *Libraries Act on Their LibQUAL+™ Findings: From Data to Action* (ed: Fred M. Heath, Martha Kyrillidou, and Consuella A. Askew) The Haworth Information Press, an imprint of The Haworth Press, Inc., 2004, pp. 59-72. Single or multiple copies of this article are available for a fee from The Haworth Document Delivery Service [1-800-HAWORTH. 9:00 a.m. - 5:00 p.m. (EST). E-mail address: docdelivery@haworthpress.com].

http://www.haworthpress.com/web/JLA
© 2004 by The Haworth Press, Inc. All rights reserved.
Digital Object Identifier: 10.1300/J111v40n03_05

general satisfaction, a positive average service superiority score, and a higher frequency of daily library use on premises response. There were no instances in the gap analysis in which the library failed to meet minimum expectations. *[Article copies available for a fee from The Haworth Document Delivery Service: 1-800-HAWORTH. E-mail address: <docdelivery@haworthpress.com> Website: <http://www.HaworthPress.com> © 2004 by The Haworth Press, Inc. All rights reserved.]*

KEYWORDS. Service quality, problem-based learning, health sciences libraries, case studies

INTRODUCTION

Mercer University School of Medicine accepted its first class of medical students in 1982, into a fully integrated problem-based curriculum with a strong community-based education component, and ranks among the top in the nation in percentage of graduates entering family medicine residencies. The mission of the school is to train primary care physicians and other health professionals who will practice in rural and underserved areas of Georgia. Other educational programs offered include graduate training in Marriage and Family Therapy, Marriage and Family Services, and Public Health.

The Medical Library and Peyton T. Anderson Learning Resources Center (LRC) serve the school's faculty, staff and students on campus and across the state. To support off-campus faculty, students and rural health care entities, the library serves as the hub of the Georgia Interactive Network for Medical Information (GaIN) and provides an active program of outreach services.[1] The library faculty and staff support the school's PBL curriculum through a variety of traditional and nontraditional services, and are actively involved in the school and its mission.

In the past, we have periodically used questionnaires and focus groups to survey our users on how we are doing and received suggestions on what they'd like us to do differently. We also have participated every year in the comprehensive statistical report compiled by the Association of Academic Health Sciences Libraries. This quantitative report not only helps us to formulate our internal annual report but also provides a mechanism for benchmarking with other health sciences libraries.

LibQUAL+™ 2002 SURVEY

The opportunity to participate through a consortial agreement of AAHSL in a national survey measuring quality was welcomed. LibQUAL+™ 2002 provided a proven, reliable instrument for us to collect data about the quality of our services, participate in a national research project and benchmark in new areas with other libraries.

Administration

Like several other AAHSL participants, we chose to administer the survey to *all* students, full-time faculty and staff.[2] There were two reasons. First, the school is small with a total on-campus population of 534: 313 graduate students, 106 full-time faculty and 213 staff (includes 17 library faculty and staff). Second, at the time the survey was administered, e-mail accounts for students and e-mail groups for students, faculty and staff were managed by the library's technology staff. We knew all addresses were valid and that groups were current. The library director sent out three e-mails on behalf of the co-chairs of the library committee and herself on Monday mornings at one-week intervals. The first message was the longest and most informational. Subsequent e-mails reiterated the key points of the first. Each message included a link to the survey itself as well as an FAQ on the library's Web site. To further market the survey, we posted flyers throughout the school, put table tents by every public computer in the library and LRC, and advertised the survey and FAQ site on the library's Web site. As an attention-getter we heavily used the image of a palm-held device (PDA) in all our announcements since two were being given away as incentives to random participants (one at the national level and one to AAHSL participants). We also solicited local prizes from the university bookstore, area restaurants and other merchants. Incentives offered at the local level included movie tickets, free lunches and dinners from area restaurants, coffee mugs, t-shirts, and promotional items from a local sports team.

Response Rates

Of the 534 faculty, students and staff invited to participate, 167 (31.3%) started the survey, and 104 (19.5%) completed it.[3] Response rates for each category are shown in Table 1.

TABLE 1. Response Rates of Mercer Medical Library and LRC Participants

Category	Invited	Completed	%
Graduate Student	313	58	18.5%
Faculty	106	25	23.6%
Library Staff	17	9	52.9%
Staff	98	12*	12.2%
Total	**534**	**104**	**19.5%**

*Includes two staff members who are also enrolled in undergraduate programs elsewhere at Mercer University and selected Undergraduate in error on the demographics question.

Survey Results

Comments

Messages on the AAHSL participants' informal e-mail discussion group indicated that a significant number of respondents provided optional comments at the end of the survey.[4] Recurring themes at the reporting libraries were the need for more journals (especially online), remote access problems, and positive comments about staff. As seen in Table 2, of those completing the survey at Mercer, 44 took the time to submit comments (42.3%). The majority of these comments (28 or 63.6%) were compliments on specific library staff members or the staff in general. Other comments dealt with circulation policies, suggestions for purchase, and a desire for longer staffed hours. A couple of comments were received about on-site technology assistance needs, but no one stated a concern about access from home or office.

Frequency of Library Use

Like other libraries participating in the LibQUAL+™ 2002 survey [ARL-Aggregate, ARL-AAHSL], most of Mercer's respondents reported using the library on a weekly basis, both on the premises (39.78%) and electronically (37.63%), followed by monthly use on premises (26.88%).[5] However, as shown in Table 3, Mercer's users reported daily use on premises as 22.58%. This is considerably higher than the norm for the entire group of 164 libraries (12.04%) and for the 35 AAHSL libraries (10.62%).

TABLE 2. Comments Received from Mercer Medical Library and LRC Participants

Category	Completed Survey	Sent Comments	%
Graduate Student	58	26	44.8%
Faculty	25	11	44.0%
Library Staff	9	3	33.3%
Staff	12*	4	33.3%
Total	**104**	**44**	**42.3%**

*Includes two staff members who are also enrolled in undergraduate programs elsewhere at Mercer University and selected Undergraduate in error on the demographics question.

TABLE 3. Analysis of Frequency of Library Use from All User Groups*

Frequency	All Libraries	AAHSL Libraries	Mercer Medical Library and LRC
Daily Use on Premises	12.04%	10.62%	22.58%
Daily Electronic Use	21.18%	31.83%	17.20%
Weekly Use on Premises	40.07%	35.93%	39.78%
Weekly Electronic Use	38.90%	34.84%	37.63%
Monthly Use on Premises	29.98%	31.42%	26.88%
Monthly Electronic Use	20.38%	15.01%	21.51%
Quarterly Use on Premises	16.02%	19.54%	9.68%
Quarterly Electronic Use	11.41%	8.98%	13.98%
Never–Use on Premises	1.89%	2.49%	1.08%
Never–Electronic Use	8.13%	9.35%	9.68%

*Excludes Library Staff

General Satisfaction

Average scores for all user groups in all libraries participating in the LibQUAL+™ 2002 survey reflect a high level of satisfaction across the three broad dimensions of service. However, we were surprised and delighted to see that Mercer's scores were above the norms for both aggregated groups (Table 4). In addition, the institutional norms tables reveal that Mercer had the only positive average service superiority score (0.029065008), indicating that overall perceptions are higher than desired.[6]

Gap Analysis

Mercer, like all other libraries participating in LibQUAL+™ 2002, identified areas for improvement by looking at the "service adequacy" and the "service superiority" gaps between respondents' minimum and perceived, and desired and perceived, levels of service quality.[7] Mercer had no negative gaps. For the AAHSL aggregate group scores, only one of the items analyzed revealed a perceived level of service quality below users' minimum expectations–or, a negative gap–(Item #5 "making electronic resources accessible from my home or office" −0.04), but this was not identified as being a particularly pressing problem by Mercer respondents (1.36). The aggregated scores for all 164 participating libraries in the survey showed perceived levels of service quality less than users' minimum expectations for Items #2 (−0.05), 4 (−0.10) and 7 (−0.03).

TABLE 4. Analysis of Average Rating of General Satisfaction Scores from All User Groups*

Area of Satisfaction	All Libraries	AAHSL Libraries	Mercer Medical Library and LRC
Satisfaction with Treatment	7.30	7.47	8.52
Satisfaction with Support	6.84	7.05	8.23
Overall Quality of Service	7.14	7.35	8.28

*Excludes Library Staff

Survey items with mean scores that fall within the zone of tolerance (above users' minimum expectations, but below their desired level of service) indicate where most of the scores should fall. Mercer's areas are comparable to those reported by other AAHSL libraries. Convenient business hours, comprehensive electronic resources, and complete runs of journal titles are included among the top items common to both lists as shown in Table 5.

In addition, Mercer had a number of items in which users' indicated that their perceived level of service was greater than their desired level of service. As shown in Table 6, all of the "Affect of Service" item scores (Items #1, 4, 11, 14, 15, 17, 18, 20, 24) and several other items (Items #9, 13, 21, 23) fell into this category, including three out of the five local questions added by the AAHSL cohort (Items #2, 3, 4).

DISCUSSION

Mercer's scores that fell outside the norms for other libraries were discussed and analyzed further by the library faculty and staff as well as

TABLE 5. Gap Analysis: Items Perceived as Above Minimum but Less Than Desired ("Zone of Tolerance") by Mercer Medical Library and LRC Participants

Item # and Text	All Libraries	AAHSL Libraries	Mercer Medical Library and LRC
#2 Space that facilitates quiet study	−0.05	0.63	1.35
#3 Complete runs of journal titles	0.20	0.08	1.27
#5 Making electronic resources accessible from my home	0.34	−0.04	1.36
#6 Modern equipment that lets me easily access the information I need	0.11	0.36	1.32
#7 A library Website enabling me to locate information on my own	−0.03	0.32	1.21
#19 Convenient business hours	0.80	0.32	0.91
#1 of AAHSL Questions: Providing health information when and where I need it	N/A	0.58	1.55
#5 of AAHSL Questions: Having comprehensive electronic resources	N/A	0.02	1.17

TABLE 6. Gap Analysis: Items Perceived Greater Than Desired by Mercer Medical Library and LRC Participants

Item # and Text	All Libraries	AAHSL Libraries	Mercer Medical Library and LRC
#1 Willingness to help users	0.32	0.98	**2.11**
#4 Employees who are consistently courteous	**−0.10**	0.74	**1.78**
#9 Interdisciplinary library needs being addressed	0.24	0.34	**1.90**
#11 Dependability in handling users' service problems	0.01	0.50	**1.70**
#13 A place for reflection and creativity	0.20	0.94	**1.90**
#14 Giving users individual attention	0.43	0.89	**2.00**
#15 Employees who deal with users in a caring fashion	0.18	0.77	**1.81**
#17 Employees who have the knowledge to answer user questions	0.07	0.49	**1.38**
#18 Readiness to respond to users' questions	0.19	0.64	**1.77**
#20 Employees who instill confidence in users	0.29	0.84	**1.85**
#21 A comfortable and inviting location	0.06	0.84	**1.91**
#23 A contemplative environment	0.22	0.91	**1.27**
#24 Employees who understand the needs of their users	0.17	0.59	**1.68**
#2 of AAHSL Questions: Employees teaching me how to access or manage information	N/A	0.82	**1.70**
#3 of AAHSL Questions: An environment that facilitates group study and problem solving	N/A	0.78	**1.21**
#4 of AAHSL Questions: Access to information resources that support patient care	N/A	0.46	**1.38**

by the library committee made up of other medical school faculty and students. We looked at how our school and library are different, and how those differences may have affected our survey participants' responses.

PBL Curriculum

Mercer's problem-based curriculum is probably the strongest contributing factor to the school's atmosphere and the relationship among students, faculty and staff. It follows that it influences every department, program and service within the school. Since it is a student-centered curriculum and libraries are service departments, PBL has a dramatic impact on the library and its services.

Students

It has been well documented that PBL students differ in several ways from their traditional counterparts, and that those differences translate to a difference in the student's role as a library user.[8] PBL students must be prepared and must attend tutorial sessions or they will answer to their peers. Traditional students frequently rely on class notes from fellow students, faculty handouts or assigned texts in lieu of faithful attendance in class. PBL students prepare *before* sessions while traditional students study *after* lectures. As a result, PBL students spend more time in the library, and use a greater variety and number of resources.

The more frequent use of the library is indicated in Mercer's LibQUAL+™ survey results by the high "Daily Use on Premises" score mentioned previously and documented in Table 3. In addition, several comments were received concerning the need for longer hours, particularly during exams. At a time when the future of the "physical library" is being debated in a progressively online environment, it is refreshing to know that our users still want to come to the library and would stay longer if we were open!

Size

Primarily because of the PBL curriculum and its mission focused on training students to be primary care givers in rural and underserved areas of the state, Mercer's student body is comparatively small. As mentioned, we have participated in the AAHSL statistics every year, and have noted from analyzing those statistics and benchmarking efforts that we fall below the mean in most quantitative categories (Table 7).

TABLE 7. Comparison of Statistics Reported by Mercer's Library and LRC with Those for All AAHSL Libraries

Area	Mercer Medical Library and LRC	AAHSL Mean
Total Annual Expenditures	$1,359,180	$2,861,636
Total Library FTEs (faculty, staff and student workers)	22.70	38
Primary Clientele–Students	313	2,174
Monographs–Print Volumes	97,200	236,150
Unique Current Serials	1,302	2,327
Gate Count	157,837	279,667
No. of Reference Questions	10,402	26,369
Circulation*	83,610	210,721
Attendance at Educational Events#	1,479	2,082

*Includes External Print, External AV, Internal Print and Internal AV
#Includes Education Programs and Orientations

Being a small institution carries with it the advantage of creating a close-knit, collegial atmosphere in which everyone knows everyone else and there can be a lot of one-on-one personal attention. Here again, several of the optional comments received from LibQUAL+™ survey respondents mentioned that they feel welcomed, special and important when they come to the library because everyone knows their name.

Library Philosophy

Serving a small, PBL school has a strong influence on the library's philosophy. Part of the reason that "everyone is known by name" comes from a conscious customer service focus by everyone on the library staff including student workers. Our "customers" may not always be right, but they are the reason we are here and we never forget that! All library faculty, staff and student workers are recruited who have a strong customer service background, excellent people skills and a demonstrated "service" work ethic. Monthly staff meetings and other staff development events emphasize these qualities also and serve to sharpen those skills. Like any library staff, our emphasis is on being friendly but professional, courteous, approachable, knowledgeable, and eager to please. We believe in being upfront about what can be provided and when. We never say we *cannot* do something without offering an alternative, and strive to be consistent in our follow-up.

This philosophy is also reflected in our "place" within the school. The library faculty have academic appointments to the medical school faculty. The faculty and staff alike are actively engaged in the administrative, academic and social activities of the school, which makes them more visible and familiar to coworkers in other departments. Anecdotal evidence over the years shows that we are perceived within the school as collegial, service-oriented, knowledgeable, collaborative, cross-trained, creative, outgoing, and–not surprisingly–a lot of fun.

Outreach Services

While the library and LRC's service philosophy may not be very unique, our long-standing involvement in the school's community-based component is noteworthy and may explain why the remote electronic access problem identified by the AAHSL group (both on the e-mail discussion group and in the "gap" analysis of desired levels of service) was not an issue in Mercer's survey results.

Students' off-campus education with preceptors prompted the development of GaIN (Georgia Interactive Network for Medical Information) early in the school's history. From its inception, GaIN was designed as a model for a statewide computer-based medical information network to provide clinical and research information to students and primary care practitioners at the hospital or practice site. Based in the Mercer Medical Library and LRC, the network was established with a National Library of Medicine grant in 1983, and is celebrating its 20th anniversary this year. GaIN has been recognized by the Association of American Medical Colleges as an example of an academic initiative to address physician supply in rural areas, by the Federal Office of Rural Health Policy as a model for rural telehealth programs, and also by the Medical Library Association's Frank Bradway Rogers Information Advancement Award, for providing information outreach to rural health care practitioners and institutions, and serving as a national model of the central role of a library in information transfer.[9] The network has evolved over the years to keep up with technological advances and answer the needs of its users. It continues to make the resources of the library and LRC accessible to our students no matter where they are, supports our volunteer faculty who act as preceptors for our students, and serves the rural health care institutions where those preceptors practice.

CONCLUSIONS AND FUTURE PLANS

The LibQUAL+™ 2002 survey was relatively easy to administer, and we were well pleased with the response rates and results. In the final analysis, we feel that the greatest determinant in the scores received by Mercer's library was the PBL curriculum and other factors that are influenced by a problem-based learning format: heavier library usage by students, a small student body size, the library's customer service philosophy, increased visibility in the school, and an active outreach program. The areas identified in the survey for improvement are being addressed, and plans are underway to participate in the LibQUAL+™ 2003 survey.

Mercer University in general and the medical school in particular are due for accreditation visits from both the Southern Association of Colleges and Schools (SACS) and the Liaison Committee on Medical Education (LCME) in 2005. Therefore, all Mercer libraries have decided to participate in the broader constituency as a four-year private institution in the LibQUAL+™ 2003 survey. It is felt that the survey can provide a reliable, dynamic assessment component that both accrediting agencies require. The medical library is the only one serving a school with a problem-based learning curriculum. The other libraries serve undergraduate schools, and graduate programs with a more traditional format. It will be interesting to see how the baseline quality performance scores established for the medical library in 2002 will be affected by surveying all libraries in 2003.

ACKNOWLEDGMENTS

The author gratefully acknowledges access to the spreadsheets of survey results provided by Bruce Thompson for the *LibQUAL+™ Score Norms 2002*, and to James Shedlock for the AAHSL statistics from *2000-2001 Annual Statistics of Medical School Libraries in the United States and Canada*. Many thanks also to Tamera P. Lee, MLS, Professor and Director of Libraries, Robert B. Greenblatt M.D. Library, Medical College of Georgia, Augusta, Georgia for her assistance in interpreting the survey results.

NOTES

1. The Georgia Interactive Network (GaIN) for Medical Information is a non-profit, university-based electronic health care information network. Centered at the Mercer University School of Medicine (MUSM) in Macon, Georgia, GaIN was established in 1983 with a National Library of Medicine grant. It is an interactive network offering a wide range of information services to member health care individuals and institutions.

GaIN is also a partner and collaborator in many statewide educational, health care and information access programs. For more information about GaIN visit <http://gain. mercer.edu/about.asp>.

2. L. Dennison, Jan H. LaBeause, K. W. Rosati, F. A. Meakin, B. J. Schorre, W. Morton, *"LibQUAL+™: Southern Style,"* poster session presented at Southern Chapter of Medical Library Association, Nashville, TN.

3. Duane Webster and Fred Heath, *LibQUAL+™ Spring 2002 Survey Results–Mercer University School of Medicine, Medical Library & LRC.* (Washington, DC: Association of Research Libraries, 2002).

4. T. P. Lee 2002. *Exploring Outcomes Assessment: The AAHSL LibQUAL+™ Experience,* presentation at Association of Academic Health Sciences Libraries Business Meeting, San Francisco, November 11, 2002.

5. Duane Webster, and Fred Heath, *LibQUAL+™ Spring 2002 Aggregate Survey Results.* (Washington, DC: Association of Research Libraries, 2002); Duane Webster and Fred Heath. 2002. *LibQUAL+™ Spring 2002 Survey Results–AAHSL.* (Washington, DC: Association of Research Libraries, 2002); Duane Webster and Fred Heath. 2002. *LibQUAL+™ Spring 2002 Survey Results–ARL.* (Washington, DC: Association of Research Libraries, 2002).

6. For more information about score norms, see Bruce Thompson's *LibQUAL+™ Score Norms 2002,* available online at: http://www.coe.tamu.edu/~bthompson/libq2002.htm.

7. Association of Research Libraries, 2003 Survey Highlights: http://www.libqual. org/documents/admin/ExecSummary1.1_locked.pdf.

8. S. Anderson, M. G. Camp, J. R. Philp, "Library Utilization by Medical Students in a Traditional or Problem-Based Curriculum," in *Teaching and Assessing Clinical Competence,* eds. W. Bender, R. J. Hiemstra, A. J. Sharpabier (Groningen, The Netherlands: Boekwerk, 1990); J. Blake, "Library Resources for Problem-Based Learning: The Program Perspective," *Comput Methods Programs Biomed* 3-4 (1994):167-73; R. S. Donner, H. Bickley, "Problem-Based Learning in American Medical Education: An Overview," *Bull Med Libr Assoc* 3 (1993): 294-8; E. K. Eaton and E. Richardson, "Strategies for Libraries Serving Problem-Based Learning Programs" in *Problem- Based Learning as an Educational Strategy,* eds. P. A. J. Bouhuijs, H. G. Schmidt, H. J. M. van Berkel (Maastricht: Network of Community-Oriented Educational Institutions for Health Sciences, 1994), 171-176; Fitzgerald D. "Problem-Based Learning and Libraries: The Canadian Experience." *Health Libr Rev 1996* 13, no. 1:13-32; J. G. Marshall, D. Fitzgerald, L. Busby, G. Heaton, "A Study of Library Use in Problem-Based and Traditional Medical Curricula," *Bull Med Libr Assoc* 3 (1993): 299-305; J. A. Rankin, "Problem-Based Medical Education: Effect on Library Use," *Bull Med Libr Assoc* 1 (1992): 36-43; K. Saunders, D. E. Northup, and S. P. Mennin, "The Library in a Problem-Based Curriculum," in *Implementing Problem-Based Education,* ed. A. Kaufman (New York: Springer, 1985).

9. M. H. Littlemeyer, and D. Martin, "Academic Initiatives to Address Physician Supply in Rural Areas of the United States: A Selected Bibliography, 1980-1989," *Acad Med* 12 (1990): S55-S84; J. P. Witherspoon, S. M. Johnstone and C. J. Wasem, *Rural Telehealth: Telemedicine, Distance Education and Informatics for Rural Health Care: Report of the Office of Rural Health Policy* (Boulder, CO: WICHE Publications, 1993); "Frank Bradway Rogers Information Advancement Award," (presentation of awards in Proceedings, Ninety-second Annual Meeting, Medical Library Association, Inc., Washington, DC, May 15-21, 1992). _____ *Bull Med Libr Assoc* 1, (1993): 113.

REFERENCES

Association of Academic Health Sciences Libraries (2002). *2000-2001 Annual Statistics of Medical School Libraries in the United States and Canada*, 24th ed., Association of Academic Health Sciences Libraries, Chicago, IL.

Association of Research Libraries/Texas A&M University (2002). *LibQUAL+™ Spring 2002 Aggregate Survey Results: 1–Summary Statistics and Graphs*, Association of Research Libraries, Washington, DC.

Association of Research Libraries/Texas A&M University (2002). *LibQUAL+™ Spring 2002 Survey Results–AAHSL: 3–Group Statistics and Graphs*, Association of Research Libraries, Washington, DC.

K. Saunders, D. E. Northup, S. P. Mennin, "The Library in a Problem-Based Curriculum," in *Implementing Problem-Based Education*, ed. A. Kaufman (New York: Springer, 1985): 71-88.

S. Anderson, M. G. Camp, J. R. Philp, "Library Utilization by Medical Students in a Traditional or Problem-Based Curriculum," in *Teaching and Assessing Clinical Competence*, ed. W. Bender, R. J. Hiemstra, A. J. Sharpabier (Groningen, The Netherlands: Boekwerk, 1990): 77-80.

LaBeause, J. H. (1999). "Health Sciences Library Programs in Problem-Based Learning Institutions: The Lessons Learned," in *Handbook on Problem-Based Learning*, ed. J. A. Rankin (Forbes, New York).

LaBeause J. H. (1999). "Implications of a Problem-Based Learning Curriculum for Health Care Libraries and Librarians: Practical Applications in Preparing for Change," in *Handbook on Problem-Based Learning*, ed. J. A. Rankin (Forbes, New York).

The Evolution and Application of Assessment Strategies at the University of Colorado Health Sciences Center

Rick B. Forsman

SUMMARY. Librarians at the University of Colorado Health Sciences Center (UCHSC) began collecting user survey data in 1984. Over time, surveys have been modified to capture new usage patterns as users shifted from walk-in use to remote electronic access of library resources. Taking advantage of the evolution of outcome measurement techniques and new tools, UCHSC librarians have incorporated user feedback into strategic planning and fiscal reallocations. Use of the LibQUAL+™ survey has confirmed past data and decisions, and points to a clear path for the future. Survey results will drive the physical design and service deployment to be showcased in a new state-of-the-art biomedical library due to open in 2006. *[Article copies available for a fee from The Haworth Document Delivery Service: 1-800-HAWORTH. E-mail address: <docdelivery@haworthpress.com> Website: <http://www.HaworthPress.com> © 2004 by The Haworth Press, Inc. All rights reserved.]*

Rick B. Forsman is Director, Denison Memorial Library, University of Colorado Health Sciences Center, Denver, CO (E-mail: rick.forsman@uchsc.edu).

[Haworth co-indexing entry note]: "The Evolution and Application of Assessment Strategies at the University of Colorado Health Sciences Center." Forsman, Rick B. Co-published simultaneously in *Journal of Library Administration* (The Haworth Information Press, an imprint of The Haworth Press, Inc.) Vol. 40, No. 3/4, 2004, pp. 73-82; and: *Libraries Act on Their LibQUAL+™ Findings: From Data to Action* (ed: Fred M. Heath, Martha Kyrillidou, and Consuella A. Askew) The Haworth Information Press, an imprint of The Haworth Press, Inc., 2004, pp. 73-82. Single or multiple copies of this article are available for a fee from The Haworth Document Delivery Service [1-800-HAWORTH, 9:00 a.m. - 5:00 p.m. (EST). E-mail address: docdelivery@haworthpress.com].

http://www.haworthpress.com/web/JLA
© 2004 by The Haworth Press, Inc. All rights reserved.
Digital Object Identifier: 10.1300/J111v40n03_06

KEYWORDS. Health sciences libraries, university libraries, assessment, strategic planning, service quality, resource management

INTRODUCTION

The University of Colorado Health Sciences Center (UCHSC) in Denver is one of the top-ranked academic health sciences centers in the United States. Recently, the campus has undertaken a physical relocation of all programs to a new site that affords space for the long-term expansion of all facilities and an expanded presence in all aspects of health science education, research and patient care. Build-out of the $1.3 billion new campus will greatly increase research space, raising the possibility that UCHSC could become one of the top ten research institutions in the country. With seventeen clinical and research buildings under construction or already completed, the campus is about to begin work on its new educational buildings, including a state-of-the-art biomedical library.

For over fifty years the existing campus has been served by the Denison Memorial Library, a medium-sized academic health sciences library with approximately 265,000 volumes, 50 FTE staff, and a concentration on biomedical databases and journals. For the past twenty-five years the library has participated in the annual collection of data conducted by the Association of Academic Health Sciences Libraries, most recently published in its 24th edition.[1] Denison's librarians began collecting data from walk-in users nearly twenty years ago, seeking to better understand who was using the traditional library services and whether there were predictable patterns of usage. With the advent of electronic resources, however, it became clear that user behaviors no longer reflected the norms familiar from in-person use of print materials. Accordingly, the librarians at Denison developed a local survey instrument to examine access to electronic resources. Availability of the LibQUAL+™ survey provided a third approach to measuring user behavior, this time with a broader perspective and a focus on client satisfaction.

INITIAL EFFORTS TO UNDERSTAND USE OF THE LIBRARY

In 1984 the UCHSC contracted with Peat, Marwick, Mitchell & Co. (now known as KPMG) to provide data documenting the services and costs incurred in supporting federally funded research programs hosted on the campus. One section of this contract required Peat Marwick to devise a reliable methodology to measure library usage, administer a paper survey instrument to gather data, and conduct a random sampling of the library's walk-in users. Each time clients entered the building, they were asked to complete a short form indicating the primary purpose for that visit, the specific services they had tapped, and their affiliation with the campus. Because surveys were handed directly to each person entering the library and because users were told their completion of the form was critical, a 90% response rate was achieved.

Results of the 1984 survey provided the library with its first clear overview of who was using the library, for what purposes, and the departments with which they were interacting. The campus subsequently hired KPMG to coordinate the same sampling of library activity in 1987, 1991 and 1998. Comparison of the results of the four survey periods produced a very consistent longitudinal picture of which groups were heavy library users (e.g., members of the general public were a significant component of walk-in users), their primary focus, and services utilized. Not surprisingly, the response rate dropped as users became inured to the paper survey forms.

The repeated surveys documented students as the most frequent walk-in users of the library and revealed that the monograph collection was of most importance to them. Not surprisingly, faculty came to the library primarily to use print journals and bibliographic indexes. Usage patterns by school and other subsets of the campus populations remained relatively stable until 1992 when the School of Pharmacy moved from the Boulder campus to the UCHSC campus, after which time pharmacy users became a central user group.

By the time the 1998 survey was administered, however, Denison's services had undergone significant changes in keeping with developments at the national level. Libraries everywhere, and academic health sciences libraries in particular, had embraced online bibliographic databases and the emerging full-text electronic information resources. Data showed that walk-in traffic was stable compared to growth in earlier years, but the librarians were aware that many users had discovered digital access as a timesaving replacement for a physical trip to the library. Besides distributing paper surveys in 1998, the library created some brief Web pages and forced users to respond to four simple questions whenever they wished to connect to Ovid, one of the library's key biomedical bibliographic databases. It was evident, however, that better data would be needed if we were to have a complete picture of changing behavior.

LOCAL ELECTRONIC SURVEY DEVELOPMENT

In 1999, Denison librarians agreed to take a new survey approach and to focus on digital access. Using commercially available survey software, a Web-based questionnaire was created to gather demographic data and query users about use of electronic resources. The software was able to capture individual responses, tabulate aggregate data, produce some basic reports, and allow data to be downloaded for more sophisticated statistical manipulation. In the spring of 2000, an e-mail message was sent to all campus users with an active address on the "UCHSC.edu" Internet domain. E-mail readers were invited to click on an embedded URL that opened the Web survey. A total of 1,344 responses were received in the first fifteen days, with a final response rate of almost 32%. Nearly 20% of all respondents reported making daily use of electronic resources, compared to 1.5% who made daily use of print materials. More than 80% of all respondents said online bibliographic databases and full-text journals were very useful to them. The majority of respondents expressed a desire for more full-text journals. A large number of free text comments indicated that users wanted more training in performing searches and retrieving relevant items.

The same methodology was used in the spring of 2001. Survey questions were pared down from sixteen to thirteen with some rephrasing. This second local survey produced 1,031 usable responses for a response rate of 22%. Results were consistent with those from the previous year and highlighted changes that had occurred in resource availability and usage during the intervening twelve months. The library had licensed new digital products, and the usage data confirmed intuitive impressions that the new resources were being well used. While 40% of respondents reported using print materials on a monthly basis, 53% reported using electronic resources weekly and another 16% used them monthly; 57% of respondents reported that they had increased their use of electronic resources in the past twelve months; 4% indicated they cancelled personal or departmental subscriptions to print journals because of online access through the library. Free text comments applauded the greater number and scope of full-text online resources, at the same time pleading for yet more digital content.

With the spring 2001 administration of its survey of electronic use, the library completed its second stage of measuring usage. Thanks to the KPMG data and its own online surveys, the librarians had a clear understanding of walk-in user behavior and a strong impression of the impact of electronic information resources. We knew what people were using, where usage was tapering off, and that the use of scholarly information in electronic format was escalating on a very steep slope. What was still lacking, however, was an understanding of user satisfaction with overall library services and expectations about specific services. Obtaining this perspective would require a new technique.

As Denison's librarians were finishing their review of all previously accumulated data, the Association of Academic Health Sciences Libraries (AAHSL) was preparing to step beyond the simple collection of annual benchmarking data. AAHSL reached an agreement with the Association of Research Libraries (ARL) and Texas A&M University to allow a subset of AAHSL libraries to participate in the planned 2002 administration to the LibQUAL+™ survey instrument. The development of the LibQUAL+™ survey methodology had been widely reported in the literature, e.g., Cook and Heath, 2001.[2]

Individual libraries participating in LibQUAL+™ can identify where their services need improvement in the eyes of their users. They also can compare their service quality with that of peer institutions in an effort to develop benchmarks and an understanding of best practices across institutions. These benefits were in keeping with the philosophy of Denison librarians, and the UCHSC committed to joining other AAHSL libraries in the next survey. This was made possible in part due to financial underwriting from the National Library of Medicine, which wished to assist academic health sciences libraries in entering into a new era of outcomes assessment. Cullen[3] has emphasized the importance of testing library assumptions in a time of rapid change in user behavior and attitudes. Health sciences librarians were in agreement and were heartened by the receptivity of colleagues at ARL and Texas A&M University.

THE LibQUAL+™ EXPERIENCE

Participation in the LibQUAL+™ survey was facilitated for Denison and its users because the administration of the instrument was very similar to the methodology employed for the two earlier, local surveys.

Once again users received an e-mail request for their cooperation. They clicked on an embedded URL, and completed a Web form. Data were tabulated at Texas A&M University and distributed to health sciences libraries in the summer of 2002, with ARL staff providing a workshop on interpretation in the fall of that year. Denison librarians received data specific to their own institution, aggregate data for all AAHSL participants, and aggregate data across all 164 libraries that took part. Although it has been helpful to compare Denison data to that of the full AAHSL cohort and somewhat helpful to compare AAHSL data to that of ARL libraries, the aggregate data of all 164 participants has been of limited interest because it mixes such different types of libraries with different missions and user populations. Even comparisons of AAHSL to ARL libraries are of limited value because of the vastly different ratios between faculty and students on specialized versus general campuses. Health sciences faculty are much more demanding than large numbers of undergraduate students.

UCHSC responses were very consistent with the results of prior surveys performed by Denison librarians. Users tended to respond within the first forty-hours after receiving the e-mail invitation. The new survey elicited a strong response rate until the greater length and complexity of the LibQUAL+™ instrument caused discouragement and significant drop-off about three quarters of the way through the questions. Whereas 1,035 people completed the first three pages of the online survey, this plummeted to only 681 individuals finishing the fourth page. The same drop-off pattern applied for AAHSL libraries as a whole, suggesting that the length of the questionnaire exceeds the patience level of health science users who work under extreme time constraints.

Denison's overall levels of user satisfaction were quite high with a score of 7.4 out of 9.0 for 'overall quality of service.' Nearly 68% reported daily or weekly use of electronic resources, and 35% reported walk-in use with the same frequency. To the chagrin of librarians, 7.8% said they never use electronic resources despite continual efforts to inform users of their availability and usefulness.

Across all user groups the library was perceived as exceeding the minimum service expectations, and in some instances the library was approaching the optimal desired level of service. Weaknesses appeared in not satisfying user desire for complete runs of print journals, comprehensive electronic resources, and convenience and reliability of remote access. In retrospect, it may have been misleading to suggest to users that it is reasonable to expect to have comprehensive electronic resources because the marketplace does not in fact offer such complete scope. Once again, users took the time to enter hundreds of free text comments, often in praise of the staff and the quality of service they provide. And they asked for yet more digital content.

COMPARING RESULTS OVER TIME

McCord and Nofsinger[4] have reported multi-year user assessment at the Washington State University libraries, and Boykin[5] has described the importance of gathering user data to validate decision-making and strategic planning. Denison librarians have approached user data from the same viewpoint, examining it for consistency over time and using it to make critical choices in a period of transmutation. It is clear that Denison user groups are stable over time, that electronic access adds tremendous benefits, and that we must continue to allocate funds towards digital products while at the same time taking every opportunity to market them to the campus at large. This is particularly true as the UCHSC migrates departments and programs from its existing site to the new campus. At a time when the Health Sciences Center straddles two locations, online access becomes the only workable strategy for providing equitable information access to all personnel.

Ahead of us lies the task of delving into our LibQUAL+™ data and earlier surveys to see if we can identify which subpopulations have yet to understand or appreciate the range and depth of electronic resources at their disposal. The aggregate data suggest that users are not keeping current with the ever-expanding digital products Denison has added to its collection. Although we do not pretend to come anywhere near the claim of having 'comprehensive' electronic resources, we believe our users underestimate what is already in place. It may be helpful to identify those groups making greatest use of the resources in hopes of learning how we can better reach the less informed.

The disparate user responses gathered over time mirror the imperfect usage data we receive from the vendors of the online products we license. More people are using a broader array of electronic resources while walk-in use of the building is going down. Data show that clinicians and researchers are making more use of electronic resources than they did of print materials. Because these two groups are often place-bound by their commitment to see patients or to oversee laboratory experiments, they have difficulty making physical trips to the library. With online access at their fingertips, however, they are enjoying a new level of information convenience, and their use of digital access is likely to jump even further when 600,000 square feet of new research space opens on the new campus in 2004. The library has rapidly become one of the major digital traffic points on the campus network, and the new library facility will need to be designed as an even greater hub of knowledge transfer.

Students remain the heaviest walk-in users of the library. Although the faculty is beginning to substitute online access for walk-in use, students continue to want to come to the library for a number of reasons. As we design the new biomedical library for 2006, this emphasis on student-centered space will influence many of our decisions about layout, study rooms, and service points. It is invaluable to have data and trend lines showing various changes in user preferences and usage patterns.

CONCLUSIONS

Denison's librarians are engaged in monumental decisions during a time of huge change. Exciting new products and services are available. User behaviors are shifting. We face the challenge of building a new, future-oriented facility. The state of Colorado is in severe economic disarray. The combination of these factors will force many changes over a relatively short period of time, making it imperative that decisions are based on facts and longitudinal evidence. Fortunately, we can bring forward the data we have collected over time to help tell our story and describe our future.

The data are also critical in the face of Colorado's current fiscal distress. In the immediacy of state budget cuts, we have used our data as evidence that the library can look at being open fewer hours each week with less negative impact on users than would have been true in earlier years. In addition, we must look at other modifications of past practice and professional attitudes in light of what the data tell us about the future. For example, reference librarians who derive great satisfaction from serving individual users must find a way to derive an equal sense of reward from supporting the burgeoning and faceless population of remote users, a group not always as immediate or direct in expressing its appreciation for good service. We must find ways to preserve and sustain our relationship with faculty who no longer come to the library in person. We cannot let them become isolated and forgetful about what we offer and the value the library contributes. When the faculty fails to come to us, we have become more assertive about going to their offices,

labs and classrooms. With clear indications that this trend will not reverse itself, outreach has taken on a new urgency.

Likewise, communication must increase in other ways. We have invited our users to tell us about their needs and expectations, and we have
listened closely to their input. Now we must speak up and sustain the di-
alogue. It has become evident, for instance, that users understand even
less than they did in the past just what the library staff does. Because we
don't tell them what we do to make electronic resources accessible, they
make simplistic assumptions about how little work this must entail. In
times of budget reductions, it is very unwise to allow patrons to underestimate our contribution and value. If they do not perceive the essential
roles and the expertise of staff, we will lose funding and be forced to reduce our most precious asset.

As the importance of online access is documented, there is also
greater impetus for working with faculty colleagues who control the
curriculum. If faculty and student success is directly tied to their ability
to retrieve pertinent information, the curriculum must incorporate basic
information competencies essential to learning, research or clinical
care. Denison librarians have been well received as we move into a
leadership position in teaching these competencies, and we have reallo-
cated more personnel to this educational role.

In summary, today's health sciences environment necessitates that
all libraries move into outcomes assessment. Beginning with simple
data gathering, the librarians at the University of Colorado Health Sciences Center have refined and reshaped measurement techniques to
gain a broad, longitudinal picture of changing user needs. Besides bol-
stering the factual basis for decision-making, participation in the testing
of instruments such as LibQUAL+™ gives the library the advantage of
greater credibility within the parent institution. Methodologies for assessment will continue to evolve and improve, allowing librarians to
better demonstrate the value of the investment in library staff and resources. New data will support librarians as they design new facilities
and revamp their services for the digital age.

NOTES

1. Association of Academic Health Sciences Libraries, *Association of Academic
Health Sciences Libraries Annual Statistics of Medical School Libraries in the United
States and Canada: 2000-2001* (Seattle, WA: Association of Academic Health Sci-
ences Libraries).

2. Colleen Cook and Fred Heath, "Users' Perceptions of Library Service Quality: A LibQUAL+™ Qualitative Study," *Library Trends,* 49 (2001): 548-84.

3. Rowena Cullen, "Perspectives on User Satisfaction Surveys," *Library Trends* 49, (2001): 662-86.

4. Sarah K. McCord, and Mary M. Nofsinger, "Continuous Assessment at Washington State University Libraries: A Case Study," *Performance Measurement and Metrics,* 3, no. 2 (2002): 68-73.

5. Joseph F. Boykin, "LibQUAL+™ as a Confirming Resource," *Performance Measurement and Metrics,* 3, no. 2 (2002): 74-77.

The LibQUAL+™ Challenge:
An Academic Medical Center's Perspective, Duke University

Richard Peterson
Beverly Murphy
Stephanie Holmgren
Patricia L. Thibodeau

SUMMARY. In March 2002, the Duke University Medical Center Library administered the LibQUAL+™ survey instrument, which measures library users' perceptions of service quality and identifies gaps between desired, perceived, and minimum expectations of service. This case study represents the Library's decisions regarding participants, approaches used to reach them, problems encountered with the survey, and the results of the data for the health care community. We will also explore how including hospital staff in the survey impacted our results. *[Article copies available for a fee from The Haworth Document Delivery Service: 1-800-HAWORTH. E-mail address: <docdelivery@haworthpress.com> Website: <http://www.HaworthPress.com> © 2004 by The Haworth Press, Inc. All rights reserved.]*

Richard Peterson (E-mail: peter073@mc.duke.edu) is Deputy Director; Beverly Murphy (E-mail: murph005@mc.duke.edu) is Assistant Director of Marketing and Publications; Stephanie Holmgren (E-mail: holmg001@mc.duke.edu) is Information Services Librarian; and Patricia L. Thibodeau (E-mail: thibo001@mc.duke.edu) is Associate Dean for Library Services, all at Duke University Medical Center Library, Durham, NC.

[Haworth co-indexing entry note]: "The LibQUAL+™ Challenge: An Academic Medical Center's Perspective, Duke University." Peterson, Richard et al. Co-published simultaneously in *Journal of Library Administration* (The Haworth Information Press, an imprint of The Haworth Press, Inc.) Vol. 40, No. 3/4, 2004, pp. 83-98; and: *Libraries Act on Their LibQUAL+™ Findings: From Data to Action* (ed: Fred M. Heath, Martha Kyrillidou, and Consuella A. Askew) The Haworth Information Press, an imprint of The Haworth Press, Inc., 2004, pp. 83-98. Single or multiple copies of this article are available for a fee from The Haworth Document Delivery Service [1-800-HAWORTH, 9:00 a.m. - 5:00 p.m. (EST). E-mail address: docdelivery@haworthpress.com].

http://www.haworthpress.com/web/JLA
© 2004 by The Haworth Press, Inc. All rights reserved.
Digital Object Identifier: 10.1300/J111v40n03_07

KEYWORDS. Academic libraries, library services, assessment, customer satisfaction, service quality, case studies

INTRODUCTION

Although the LibQUAL+™ tool has been developed for academic library users, academic health science libraries have chosen to test the tool to see how effectively it measures service quality in the more multi-faceted environment of an academic health center. In addition to the traditional academic community of faculty, students and general administrative staff, a diverse mix of other health professionals and research staff usually exists within the health care community served by the library. Some universities also own their hospitals, thus increasing the complexity of the immediate patron populations served by the health sciences library.

Duke University Medical Center Library (DUMCL) serves such an environment, requiring us to address the information needs of practicing health professionals, as well as the expectations of the teaching and research programs within the university. This paper will discuss the challenges we faced in making decisions regarding whom to survey, the approaches used to reach the targeted participants, problems encountered with the survey, and finally, the results for the Duke Medical Center and Hospital communities.

THE MEDICAL CENTER LIBRARY
AND ITS USER POPULATION

Duke University Medical Center Library supports the teaching, research and patient care missions of the Duke University Medical Center and Health System. The 300,000-volume collection focuses on current clinical and research information, while maintaining older volumes of major journals and textbooks for research and scholarly pursuits. Given the dispersed nature of the campus facilities and hectic schedules of clinicians and researchers, many users rarely enter the physical library. As a result, electronic resources have become an essential part of our collection. Determining satisfaction with services and resources of these virtual patrons has become an increasing challenge.

Within the Medical Center, the Library serves the School of Medicine, with approximately 400 medical students and over 800 residents and fellows. Traditional medical school training is compressed into three years in order that medical students may spend their third year working on special projects, in research laboratories, or pursuing MBA, MPH, or doctoral degrees. In addition, the School supports the Physician's Assistant program, a doctoral program in Physical Therapy, and a master's-level clinical research-training program.

The faculty that supports the School of Medicine and its related training programs is distributed among 7 basic sciences and 11 clinical departments. The latter have over 75 divisions representing subspecialties. Among the 1,515 faculty members, there are many that cross the borders of basic sciences research, clinical practice and teaching–performing two or more of these functions every day.

The School of Nursing (SON), although smaller, is highly active and developing new degree programs and tracts. At the time of the survey, SON offered on- and off-campus master's degrees in nursing, and had received approval for a new accelerated bachelor's degree and a program for doctoral candidates.

The Medical Center also has a large population of over 6,000 support staff representing clerical, research, and administrative positions. While not classified as traditional library users, many of these employees regularly use the Library. For example, clerical workers often track down articles and citations for faculty. Similarly, research associates and administrators use our resources to monitor new developments and trends in their specialty areas.

The Library has the perfect location for serving Duke's clinical community as well. It sits almost in the center of the large walkway between Duke Hospital and the Duke Clinics. The hospital has more than 3,000 health professionals (nurses, pharmacists, etc.) in addition to basic support services staff. It also serves as a primary training site for medical students as well as residents. In addition, numerous collaborative training programs exist that use the hospital for educational rotations. The Duke Clinic not only provides a patient referral base for the hospital, but also offers ambulatory care training for residents, medical and other students.

Over the years, Duke has developed a health system through acquiring, managing, and collaborating with other hospitals and other types of health agencies. Two hospitals are part of the health system. Durham Regional Hospital has its own library services and relies on the Medical Center Library only for backup. However, Raleigh Community

Hospital and other health system members do not have on-site library services and access health information through the Medical Center Library.

DEFINING THE SURVEY POPULATION

The Library's first challenge was to identify and clearly define the participants for LibQUAL+™. As mentioned above, significant crossover exists among the different worlds at Duke. For example, a faculty member may deliver care in the clinic, maintain a research lab, as well as have admitting privileges at Duke and Durham Regional Hospitals. A health care worker may work at Durham Regional, but be paid by Duke Hospital or another clinical department. Given the complexities of our user population, it was critical to clearly define our targeted participant groups in order to generate meaningful survey results.

We knew that our community would not endure repeated surveys, so we decided to cast as wide a net as possible for our first survey and include not just heavy core users but also the occasional and virtual users. We also wanted to ensure that some user groups, such as hospital staff, would not be disenfranchised if they were not given a chance to voice their opinions. The next issue was to decide which groups to include to have a valid profile of our primary users.

Our core user population was easy to identify–Medical Center students, residents, faculty, and staff. We assumed that these groups would be fairly easy to reach through existing e-mail routing lists within the schools or our own patron files.

Another targeted survey group was Duke Hospital and the Duke Clinics. Since the hospital represents 41% of our user base, and because the Library serves as the hospital's primary information resource, we hoped that the data would help counter recent budget challenges made by the Hospital. Given the different work environment for hospital staff, as compared to our other users, we were also interested in seeing how satisfied they were with our services.

The decision whether to include the Duke Clinic staff (non-physicians) was difficult. While this population does not use the Library as much as other groups, due to busy schedules, they do have teaching and research responsibilities that would necessitate using our resources. Therefore, we chose to include them in order to solicit potentially informative feedback. Our last decision was to exclude Health System members. While the Library provides support to our affiliate hospitals, they do not influence the allocation of resources and development of services.

Fitting all these groups into the position and affiliation categories of the survey's demographic profile proved difficult for several reasons. First, data was not available from either human resources or the departments identifying exact numbers of employees in each category. As a result, we made best guesses based on existing staffing patterns or old data. The other concern with completing the profile was the potential for double counting staff due to the multiple roles of our employees. Take, for example, a research nurse who works part-time in the hospital, but also assists in a research lab. With the survey population defined, the next task was to determine the best mechanisms for reaching our target audience.

THE PROCESS

Institutional Review Board Approval

Since the LibQUAL+™ survey involves human subjects, one of our first steps in the process was to obtain Institutional Review Board (IRB) approval to conduct the survey. Because the risk to participants was minimal, the survey was routed through the expedited review process rather than the lengthier scheduled review of the entire IRB membership. Despite being off to a good start, we faced several unanticipated requirements. First, the Library's Associate Dean and Deputy Director needed to complete training related to human subject research and to successfully pass the post-training test. Second, we were also asked to edit some of the wording in our messages to survey respondents. This included changing the word "invite" to "ask" in the survey e-mail message and adding wording to clarify the steps that would be taken to ensure confidentiality. While we felt the confidentiality issue was more than adequately covered in the documentation submitted, we made the changes and received approval to conduct the survey. Future surveys will require only that we renew the initial approval.

Mass Mailing

Because of the diversity of programs at Duke and our desire to have those broad-based opinions represented in the survey, we decided to do a mass mailing to our primary user population of approximately 12,500.

This included students and staff in the Schools of Medicine and Nursing; faculty and staff in the clinical and basic sciences departments; clerical, clinical, and administrative staff in the Hospital, including residents, nurses, and other health professionals; and clerical, clinical, and administrative staff in the Private Diagnostic Clinic (PDC).

Meeting with Office of Information Technology

Since Duke has a policy for large-scale e-mailing to more than 500 people, we decided to meet with representatives from the Office of Information Technology (OIT). The greater part of this meeting was devoted to discussing the process and reviewing options for mass e-mailing to the selected Medical Center and Hospital user groups.

We were surprised to find that OIT did not already have e-mail lists readily available for the user groups we were targeting. While they could create some specific lists only for faculty and students in the Schools of Medicine and Nursing, they were able to provide broader lists for other groups. We still faced the challenge of being able to exclude specific employee categories from these generated lists. We had hoped to eliminate certain support staff like Housekeeping and Engineering and Operations and Operations. However, due to technical complexities, such groups could not be eliminated.

In order to generate these targeted lists, relevant addresses would be retrieved from records with Duke Medical Center box numbers or those with appropriate e-mail address endings (i.e., name@.mc.duke.edu). Since OIT would not be able to retrieve a list for residents and interns, the Library would need to retrieve that list from the Associate Dean for Graduate Medicine Education and forward it to OIT.

Due to the nature and size of this mailing, all messages would be sent by OIT. The Library would provide the specific text for the messages, the dates when they were to go out, and the reply-address (mailbox). We also discussed the types of return mail the Library would receive including out of office, delivery failure/retry notice, and bounced mail from bad addresses. Although we were advised not to take action on these messages, we were encouraged to explore them for inquiries, comments, and other concerns requiring replies.

Permissions Needed

Since large-scale e-mail communications within groups or units require their implicit or explicit prior approval, we also needed to get permissions from the various groups before the e-mails could be sent. A letter had already been sent in January 2002 by the Library's Associate Dean seeking permission from the deans and administrators to send e-mail messages about the survey to Medical Center and Hospital faculty, staff, and students. To effectively coordinate plans for distribution of the survey in March 2002, we had asked to be notified of all permissions granted by February 8, 2002. After our meeting with OIT in February, this letter was modified and sent to additional parties that needed to be notified.

Messages Sent

Once permissions were secured, we were ready to launch the survey. A total of four plain text messages were sent to Duke's faculty, staff, and students and were strategically timed to arrive in their mailboxes on each Monday in March, 2002 (see Figure 1).

Since it took several hours to disseminate the messages, OIT sent them on Sunday evenings. Rather than regenerate the list prior to each

FIGURE 1. E-Mail Message Sent to Respondents on March 4, 2002

TO: Duke Faculty, Staff and Students

FROM: Pat Thibodeau, Associate Dean for Library Services

SUBJECT: LIBRARY QUALITY SURVEY COMING

Your opinion counts! And, it means a lot to the Duke Medical Center Library!

As we plan for the future of the Medical Center Library, it is important that we understand our users' perceptions and expectations so that we can provide the services that you need.

In a few days, you will receive an e-mail providing you with a link to a library service quality survey, known as LibQUAL+™. By responding to the survey, you will provide essential information for us to use in planning our future. The survey is part of a North American effort led by the Association of Research Libraries, American Association of Health Science Libraries, and the National Library of Medicine to measure library service quality and identify best practices among health sciences libraries.

We would greatly appreciate your help. When you receive the e-mail, please take the time to go to the Web-based survey and complete it.

Thank you for your participation.

[For more information about the survey, visit our "Frequently Asked Questions" page at http://www.mclibrary.duke.edu/limited/libqual.pdf]

new mailing, the same list was used for all four mailings. The first e-mail sent on March 4 consisted of a general message announcing the survey and its purpose, and an alert that an e-mail message would soon arrive with a link to the survey. The second message sent on March 11 was a request to complete the survey which included the Website URL, and urged participants to respond no later than ten days after receiving the e-mail. The third e-mail sent on May 18 was a reminder-message to complete the survey, along with a "thank you" and a "disregard" expression if it had already been done. The e-mail sent on May 25 was a final reminder of the last chance to complete the survey.

Marketing

The Library publicized the 2002 LibQUAL+™ survey using the following venues:

- *We Need Your Help*! Announcement promoted on the front page of the Library's Website during the month of March. The message was modified appropriately on March 4, 11, 18, and 25 to correspond with the timing of the e-mail messages.
- Article in February issue of Library's newsletter, *Medical Center Library News*.
- Article in March 18 issue of *Inside DUMC*, Medical Center's newsletter.
- Poster display in Library lobby for the month of March.
- PDF version of LibQUAL+™ FAQ available on Library's Website.
- Various meetings outside the Library attended by staff.

Problems Encountered and Lessons Learned

Despite all the planning that goes into implementing a survey, there are always unexpected technical and human challenges that may affect survey results. Highlighted below are four of the issues we encountered.

Lotus Notes Browser

The Duke University Medical Center uses Lotus Notes for electronic mail, which defaults to the Notes Web browser when loading a link from e-mail. While successfully tested at the Library prior to release of the survey, we received numerous reports of memory allocation error messages and distorted formatting of the survey. Despite a high return of over 800 surveys, this technical problem unfortunately contributed to the low 35% completion rate. We conducted site visits where the problems were being reported and were able to conclude that previously unknown incompatibility issues existed with the Notes browser. We subsequently advised respondents to either copy and paste the survey link, or manually type it into the URL window of Netscape or Internet Explorer. This message was also added to the LibQUAL+™ FAQ and as a link from the Library's main page. For the 2003 survey, we will emphasize the incompatibility issue and suggest alternatives for accessing the survey in our promotional publicity.

Returned Mail

While finalizing arrangements with the Medical Center's Office of Information Technology to develop a mass mailing list, we were advised to expect some returned mail due to activation of "out of office" messages, delivery failures, and automatic forwarding to an invalid address. Of the approximately 12,500 messages sent, we received a total of 1,840 returned mail messages. This means approximately 15% of the potential respondents never received the survey e-mail. Future surveys may be sent to a smaller, more well-defined group of approximately 5,000 individuals.

Respondents Who Did Not Want to Complete the Survey

Many respondents indicated that they would not be completing the survey since they rarely, if ever, use the Library. Although these respondents may not physically visit the Library, we suspect that some of them are remotely using our online resources. While these individuals decided not to complete the survey, we feel that, at the least, we increased their awareness of the Library and its services.

Questions About Study Design

Several respondents told us they did not complete the survey because they became frustrated with the number and similarity of the questions, while others felt that the survey was too complicated, cumbersome, and vague. Even researchers familiar with research methodology found some of the questions too redundant. We also learned that some respondents did not understand how to apply the concepts of minimum, perceived, and desired levels of service. Lastly, several respondents were confused with how to select the demographic user group that best described them. We will address the logic behind the redundancy and length and other concerns in our publicity for the 2003 survey. The Association of Research Libraries may also address these concerns in their design of the 2003 survey.

THE RESULTS

Aggregate Overview

Much of DUMCL's aggregate-level results mirror the overall Association of Academic Health Sciences Libraries' (AAHSL) data. Issues of "Personal Control" and "Access to Information" were more important to users, and composed the greatest areas for improvement by the library. As with other AAHSL libraries, the only negative result (perceived performance falling below minimum level expectations) was associated with providing remote access to electronic resources (Q5).

While "Affect of Service" and "Library as Place" ranked lower than the other dimensions in terms of importance or desired level of satisfaction, the Library had strong aggregate performance ratings in these two areas.

Responses to the five local questions further highlighted additional areas for improvement. Although our comprehensive print collection score was high, the Library faces the challenge of expanding its electronic collection (see Table 1 and Figure 2).

Respondent Profile

Two of the striking differences between our library and other participating AAHSL members' results were caused by variations in the user groups. While our aggregate results may have been similar to the AAHSL average, our user groups varied widely in their responses compared to our counterparts. Our Faculty and Graduate scores tended to be out of range in relationship to the AAHSL average. Graduates consistently had higher minimum expectations and usually lower perceived gap scores than graduates at similar health science institutions. By contrast, the DUMCL Faculty gap scores were usually higher than the AAHSL average.

TABLE 1. LibQUAL+™ Survey Results–Item Analysis–All User Groups

No.	Question Text	Minimum	Desired	Perceived	Gap
	Access to Information				
3	Complete runs of journal titles	6.92	8.14	7.28	0.36
8	Timely document delivery/interlibrary loan	6.44	7.68	6.92	0.49
9	Interdisciplinary library needs being addressed	6.38	7.44	6.83	0.45
19	Convenient business hours	6.99	8.13	7.56	0.57
22	Comprehensive print collections	6.52	7.70	7.26	0.74
	Affect of Service				
1	Willingness to help users	6.44	7.92	7.33	0.89
4	Employees who are consistently courteous	7.16	8.23	7.76	0.60
11	Dependability in handling users' service problems	6.89	8.07	7.50	0.61
14	Giving users individual attention	6.38	7.63	7.25	0.87
15	Employees who deal with users in a caring fashion	6.72	7.93	7.45	0.73
17	Employees who have the knowledge to answer user questions	7.14	8.25	7.67	0.53
18	Readiness to respond to users' questions	7.07	8.22	7.68	0.60
20	Employees who instill confidence in users	6.42	7.54	7.23	0.81
24	Employees who understand the needs of their users	6.80	7.99	7.43	0.63
	Library as Place				
2	Space that facilitates quiet study	6.19	7.34	7.25	1.06
10	A haven for quiet and solitude	6.05	7.22	7.19	1.15
13	A place for reflection and creativity	5.54	6.74	6.68	1.14
21	A comfortable and inviting location	6.24	7.70	7.23	0.99
23	A contemplative environment	5.77	7.04	6.92	1.15
	Personal Control				
5	Making electronic resources accessible from my home or office	7.05	8.30	7.04	−0.01
6	Modern equipment that lets me easily access the information I need	6.84	8.12	7.20	0.36
7	A library Website enabling me to locate information on my own	7.09	8.32	7.38	0.29
12	Easy-to-use access tools that allow me to find things on my own	6.98	8.24	7.31	0.33
16	Making information easily accessible for independent use	6.99	8.21	7.42	0.43
25	Convenient access to library collections	6.94	8.11	7.50	0.56

Second, unlike most other AAHSL members, we chose to include hospital employees in our survey group. Of the 891 completed surveys, 39% represent hospital staff. This participation is much higher than the 12% AAHSL average. The hospital's inclusion in the LibQUAL+™ study accounts for the strong Staff category representation–54% of survey respondents. This result is significantly higher than AAHSL's 23%.

FIGURE 2. LibQUAL+™ Survey Results–Item Analysis–All User Groups

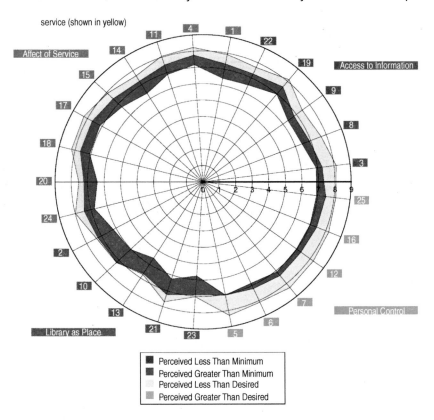

Hospital Staff's Impact on the Results

How did the addition of hospital staff in the survey affect the final results? What issues were they most concerned about? Overall, Staff was pleased with our level of service. The Library performed above its expected minimum level of service on all four parameters, as well as on the five local questions. In fact, Staff ratings acted as the median score between the typically lower graduate and higher faculty ratings. This was true not only for the Staff's minimum level of service ratings but also for their perceived performance rankings (see Table 2 and Figure 3).

Despite the predominant middle-of-the-road ratings, the survey results highlighted a number of areas where the minimum performance gap for Staff was lower compared to the other two user groups.

TABLE 2. LibQUAL+™ Survey Results–Item Analysis–Staff

No.	Question Text	Minimum	Desired	Perceived	Gap
	Access to Information				
3	Complete runs of journal titles	6.91	8.08	7.32	0.41
8	Timely document delivery/interlibrary loan	6.70	7.86	7.13	0.44
9	Interdisciplinary library needs being addressed	6.54	7.59	6.94	0.40
19	Convenient business hours	7.10	8.17	7.69	0.58
22	Comprehensive print collections	6.61	7.72	7.29	0.69
	Affect of Service				
1	Willingness to help users	6.60	8.04	7.36	0.76
4	Employees who are consistently courteous	7.26	8.29	7.73	0.47
11	Dependability in handling users' service problems	7.03	8.11	7.57	0.54
14	Giving users individual attention	6.57	7.79	7.25	0.67
15	Employees who deal with users in a caring fashion	6.95	8.07	7.48	0.53
17	Employees who have the knowledge to answer user questions	7.21	8.28	7.69	0.49
18	Readiness to respond to users' questions	7.16	8.26	7.65	0.50
20	Employees who instill confidence in users	6.64	7.66	7.26	0.62
24	Employees who understand the needs of their users	6.96	8.05	7.46	0.50
	Library as Place				
2	Space that facilitates quiet study	6.50	7.59	7.41	0.90
10	A haven for quiet and solitude	6.58	7.64	7.40	0.81
13	A place for reflection and creativity	5.92	7.05	6.86	0.94
21	A comfortable and inviting location	6.53	7.83	7.36	0.83
23	A contemplative environment	6.21	7.43	7.14	0.93
	Personal Control				
5	Making electronic resources accessible from my home or office	6.84	8.17	6.96	0.13
6	Modern equipment that lets me easily access the information I need	6.90	8.05	7.23	0.33
7	A library Website enabling me to locate information on my own	7.08	8.28	7.33	0.25
12	Easy-to-use access tools that allow me to find things on my own	7.05	8.23	7.36	0.31
16	Making information easily accessible for independent use	7.05	8.17	7.42	0.38
25	Convenient access to library collections	7.07	8.15	7.56	0.49

The most prominent concern was Staff's high regard for Affect of Service issues. Of the four categories, Staff ranked Affect of Service almost as equally important as Personal Control. They also set a higher minimum level for Affect of Service than did Faculty or Graduates. At the question level, Staff consistently demanded higher minimum ser-

FIGURE 3. LibQUAL+™ Survey Results–Item Analysis–Staff

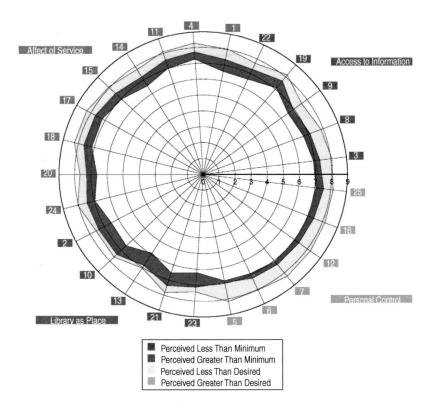

vice levels and consistently rated lower perception levels compared to
the Faculty and Graduate respondents. The lowest gap ratings were for
consistently courteous employees (Q4), dealing with users in a caring
fashion (Q15), readiness to respond to users' questions (Q18), instilling
confidence in users (Q20), and understanding needs of users (Q24).

Staff concern for service-oriented performance was also evident on
the general satisfaction questions. Although their scores were high for
all three questions, their rating for treatment was well below the Graduate and Faculty scores, as well as below the AAHSL average. In addition, Staff awarded a higher priority to the second local question on
teaching how to access information, but of the three groups, they gave
the Library the lowest gap score.

Compared to Faculty and Graduates, Staff also had lower perceptions
of the Library's performance on some questions associated with Per-

sonal Control and Access to Information. Staff had significantly lower gap ratings related to the library having an effective Website (Q7) and convenient collection access (Q25). In terms of Access to Information, Staff had lower gaps for interdisciplinary needs being addressed (Q9) and having a comprehensive print collection (Q22).

Making Sense of the Staff Results

Two issues confound our ability to meaningfully interpret the results for Staff–the LibQUAL+™ demographic category labels and the frequency of Library and electronic resource use. Since Staff includes not just hospital staff, but also research and clerical staff from the School of Medicine, it is difficult to ascertain the specific information needs of just the hospital employees. We will be designing focus groups and targeted surveys to elicit more detailed understanding of how the hospital staff's information needs may differ from the rest of the Library's primary users. Another alternative would be to develop additional demographic categories for academic health centers within the survey instrument.

The survey statistics revealed that Staff used the Library and its electronic resources less frequently compared to Faculty and Graduates. Staff was also less likely to visit the Library or use electronic resources on a daily or even weekly basis. Their usage was limited to a monthly or quarterly time period, which was similar to other AAHSL members and not particular to Duke.

However, given the low library usage by Staff, it is unclear why they responded with such low Affect of Service ratings. The Library needs to explore the reasons for these ratings to see if there are customer service issues for this user group. Possible explanations could be they have more difficulty using the Library due to their infrequent use, and the Library does not target them for training programs. An additional survey of the clerical and administrative staff may be warranted.

CONCLUSION

As a result of the 2002 survey, we have general data to guide us in continuous improvement of our resources and services. The challenge of the academic health center is identifying the unique information needs of the various user categories. For example, residents, interns, and hospital employees are significant user groups. It would be beneficial to track and analyze their data separately. For the 2003 launch, we plan to address some of the demographic problems through the use of more targeted mailing lists. We expect the second implementation of the survey to be smoother for the Library and patrons due to the lessons that we have learned.

An Academic Medical Library Using LibQUAL+™: The Experience of the Galter Health Sciences Library, Northwestern University

James Shedlock
Linda Walton

SUMMARY. The Galter Health Sciences Library has used the LibQUAL+™ survey in two consecutive years. Both sets of survey results provided useful information to understand how users perceive the quality of Galter Library services. The first year's relatively positive results offered a useful and hopeful benchmark. The second year's results provided more of a "wake up" call to explore in depth what users want and need from the library. Peer comparison also offers an additional insight as to where Galter staff can look to find models and/or best practices when exploring specific remedies that would improve services to Galter users. *[Article copies available for a fee from The Haworth Document Delivery Service: 1-800-HAWORTH. E-mail address: <docdelivery@haworthpress.com> Website: <http://www.HaworthPress.com> © 2004 by The Haworth Press, Inc. All rights reserved.]*

James Shedlock (E-mail: j-shedlock@northwestern.edu) is Director and Linda Walton (E-mail: ljwalton@northwestern.edu) is Associate Director, Galter Health Sciences Library, Northwestern University, Chicago, IL.

[Haworth co-indexing entry note]: "An Academic Medical Library Using LibQUAL+™: The Experience of the Galter Health Sciences Library, Northwestern University." Shedlock, James, and Linda Walton. Co-published simultaneously in *Journal of Library Administration* (The Haworth Information Press, an imprint of The Haworth Press, Inc.) Vol. 40, No. 3/4, 2004, pp. 99-110; and: *Libraries Act on Their LibQUAL+™ Findings: From Data to Action* (ed: Fred M. Heath, Martha Kyrillidou, and Consuella A. Askew) The Haworth Information Press, an imprint of The Haworth Press, Inc., 2004, pp. 99-110. Single or multiple copies of this article are available for a fee from The Haworth Document Delivery Service [1-800-HAWORTH. 9:00 a.m. - 5:00 p.m. (EST). E-mail address: docdelivery@haworthpress.com].

http://www.haworthpress.com/web/JLA
© 2004 by The Haworth Press, Inc. All rights reserved.
Digital Object Identifier: 10.1300/J111v40n03_08

KEYWORDS. LibQUAL+™, library service quality, health sciences libraries, consortia, peer comparisons, Association of Academic Health Sciences Libraries, benchmarking

INTRODUCTION

Northwestern University's Galter Health Sciences Library serves the information needs of the faculty, staff and students of the Feinberg School of Medicine. The school awards professional degrees in medicine and physical therapy and the PhD in basic medical sciences and clinical psychology. Various Master's degrees and certificates are offered as well. Since all medical schools collaborate with local hospitals for clinical education, the Galter Library is also the primary resource library for the McGaw Medical Center of Northwestern University. The medical center is composed of various clinical institutions, each with its own library or learning resource center, and the Galter Library provides a variety of services to each institution depending on their specific need. In this way the Galter Library staff extends support to its faculty and students through the hospital librarians.

Given this unique set of users, understanding how well the library fulfills its mission is critically important. Because the primary concern of the medical school and the academic medical center focuses on timely, current and quality information for health education, biomedical research and patient care, knowing whether the Galter Library is meeting users' expectations for information service in this intensive environment is a primary issue for the library staff. Previous attempts to measure the success of various library programs and services have been limited. The availability of the LibQUAL+™ survey now offers staff a new tool to gain insight into how users view the library in terms of quality service.

The Galter Health Sciences Library has been an early user and proponent of the LibQUAL+™ instrument. This article highlights two years' experience with LibQUAL+™ from the perspective of an academic health sciences library. The success in using LibQUAL+™ and the satisfaction with the results provides several challenges to library staff in how they view their own work. These challenges are being addressed, and they motivate us toward improvements that will be measured again in 2003.

BACKGROUND

The medical center's organizational structure and its institutional relationships have a tremendous impact on the mission and services of the academic health sciences library. Above all else, the medical environment is most concerned about treating human disease conditions and restoring health. Because treating disease and restoring health is intensely human and time critical, these facts alone separate health science schools and their libraries from the traditional concerns of scholars in a typical university or college. Second, the medical community is committed to research as a means of treating, if not eradicating, disease conditions in the future and preventing human disease from occurring. Third, there is a commitment to education and community service: to prepare professionals for future practice and research and to teach the community about health promotion and disease prevention. These environmental conditions influence the perceptions of library services that are vastly different from the perceptions of other scholarly disciplines within the broader academic community.[1]

In addition to the factors of the health care environment, all librarians, to some degree or other, face an additional set of professional and environmental conditions. Chief among these conditions is the transformation of libraries from traditional warehouses of knowledge into active service centers for information access. The Galter response to both sets of environmental challenges has been to place special emphasis on using information technologies as a means of serving users. We have done so for two reasons. First, we have continuously assessed our collections' strengths and weaknesses and estimated that we could not be strong in traditional collections building. This is due primarily to the high cost of scientific-technical-medical subscriptions and the broad array of journals needed to satisfy user demand. In other words, a great deal of financial support is required to build the collections to a degree that would satisfy user demand, make a significant impact on users' perception of the quality of the Galter collections, and improve our collections' standing among our peers. Second, we managed over the years to attract talented staff possessing the technological skills and interests to make a strong electronic library a reality.

While this focus is similar to that of many other academic libraries, the Galter staff have chosen to pursue technology as a means of improving service through innovations in managing the library's resources more efficiently. For example, staff have gone beyond Web design as the means of organizing the electronic library. Behind the interface design are many successful internal databases that make it easy for users to find and manage their own information needs. A completely paperless interlibrary loan process is but one example. At the same time, several back-end processes are totally automated for staff use. In addition, this technological approach to library service often extends directly to users. Under current development is a series of tools that will become the focus of a new Health SmartLibrary. Targeting the busy clinician for improved information service and designed to push information to the user before the need is recognized, these tools include several innovations: an alert service that keeps the user current with the latest health information by linking database citation to electronic full-text; a personal database for storing electronic information deemed too important to discard; a meta search engine to tell users what resource has the information they need; discipline-based resources pre-selected for faster searching; and an interface to assist the user in managing their personal Health Smart-Library for current awareness of new information and self-selection of critical resources. These tools are what make the My Library concept smarter and showcase the role of the medical librarian as a technology innovator.

In whatever conditions a library finds itself, the need to know whether its work is valued by meeting actual information needs is paramount, evaluation and assessment of services a *sine qua non* no matter what program a library offers its users. This is why the LibQUAL+™ tool is important: can we measure the quality of what we do for users?

MOTIVATION FOR USING LibQUAL+™

There were several motivational factors that influenced the Galter Library staff to volunteer to start using the LibQUAL+™ survey in 2000. These factors included:

- *Measuring the Effect of a Strategic Plan.* As for other LibQUAL+™ participants, the primary motivating factor in the Galter Library's participation was the conclusion of the library's five-year strategic plan in 2000.[2] In the original plan, library staff committed themselves to measure the effect of their programs and services, mostly through traditional paper-based surveys on satisfaction. The LibQUAL+™ announcement of its availability for testing beyond the original Association of Research Libraries (ARL) core group provided Galter staff with an easy means to measure the overall effect of the library's strategic plan. Staff also hoped that participation in a national test would improve user response as would the ability to offer a completely Web-based survey. Timing being right, Galter staff seized the opportunity and volunteered for the 2001 test. Though the Galter Library was the only stand-alone academic health sciences library participating in this test and true peer comparison data would be lacking, access to valuable user feedback was of primary importance and the cost to participate was considered very worthwhile.

- *Recognizing the Need to Evaluate Library Programs and Services*. Galter staff formed their own Assessment Committee during the strategic plan's time frame. This committee's goal is to better understand whether and how well staff fulfill the mission of the library. Assessment projects have included a Web site usability study, measuring user preferences for MEDLINE interfaces (e.g., using Ovid Technologies vs. National Library of Medicine (NLM) PubMed), assessing the types of questions presented at the main reference desk to determine levels of staffing and need for professional vs. paraprofessional staff, etc. Participating in LibQUAL+™ provides data that adds to staff self-knowledge and encourages development of new assessment projects.
- *Linking Quantitative Statistics to Qualitative Measures*. The library director chairs the Editorial Board of the Association of Academic Health Sciences Libraries (AAHSL) *Annual Statistics*,[3] an equivalent to the *ARL Statistics Survey*.[4] As chair, the director seeks better ways to assess academic health sciences library programs and services that would use and/or complement the association's effort in producing quantitative measures. In other words, can academic medical library directors find a means of moving beyond quantitative measures toward understanding how to measure quality? Again, LibQUAL+™ participation would provide a learning opportunity to explore possible relevance in transforming quantitative measures into qualitative ones.
- *User Feedback*. Another motivating factor was the need for objective user data that could be applied toward the next strategic plan. The hope and desire was that any user feedback is positive information and would be used by staff in formulating a new set of goals and objectives for the next strategic plan.

The procedures for participating in LibQUAL+™ are very easy. Because LibQUAL+™ is completely Web-based, the central task is gathering users' e-mail addresses. Once obtained, managing the LibQUAL+™ survey is a matter of sending e-mail messages to users. In some institutions that lack any centralized e-mail administration, gathering a sufficient number of addresses to meet the minimum levels of LibQUAL+™ participation may be troublesome but not overly difficult. In Northwestern's medical school environment, e-mail addresses were obtained without difficulty for 49% of the faculty and all of the professional and graduate students and residents. E-mail addresses for the remaining 51% of faculty are currently unknown to school administrators because they are primarily volunteers who donate teaching time to the medical school.

As indicated above, at Northwestern's medical school all known users were sent e-mail messages asking them to complete the LibQUAL+™ survey. Because academic medical schools have a much smaller population than the whole university, sampling was unnecessary and casting as broad a net around available users was essential.

The primary contact for the 2001 and 2002 LibQUAL+™ surveys was the library director. This direct communication between the director and library users confirms the importance of the survey. By direct appeal to all users, the library director can "make the case" as to why users should contribute their time toward improving library services that could ultimately benefit them. Adding incentives such as a drawing for gift certificates does not hurt the effort either.

LibQUAL+™ RESULTS: A COMPARISON

The 2001 survey results were important because they established a benchmark as to what can be expected from the LibQUAL+™ survey. These first survey results also allowed us to start to learn from users. By listening to their views through the minimum, desired and perceived expectations for library service, staff begin to understand how the user views services or library features that are important to them.

The overall assessment of the Galter Library in 2001 was a positive one. In the 2001 survey, nine dimensions were used to group 56 questions. Out of this set, only three questions received a negative gap score. Because negative gap scores measured perceptions that were less than minimum expectations, those scores received the most attention. Not unexpectedly, these three questions targeted: "comprehensive print collections," "convenient business hours" and "complete run of journal titles." As predicted, these were the very topics that staff expected to receive the most criticism and the first LibQUAL+™ results came as no surprise. Having objective data to verify anecdotal comments received over the years was actually good news to the library staff. However, in truth, these negative scores were not unique to the Galter Library even though staff thought they were. In follow-up sessions with other 2001 participants, all libraries were marked negatively for these same three items.

Because the Galter Library stood alone among the 2001 participants as the only distinct academic health sciences population, peer-to-group and peer-to-peer comparisons were not warranted or available. Though some 2001 participants did include user response from various health sciences schools or programs in their survey population, these data could not be extracted to allow for any comparison among health sciences peers. Overall, and based only on assessing the raw scores, Galter Library staff were generally pleased with this initial report. The areas needing improvement were already known to library administration and efforts to improve these services had already appeared in several budget proposals prior to the introduction of the LibQUAL+™ survey.

Consequently, the 2002 survey results were viewed more critically because they could be benchmarked against the 2001 scores and they provided Galter staff with the opportunity for true peer comparison. In the 2002 test, 23 peer libraries from the Association of Academic Health Sciences Libraries (AAHSL) provided the necessary data to do a realistic comparison.[5] Also, these new scores would allow staff to see how LibQUAL+™ measured performance from year to year and whether there was any difference in the scores.

The year-to-year comparison was revealing. Theoretically, staff expected raw mean scores to be relatively the same in year two given no major changes to programs or services. This proved not to be the case. Overall satisfaction lowered in the second year compared to the first is enumerated in Table 1.

Another view is to look at the raw scores for each dimension of survey topics. Again, there is the decline in mean values from one year to the next as illustrated in Table 2. Clearly, access to information (which covers the topics of "complete runs of journals," "timely document delivery," "interdisciplinary needs being addressed," "convenient business

TABLE 1. Overall Satisfaction Mean Scores

Overall Satisfaction	2001	2002
Quality	7.10	6.30
Services	7.25	6.84
Support	6.88	6.01

TABLE 2. Dimension Mean Scores

Dimension (Perceived, All Users)	2001*	2002	Difference
Access to Information	6.64	5.86	.78
Affect of Service	6.81	6.58	.23
Library as Place	6.56	6.10	.46
Personal Control	7.00	6.88	.12

Note: These dimensions are singled out from the total set of nine to make a comparison with 2002 data.

hours," and "comprehensive print collections") is where users are speaking most loudly about the lack of or at least concerns about quality.

One way to explain the change in scores is by examining survey participants. In the first survey, the library's user population was more evenly distributed among the three groups of faculty, staff and students. However, students made more of an effort to respond to the survey in the second year than did the other user groups (Table 3). One conclusion, then, is that students used the LibQUAL+™ survey to be more vocal about their issues with library services.

For the most part, the same negative issues that were identified in the first LibQUAL+™ survey repeated in the second year: namely, "convenient business hours" and "complete runs of journals." In year two, however, new negative issues are identified: "making electronic resources accessible from home or office" and "modern equipment that lets me easily access the information that I need." These two new issues reflect specific library problems that occurred in late 2001: proxy maintenance issues and excessive downtime for many of the library's internal computers and frequent printing problems. Here we see how LibQUAL+™ results specifically reflect known service problems.

Comparison of the local library's LibQUAL+™ scores with its peers establishes an additional set of useful information for internal assess-

TABLE 3. Survey Participation by User Group

Survey Participation	2001	%	2002	%
Faculty	164	34	99	24
Staff	186	39	120	28
Students	126	27	198	47

ment. By relying on peer information, LibQUAL+™ data leads eventually to an understanding of best practices. For example, Table 4 shows the raw score comparison of Galter to its peers.

Using only a surface comparison, we see that the Galter Library has lower mean scores than its peer group. What does this mean for library staff? Again, just from a surface view, a lower score provides the impetus to start asking questions. For many questions that make up the Access to Information dimension, we know from quantitative statistics that many individual peers are more information-rich libraries. They have bigger collections of electronic journals and books suggesting perhaps that these libraries are better equipped to satisfy local information needs. We know this is not the case for the Galter Library, and we already know from investigating best practices that variations in funding patterns and consortial alliances explain much of the difference in creating an information-rich environment for users.

Besides raw score comparison, the LibQUAL+™ team provides access to norm scores. Norm scores allow staff to see how a library's scores "stack up" to its peers.[6] Using the norm tables provided to participants, for the 2002 survey Galter scores did not "stack up" very well. For example, none of the Galter dimension scores at the institution level reached above the 50th percentile. As norm scores give factual information, they provide indication of where to look further to investigate differences among library programs and services. To know that we did not "stack up" very well with our peers was the observation that we wanted from the beginning of the library's participation in LibQUAL+™ testing. We needed to know how well we were doing using peers as a gauge, and now that we know, we have much work to do in understanding both our users' needs and how our peers meet their users' needs.

To reinforce this view, we reviewed the difference between what users desire in terms of quality service against what they actually perceive. The gaps scores in Table 5 give an indication of how much work

TABLE 4. Raw Score Comparison of Galter Library to Its Peers

Dimension (Perceived, All Users)	AAHSL Score	Galter Score
Average	7.05	6.78
Access to Information	6.92	6.46
Affect of Service	7.34	7.02
Library as Place	6.79	6.59
Personal Control	7.15	7.08

TABLE 5. Gap Scores for Dimensions Measured by the 2002 LibQUAL+™ Survey

Dimension (Perceived vs. Desired, All Users), 2002	Desired	Perceived	Gap
Access to Information	7.99	6.46	1.53
Affect of Service	7.91	7.02	.89
Library as Place	7.49	6.59	.90
Personal Control	8.20	7.08	1.12

is needed to reach users' expectations for quality. The desired scores serve as a guide that can be incorporated into the strategic planning process as targets for improving services.

To further understand the meaning of both raw scores and norm scores, library staff explored how users viewed some of the issues measured in the survey via focus groups. Instead of trying to address the fluctuations in scores between the two years, only one topic was examined: "complete runs of journals." Different sets of faculty were invited to two lunch meetings. Faculty were prepped ahead of time with handouts and e-mail messages and knew they were expected to discuss the quality of the library's journal collection. One group included only basic science faculty while the other group attempted to attract clinical sciences faculty. The goal was to understand faculty perception of journal collection quality. We asked, "How do you define a quality journal collection," and "What does the phrase 'complete run of journals' mean to you."

As expected, each group commented on the need to improve the collection. New faculty, recently arrived from other institutions, were vocal about the lack of titles to be found in the Galter library compared to where they just left. For years library staff heard from faculty that the collection lacked breadth–not enough journals–and depth–not the right journals in specific disciplines. The lunch conversations verified this assumption once again. However, with the availability of electronic formats, faculty stressed the importance of format more than anything else. The library still needs more breadth–more journals–especially in interdisciplinary areas, but new titles must be "electronic only." Even if the library added more journals in print format, this would not satisfy users' needs, according to the focus groups. Basically, these new titles would go unused. As for understanding depth, faculty understood this concept less in terms of collecting all the journals in a particular discipline or collecting the right journals. Faculty see collection depth in terms of backfiles for an online journal: how far back in time does the library provide access to an electronic journal. Faculty seemed more interested in additional electronic backfiles of the most important titles than more titles in the same topical area.

Another conclusion from the focus group is that faculty do not want to work too hard to find information. For example, they are not inclined to support an online catalog. They know this database is useful to identify what books, journals and audiovisuals the library owns, but they do not want to use it–especially for tracking journal titles. They simply want a list of journals with coverage dates. Explanations in the form of notes are unnecessary because the library should own a whole title and it should be available to them when and where they need it. In other words, they appear to say, "Please do not make me look for more helpful information about what I need–just give it to me right up front." These observations are critical for librarians to understand the personal control issues measured by the LibQUAL+™ survey.

In general, the use of focus groups proved very beneficial in combination with the LibQUAL+™ results. Focus groups extend the market research survey by concentrating on user opinion. Through this method, librarians reach a greater depth of understanding than what raw scores or norm scores provide by themselves. Raw scores lead library staff toward new investigations that provide the framework for improving services to users.

CONCLUSION

The Galter Health Sciences Library has used the LibQUAL+™ survey in two consecutive years. Both sets of survey results provided useful information to understand how users perceive the quality of Galter Library services. The first year's relatively positive results offered a useful and hopeful benchmark. The second year's results provided more of a "wake up" call to explore in depth what users want and need from the library. Peer comparison also offers an additional insight as to where Galter staff can look to find models and/or best practices when exploring specific remedies that would improve services to Galter users. Even relying on just raw scores and norm scores for peer comparison gives local library staff insight as to how they "stack up" and where they can start to make plans for improving services. Using focus groups to extend the LibQUAL+™ market research is another valuable tool to better understand what users want the library to provide. Galter staff consider the LibQUAL+™ instrument a valuable resource and will use it again in 2003 to see if it can detect a positive user response to actual changes made in library services and programs as a result of two years of LibQUAL+™ scores. We look forward to examining these results as we did in 2001 and 2002.

NOTES

1. K. Ann McKibbon et al. "The medical literature as a resource for evidence based care." Working Paper from the Health Information Research Unit, McMaster University, Ontario, Canada. 1995. This paper is also available on the Web at http://hiru. mcmaster.ca/hiru/medline/asis-pap.htm.

2. Wanda Dole, "LibQUAL+™ and the small academic library," *Performance Measurement and Metrics*, 3, no. 2 (2002): 86. Sessions, Judith A., Schenck, Alex and Shrimplin, Aaron K.. "LibQUAL+™ from Miami University: A look from outside ARL," *Performance Measurement and Metrics*, 3, no. 2 (2002): 59.

3. Association of Academic Health Sciences Libraries. *Annual Statistics of Academic Medical Libraries in the United States and Canada*. Seattle: The Association. 24th ed: 2002. The *Annual Statistics of Medical School Libraries in the United States and Canada* is a publication of the Association of Academic Health Sciences Libraries. Published since 1978, the *Annual Statistics* provides comparative data on significant characteristics of collections, expenditures, personnel and services in medical school libraries in the United States and Canada.

4. The Association of Research Libraries (Washington, D.C.) publishes the *ARL Statistics* annually for its membership. The *ARL Statistics* datafiles, with accompanying documentation, are available at <http://www.arl.org/stats/>.

5. Duane Webster and Fred Heath, *LibQUAL+™ Spring 2002 Survey Results–AAHSL*. (Washington, DC: Association of Research Libraries, 2002).

6. Bruce Thompson, "*LibQUAL+™ Spring, 2002 Selected Norms*," see: http://www.coe.tamu.edu/~bthompson/libq2002.htm.

UNIVERSITY/COLLEGE LIBRARIES

Quantifying Qualitative Data: Using LibQUAL+™ Comments for Library-Wide Planning Activities at the University of Arizona

Wendy Begay
Daniel R. Lee
Jim Martin
Michael Ray

SUMMARY. University of Arizona Library used the LibQUAL+™ comments to inform its strategic direction. The 303 comments received

Wendy Begay (E-mail: Begayw@u.library.arizona.edu) is affiliated with the Materials Access Team, Daniel R. Lee with the Undergraduate Services Team, Jim Martin (E-mail: Martinj@u.library.arizona.edu) with the Science-Engineering Team, and Michael Ray (E-mail: Raym@u.library.arizona.edu) with the Staff and Organization Systems Team, all at the University of Arizona, Tucson, AZ.

[Haworth co-indexing entry note]: "Quantifying Qualitative Data: Using LibQUAL+™ Comments for Library-Wide Planning Activities at the University of Arizona." Begay, Wendy et al. Co-published simultaneously in *Journal of Library Administration* (The Haworth Information Press, an imprint of The Haworth Press, Inc.) Vol. 40, No. 3/4, 2004, pp. 111-119; and: *Libraries Act on Their LibQUAL+™ Findings: From Data to Action* (ed: Fred M. Heath, Martha Kyrillidou, and Consuella A. Askew) The Haworth Information Press, an imprint of The Haworth Press, Inc., 2004, pp. 111-119. Single or multiple copies of this article are available for a fee from The Haworth Document Delivery Service [1-800-HAWORTH, 9:00 a.m. - 5:00 p.m. (EST). E-mail address: docdelivery@haworthpress.com].

http://www.haworthpress.com/web/JLA
© 2004 by The Haworth Press, Inc. All rights reserved.
Digital Object Identifier: 10.1300/J111v40n03_09

from the LibQUAL+™ survey in 2002 were coded using a "Grounded Theory" approach. Using the qualitative statistical software QSR's N6, all comments were coded demographically and by categories around Library access, environment and service. N6 assisted the research and analysis of comments, providing a base for both quantifiable and qualitative development of data into useful information. The comments were used to determine strategic direction at the organizational and individual team level by triangulating the qualitatively organized comments with the quantitative LibQUAL+™ data, as well as other sources of customer data. This approach provided a focused method to organize and understand information in order to meet and address Library customer needs. *[Article copies available for a fee from The Haworth Document Delivery Service: 1-800-HAWORTH. E-mail address: <docdelivery@haworthpress.com> Website: <http://www.HaworthPress.com> © 2004 by The Haworth Press, Inc. All rights reserved.]*

KEYWORDS. LibQUAL+™, NUD*IST, strategic planning, library service quality, academic libraries

The University of Arizona Library has participated in LibQUAL+™ since its pilot phase in spring 2000. Each year the results have been an important element in the library's Strategic Long Range Planning (SLRP) team's deliberations; and each year the instrument has improved and provided more useful information. In 2002, one such improvement was the inclusion of the opportunity for respondents to provide open comments as part of the survey instrument. This opportunity was welcomed by both the library-planning group and by our customers, as indicated by the 303 comments provided by them.

However, the existence of a large number of comments also raised questions about how to interpret them in a way that would provide valid information for decision-making purposes. As individual members of the library staff reviewed the many comments, different themes stood out as important for each reader. For one reader, the key issue was a consistent criticism of the quality of service provided by student employees. For another, the top concern was the level of noise in the quiet study areas of the library. In order for SLRP and the other library teams to make the best use of this gold mine of information, a systematic, objective analysis of the comments needed to be conducted.

METHODOLOGY

An ad hoc working group was formed to organize the comments and provide an initial analysis of the qualitative data collected. Michael Ray, the library's Assistant to the Dean, was asked to advise the group. He led the group through a methodology he had used in his dissertation research–the "open coding" method described by Strauss and Corbin.[1] The group began by analyzing a small sample of the comments sentence-by-sentence and labeled the activities, actions, and events described in those responses. These were coded as concepts (see example in Table 2). Similar concepts were, in turn, grouped together into larger categories. This work on an initial set of concepts and categories provided training in coding, and the resulting categories served as an iterative guide for continuing coding. The comments were then divided among the working group to code the entire set of comments.

As a result of having multiple people involved, each person coding only a subset of the comments, this first attempt at open coding lacked a consistent approach and terminology. After reviewing the various lists of terms presented, the group decided to conduct a second reading of the comments and to re-code the comments using an agreed-upon list of major categories and sub-categories. The labels for the categories and sub-categories came out of the language used by respondents in the comments. The headings used to direct our analysis are listed in Table 1. Not surprisingly, our open coding in many ways paralleled the structure of the LibQUAL+™ survey. The main category headings also closely parallel the activities of the library staff. For an example of a coded comment see Table 2.

In order to assist with the organization of the data by both categories and demographics, the coded comments were entered into the text analysis software N6, the latest version of NUD*IST from QSR. One of the work group members had recently been trained in this software in her regular coursework, which allowed the library to make use of existing, but often underutilized, skills within the organization.

Each message from a survey participant was divided into comments about individual topics. For example, one comment might address noise in the library and then shift to talking about the benefits of remote access to electronic collections. This comment would be categorized twice: once for noise in the library and again for the remote access. Once the classifications, or codes, were agreed upon and entered into N6, the coding in the database of each of these comments went quickly. The

TABLE 1. Labels Used for Categories and Sub-Categories

Access		
To electronic	To print collections	To journals
Remote	By Discipline	By discipline
To hardware and/or software	Remote	Enforcement
Organization (the way access is organized)	Suggestions/ Recommendations	
Environment		
Facility	Lighting	Enforcement
Cleanliness	Noise	Temperature
Furniture	Hours	Suggestions/ Recommendations
	Study Rooms	
Service		
Staff	Photocopy	ILL
Affect	Suggestions/ Recommendations	Enforcement
Competence		

TABLE 2. Example of a Coded Comment

Statement	Concept	Category/ Sub-Category
As it pertains to the environment and comfort level at the library, I am continuously annoyed by the loud carts used to wheel around and shelve books! The wheels clatter too loudly.	Annoyed by shelving cart noise	Environment– Noise

topic code, and the users' demographic information are then associated with the comment in the database. N6 provides for a range of reports from simple reports such as the number of comments in a category, to viewing all the comments in a particular category, to more sophisticated reports such as a listing of all the comments from a specific age group that address both access issues and service quality.

As stated above, one of the key reasons for taking on this project was to be able to determine in a systematic, objective manner what issues were of greatest concern to our customers. At a basic level, this was to be done by quantifying the number of customers who took the time to address each area. These figures are represented in Table 3.

It is worth noting that access, in its various topical forms, drew the largest response. It also became clear that, at the sub-category level, although noise and staff competence were important, access to electronic resources brought out the most comments. When these numbers were looked at for each of the core campus groups, it was also true that access was the most important with 70 comments from faculty, 97 comments from graduate students, and 63 comments from undergraduates that were classified as concerning access. There was an expected contrast in the number of comments about the library environment with 61 comments coming from undergraduates, a close second to access, and only 13 comments about the library environment coming from faculty.

Having quantified the responses in each category, the real value was still to be demonstrated. It is one thing to note that 27 people commented on staff competence, for example, but numbers alone did not tell us the values implied by the judgments and observations contained in the responses.

The next step was to determine the relationships, if any, between categories or sub-categories and investigate the range of opinions and ex-

TABLE 3. Number of Customers Addressing Identified Areas

Access (n = 290)   **Environment** (n = 156)   **Service** (n = 161)

Access		Environment		Service	
To electronic	66	Facility	11	Staff	41
Remote	10	Cleanliness	5	Affect	27
To hardware and/or software	12	Furniture	11	Competence	27
Organization (the way access is organized)	23	Study Rooms	17	Photocopy	11
To print collections	32	Lighting	6	Suggestions/ Recommendations	9
By Discipline	8	Noise	38	ILL	23
Remote	5	Hours	25	Enforcement	3
Suggestions/ Recommendations	34	Enforcement	14		
To journals	32	Temperature	5		
By discipline	10	Suggestions/ Recommendations	11		
Enforcement	26				

periences represented in the comments. This was done by developing the properties (attributes or characteristics), and examining the dimensions (the location of properties along a continuum) for each category. Using this approach, we began to characterize the data in ways that would allow us to make comparisons and ask questions. This represents a second phase called Axial Coding, so-named because the dimensional data can be compared to each other as x and y axes. After seeing the range of responses within a category, we hypothesized relationships that might explain the differences in the judgments rendered or the experiences described in the comments. The final step was to return to the comments to verify the hypotheses.

Following the example of staff competence, it was determined that 17% of the comments in that sub-category were negative, 77% were positive, and 6% were neutral. A number of librarians were lauded by name for their abilities and service. The negative comments were mostly about part-time student staff. We hypothesized a relationship between staff training and experience to customers' satisfaction with staff competence. We also hypothesized a relationship between the personal relationship built between a customer and a librarian and the level of customer satisfaction with library staff competence.

These hypothesized relationships were then verified against actual data. There is a constant interplay between proposing hypothesis and checking. This process continued as several profiles were grouped together to give patterns, and the relationships among patterns explored. Connections were seen between the comments about staff competence and those about service affect, for example. In both sets of comments, there is a relationship between the customers' expectations and their perception of service quality. There is also a correspondence between customers' perception of staff competence and customer satisfaction with the affective qualities of service, as the respondents many times started addressing staff competence, eventually commenting on their satisfaction with the services received.

Analysis of the comments is ongoing. The final theory about what was being said by survey participants will be built upon and limited to the categories employed, their properties and dimensions, and statements of relationships that exist in the actual data collected. This is what Strauss and Corbin call a "Grounded Theory"[1] because the stories that are told with the data are grounded not in some imported abstract notion of what is happening or in preconceived notions of what concerns customers, but in the data provided by the customers and their comments.

USING THE DATA

Strategic planning is part of the regular, ongoing work of the library. Given the timing of the work done with the 2002 survey comments and the library planning calendar, the information gained from the comments and this analysis was folded into the work of SLRP, the library-wide planning team, as part of the planning effort for 2003-2004. The library has agreed upon three core goals centering on access, education, and infrastructure. We have also defined the critical processes the library will perform to meet these goals. As part of their work, SLRP used the resulting analysis of the comments to inform their deliberations regarding the relative importance of these processes for the next three years. SLRP also used the results to help them develop their current situation analysis.

The library uses a number of tools to solicit customer feedback about the collections and services offered, including an ongoing "Library Report Card" on the Web page, focused surveys aimed at particular demographic groups or about specific services, and previous LibQUAL+™ data. The data derived from these various efforts are not looked at in isolation, but rather are compared to previously derived available data. In this context, SLRP found nothing "earth shattering" in the conclusions drawn from these comments. For the most part, they provide important support and verification for patterns already observed. A matrix was created from the results that indicated customer ranking of importance of library work according to demographic group (see Table 4). This matrix was considered along with other information SLRP had from the other customer feedback mechanisms, readings on current trends, and studying the current campus situation. From this discussion, SLRP will further define a few important projects that should be funded in the next year in order to move the library towards its goals.

From a library-wide perspective, SLRP's use of the 2002 LibQUAL+™ comments is very important. However, planning in the library also takes place in each functional team, and each of these teams is also using these comments to inform their efforts for 2003-2004. The Science-Engineering Team, for example, has conducted several information-gathering projects in recent years. These efforts include a survey of faculty and students in the relevant colleges and departments, a citation analysis of student dissertations and faculty journal articles, and an analysis of interlibrary borrowing activity. Certain themes have emerged from these efforts, such as the need for reliable access to electronic journals

TABLE 4. Customer Ranking of Library Work

User Group	Access	Environment	Service
Undergraduate	63	61	30
Graduate	97	70	69
Faculty	70	13	36
Staff	60	12	26
Total	290	156	161

and the interdisciplinary nature of the resulting scholarly work. The 2002 LibQUAL+™ comments from customers in the relevant disciplines are being used along with the other data in determining team projects and other planning for next year.

Other subject-oriented teams are looking at the comments from their relevant demographic groups in similar ways. Rather than looking at the comments from a particular demographic group, the Materials Access Team (MAT) examined comments focusing on service affect, staff competency, access organization, and access to the print collection. They are using these comments, along with user comments received from the Library Report Card and from their own "AskCirc" e-mail account, to confirm which issues require immediate attention and to better anticipate customer needs. MAT has defined the competencies needed for each member of the team. The comments received from LibQUAL+™ have helped to test whether these competencies have been met, and have helped determine what projects need to be undertaken in order to address deficiencies. Other projects are being considered to address needs expressed regarding the availability of material from the print collection, especially in the smaller branch libraries. The three sets of comments are now being regularly entered into N6 and coded according to the categories used in the 2002 LibQUAL+™ project. This combined set of customer feedback will be the driving force in deciding strategic directions and team projects for 2003-2004.

CONCLUSION

The University of Arizona Library is a data driven, customer-centered library. As such, this project has been fruitful and will benefit the library in several ways. The comments we now get from LibQUAL+™ are yet another piece of customer feedback that can be used along with other information to gauge the needs of our campus customers and to plan new services and new approaches to meeting their needs. Further, the tools the working group has developed in this project can be applied to a wide range of other data sets to help the library understand what our customers are telling us. The project to analyze the 2002 comments has been a learning experience for the entire working group. As this article is being completed, we are starting to receive the comments from the 2003 survey. The work of this group will serve as a starting point for a systematic analysis of the 2003 comments.

NOTE

1. Anselm L. Strauss and Juliet M.Corbin, *Basics of Qualitative Research: Grounded Theory Procedures and Techniques*. (Newbury Park, California. Sage Publications, 1990): 23-24.

Another Tool in the Assessment Toolbox: Integrating LibQUAL+™ into the University of Washington Libraries Assessment Program

Steve Hiller

SUMMARY. The University of Washington is one of five institutions that participated in the LibQUAL+™ surveys conducted each year since its pilot phase in 2000. These surveys are sponsored and administered by the Association of Research Libraries (ARL) and Texas A&M University. This paper reviews the administration, methodology and results from the LibQUAL+™ surveys in the context of an existing assessment program at the University of Washington Libraries that employs a suite of assessment tools. It also compares our LibQUAL+™ experience with the set of expectations we articulated in 1999 for participating in the LibQUAL+™ project. *[Article copies available for a fee from The Haworth Document Delivery Service: 1-800-HAWORTH. E-mail address: <docdelivery@haworthpress.com> Website: <http://www.HaworthPress.com> © 2004 by The Haworth Press, Inc. All rights reserved.]*

Steve Hiller is Head of Science Libraries/Library Assessment Coordinator, University of Washington Libraries, Seattle, WA (E-mail: hiller@u.washington.edu).

[Haworth co-indexing entry note]: "Another Tool in the Assessment Toolbox: Integrating LibQUAL+™ into the University of Washington Libraries Assessment Program." Hiller, Steve. Co-published simultaneously in *Journal of Library Administration* (The Haworth Information Press, an imprint of The Haworth Press, Inc.) Vol. 40, No. 3/4, 2004, pp. 121-137; and: *Libraries Act on Their LibQUAL+™ Findings: From Data to Action* (ed: Fred M. Heath, Martha Kyrillidou, and Consuella A. Askew) The Haworth Information Press, an imprint of The Haworth Press, Inc., 2004, pp. 121-137. Single or multiple copies of this article are available for a fee from The Haworth Document Delivery Service [1-800-HAWORTH, 9:00 a.m. - 5:00 p.m. (EST). E-mail address: docdelivery@haworthpress.com].

http://www.haworthpress.com/web/JLA
© 2004 by The Haworth Press, Inc. All rights reserved.
Digital Object Identifier: 10.1300/J111v40n03_10

KEYWORDS. LibQUAL+™, academic libraries, assessment, library service quality, Web-based surveys, peer comparison

INTRODUCTION

The University of Washington Libraries (UW Libraries), located in Seattle, Washington, supports the teaching, learning, and research needs of its academic community of nearly 4,000 teaching and research faculty, 10,000 graduate and professional students, and 26,000 undergraduates. The University of Washington (UW) is one of five institutions that has participated in the LibQUAL+™ surveys since its pilot phase in spring 2000.

The UW Libraries has an extensive record of assessment activities highlighted by the use of large-scale library surveys administered on a triennial cycle since 1992. These triennial surveys are sent to all faculty members and a random sample of graduate and undergraduate students. Surveys measure user satisfaction with library services and resources and have also included questions on the reasons faculty and students use (or don't use) libraries, use and application of electronic information, importance of information resources, and their priorities for library services and resources. The triennial survey results comprise a rich lode of information about library use and needs during a period of rapid change in the information environment.[1] This extensive survey history with its large number of responses (more than 1,300 faculty returns in each of the last three surveys) also provides excellent grounding for comparing the LibQUAL+™ surveys with its much smaller sample size and response rate. Other assessment measures used by the UW Libraries include in-library use surveys, focus groups, usability studies and guided observation. A more complete description of the program, including survey instruments, results, and analysis can be found at: http://www.lib.washington.edu/assessment/.

UW Libraries Assessment Efforts Have Found Among Our Users

- High satisfaction with the Libraries, its services, and collections
- Substantial changes in library use patterns since 1992
- A marked preference for desktop access to information resources
- Differences in library use patterns, priorities and needs between academic subject areas

- Undergraduates use libraries very differently than faculty
- Library as place remains important to undergraduates *while declining for other groups*
- Information technology and online information resources enhance research and teaching
- UW Libraries considered the most important information resource for faculty and students

LibQUAL+™ at the University of Washington

Given an existing, reasonably robust assessment program, why did the University of Washington Libraries decide to participate in the LibQUAL+™ effort? Initially the reasons were to:

- Gain experience with a Web-based survey tool
- Work with a less costly survey method utilizing a standardized survey instrument
- Identify service gaps
- Track user satisfaction and needs during non-triennial survey years
- Complement existing assessment program and activities
- Compare results with peer institutions

An earlier paper[2] reviewed the LibQUAL+™ 2000 process and results at the University of Washington and found that while the response rates were substantially lower than the UW triennial surveys, they were still representative of the population, and results meshed well with triennial survey findings. The LibQUAL+™ 2000 survey results identified many of the priorities, issues and concerns that came up in the triennial survey conducted in 1998 and LibQUAL+™ was run at a fraction of the cost.

LibQUAL+™ 2001

The 2001 LibQUAL+™ survey was administered in February so as to avoid a conflict with the UW triennial survey scheduled for Spring 2001. The University of Washington was the first institution site to launch the 2001 LibQUAL+™ survey. A flawed faculty sample, changes in survey methodology and a major earthquake in Seattle one day after the initial survey launch all had major impacts on survey administration and in obtaining useful results. The faculty survey was dropped (a new sample was not drawn and no reminder notices were sent, surveys returned by faculty were not counted) but the survey continued for graduate and undergraduate students.

2001 Survey Design and Methodology

There were several changes made in survey design and methodology that affected results, the most important being the use of a one-column rating (perceived level only) that was offered to about half the survey participants. Another change for UW survey takers was the absence of a "not applicable" category, making respondents provide ratings for each question (a "not applicable" button was provided on surveys to institutions that followed). The use of a one-column response appeared to have a noticeable impact on survey results. While the overall student response rate was similar to 2000 (Table 1), only 47 graduate students (32%) and 29 undergraduates (23%) completed the three-column survey and thus the groups that provided minimum and desired expectations were of limited size. These low numbers by themselves complicated statistical analysis and comparison of the 2001 data with results from 2000 and those of other institutions. In addition, the perceived scores of those completing the three-column survey were generally higher, sometimes substantially higher, than those responding to the single column one. Changes in the composition of the graduate student respondents also limited the ability to use results (Table 2).

LibQUAL+™ 2002

Administration of the LibQUAL+™ survey in 2002 proceeded smoothly, especially in comparison with 2001. The number of core survey items was reduced to 25 plus three overall satisfaction items and two frequency of use items. There were few technical or computer compatibility problems reported and just a handful of comments from respondents about methodology and survey design. (Fortunately, the Seattle area was not visited by any natural disasters during the survey period.) The central support provided by the LibQUAL+™ technical team was excellent and the ability to track responses was helpful in targeting reminder notices.

TABLE 1. Response Rates to LibQUAL+™ and UW Triennial Surveys

Group	2002 LibQUAL+™	2001 LibQUAL+™	2000 LibQUAL+™	2001 UW Triennial	1998 UW Triennial
Faculty	22.2%		21.6%	36.2%	40.0%
Graduate Students	21.3%	24.5%	22.7%	39.8%	45.7%
Undergraduates	15.4%	14.1%	16.1%	24.9%	39.4%

TABLE 2. Graduate/Professional Student Population and Survey Respondents by Academic Area

Academic Area	2002 LibQUAL+™ n = 128	2001 LibQUAL+™ n = 147	2000 LibQUAL+™ n = 136	2001 UW Graduate Pop n = 9158	2001 Triennial UW Survey n = 597
Health Sciences	24.2%	15.6%	22.1%	28.6%	26.3%
Sciences/Engineering	32.8%	56.5%	28.2%	27.0%*	27.8%*
Humanities/Arts/Social Sciences	26.6%	19.0%	45.0%	37.4%*	40.0%*
Other	16.4%	8.8%	4.6%	7.2%	5.9%

*Psychology moved from Science to Humanities/Arts/Social Sciences to provide comparison with LibQUAL+™ results.

Response rates were similar to previous LibQUAL+™ surveys and the breakdown by academic area for faculty and graduate students continued to show graduate students in the humanities/arts and social sciences underrepresented and faculty in the same area over-represented (Table 3). The differences in graduate student academic area affiliation may represent a mapping problem as a number of large graduate student programs such as public affairs, information, and social work may not identify with social sciences or health sciences and, instead, choose, "other." Undergraduate representation by class year was similar to the 2000 survey (Table 4).

LESSONS LEARNED

As the LibQUAL+™ project nears the end of its pilot phase, this is an appropriate time to review and compare our expectations for our LibQUAL+™ participation with our experiences and results.

TABLE 3. Faculty Population and Survey Respondents by Year

Academic Area	2002 LibQUAL+™ N = 133	2000 LibQUAL+™ N = 127	2001 Faculty Population N = 3720	2001 Triennial UW Survey N = 1345
Health Sciences	40.6%	43.0%	48.6%	47.7%
Sciences/Engineering	23.3%	25.8%	24.3%*	24.5%*
Humanities/Arts/Social Sciences	32.3%	31.2%	23.4%*	24.5%*
Other	3.8%	4.6%	3.7%	3.3%

*Psychology moved from Sciences to Humanities/Arts/Social Sciences to provide comparison with LibQUAL+™ results

TABLE 4. Undergraduate Student Population and Survey Respondents by Year

Class	2002 LibQUAL+™ n = 139	2001 LibQUAL+™ n = 127	2000 LibQUAL+™ n = 145	2002 UW Undergrad Pop. n = 23858	2002 Triennial UW Survey n = 497
Freshman	23.0%	14.2%	22.6%	16.7%	14.5%
Sophomore	13.7%	13.4%	13.9%	19.0%	12.1%
Junior	32.4%	28.3%	27.7%	26.2%	29.8%
Senior and 5th year	30.9%	44.1%	35.8%	37.0%	43.0%
Other				1.0%	0.6%

Gain Experience with a Web-Based Survey Tool

The University of Washington Libraries had not used Web-based survey tools beyond course evaluations or other targeted efforts. We were specifically interested in the ability to pull a large sample of faculty and students that included current e-mail addresses, the community's receipt and response to an e-mail invitation to take a Web-based survey, and the technical issues associated with a Web-based survey accessed through multiple mediums.

Another campus agency drew our faculty and student samples and they had no difficulty in coming up with the sample size numbers and e-mail addresses. The number of incorrect or invalid e-mail addresses remained relatively low (ranging from less than 1% of faculty up to 3% for undergraduate students) and comparable to the resultant number of invalid mail addresses in our triennial surveys. Although an Autumn 2002 Educational Technology survey found that 40% of UW students used a non-university e-mail account as their primary e-mail service,[3] the percentage of undergraduates who opened the 2002 LibQUAL+™ survey was only slightly lower than for graduate students and faculty. However, the percentage of undergraduates who completed the survey after it was opened was only 70%, compared to 80% for graduate students and 85% for faculty.

The response rate for all three years has been remarkably consistent and we have used the same approach each year: an e-mail invitation and two follow-up reminder messages. The response rate is substantially lower than what is received with our triennial surveys, although not as low if the same criteria were applied to determine a valid survey. If we applied criteria similar to what we use to define a valid returned survey for the UW triennial surveys to the LibQUAL+™ surveys, the nominal response rate for LibQUAL+™ 2002 would increase as follows: undergraduates from 15% to 18%; graduate students from 21% to 23%; faculty from 22% to 27%. There is some evidence that response rates for Web-based surveys continue to be lower than for print surveys. For example, two recent surveys conducted by the UW Office of Educational Assessment on educational technology revealed that participants were more likely to complete paper surveys than the online version. For a 2002 student survey, 59% of the completed surveys were paper, and 41% were done online. Among the completed surveys returned by faculty in 2001, 68% were paper and only 32% were online.[4]

Technical problems with users opening and completing the LibQUAL+™ survey have decreased substantially from the first year (2000). Known problems from the user end (such as using Internet Explorer with a Mac) were addressed and backend support grew more robust. User annoyance at having to complete a small number of questions on each screen before proceeding were also addressed by format changes that enabled them to view more of the survey at a given time.

Work with a Less Costly Survey Tool and Use a Standardized Survey Instrument

The 1998 UW Libraries triennial survey had direct costs of $19,000 (30% printing, 30% mailing, 30% data entry, 10% other). Increased mailing and printing costs for the 2001 triennial survey pushed the direct costs closer to $22,000. The $2,000 participation fee for LibQUAL+™ saves 90% of the direct costs and as a "turnkey" delivered Web-based survey, LibQUAL+™ virtually eliminates the staff time associated with survey design and development. While an eventual move to a Web-based triennial survey will eliminate the printing, mailing and direct data entry costs, there will be other costs associated with design and development for a Web-based environment including systems support. However, the consistently lower response rate for LibQUAL+™ and other local Web-based surveys presents us with an interesting challenge for our 2004 triennial survey. We had planned to do this as a Web-only survey, but may use a hybrid method to maximize potential returns.

The triennial surveys are developed, designed, tested and distributed by UW Libraries staff with some assistance from other campus units. Surveys are adapted to the local environment and many questions deal with issues of concern to the Libraries and/or the campus community. After the initial survey in 1992, the survey design and development process now takes about 3 months and averages about 500 hours of staff time. LibQUAL+™ offered the opportunity to use a well-proven methodology (ServQUAL) with the survey design and development done externally and grounded in qualitative theory.

Identify Service Gaps

The LibQUAL+™ methodology exerts a powerful, seductive appeal in its ability to measure the differences or "gaps" between a user or customer's service expectations and actual perceived level of service. In our other surveys we could learn about perceived levels of importance, use, and satisfaction but did not have a way to frame this level against user expectations and needs.

The 2000 LibQUAL+™ survey showed few negative service adequacy gaps (perceived level of service below minimum expectations) among UW faculty and students. The largest negative gaps occurred with the faculty response to the question "full-text delivered electronically" and graduate student and faculty ratings of "complete runs of journal titles." There were no negative gaps among undergraduates.

While there were few negative gaps in 2000, there were a number of large positive service adequacy gaps. On nearly half the questions, the mean faculty score for perceived level of service was at least .9 higher than their minimum level. Students were more measured but generally had healthy positive gaps in all dimensions (Figure 1). Further analysis of the data found that gap size did not necessarily correlate with perceived levels of service, where outside of library as place, the difference in perceived levels was relatively small. In the library as place dimen-

FIGURE 1. UW LibQUAL+™ 2000 Service Adequacy Gaps by Dimension and Group

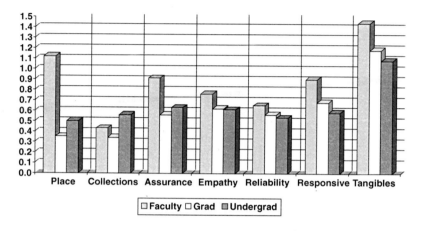

sion, the faculty positive gap was substantially larger than for students, although undergraduates had a much higher perceived score (Figure 2).

It is interesting to note that in our LibQUAL+™ 2000 survey (and in the ensuing surveys at other institutions), faculty and student results showed far larger positive service adequacy gaps for the service affect dimension than did library staff, where there were often negative gaps. Seeing our users identify librarians and library staff as strengths, and one that they valued, was important not only for our staff to know, but also for our University administration to know.

The 2002 LibQUAL+™ survey data results showed only a few small negative gaps among faculty and graduate students and none among undergraduates. While gaps can be presented in tabular data, it is easier to grasp the perceived level of service in relationship to both the minimum and desired, in addition to relativity to the other groups by viewing results in a chart showing the "zone of tolerance"–the area between minimum and desired levels. For example, while the undergraduate perceived score on the access to information dimension was similar to the other groups, undergraduate expectations were much lower, leading to a larger positive service adequacy gap (Figure 3).

There were few surprises in the questions that resulted in negative service adequacy gaps, as we knew from our triennial surveys and other qualitative data that faculty and graduate students placed a premium on remote access to information with journals being the most important in-

FIGURE 2. UW LibQUAL+™ 2000 Perceived Service Levels by Dimension and Group

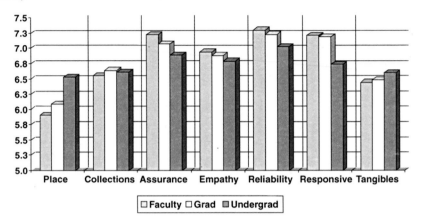

FIGURE 3. LibQUAL+™ 2002–UW Scores by Dimension and Group

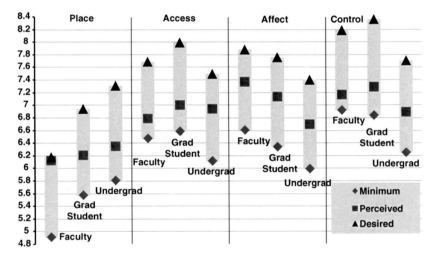

formation resource. While we initially thought that finding negative service gaps would prove valuable in identifying service deficiencies, generally that was not the case. Instead it was the large positive service gaps, especially the affective ones, that provided a dimension of user input that we had not measured before. These questions were not asked on our own surveys, and we had not looked at this area in any systematic manner before.

Track User Satisfaction and Needs During Non-Triennial Survey Years

The UW Libraries triennial surveys provide user satisfaction scores in three categories using a five-point Likert scale: satisfaction with services; satisfaction with collections; and overall satisfaction. We are also able to track user needs, satisfaction with hours and more specific services such as library instruction and access to computers in the library. Our 2001 triennial survey showed that user satisfaction was highest for faculty (although unchanged from 1998), with student satisfaction slightly lower although showing a measurable increase from 1998. The LibQUAL+™ survey ranks general satisfaction on a nine-point scale in three categories: overall; library support for learning, research and teaching needs; and affective treatment. While the more specific satisfaction questions differ and respondents will react differently to a nine-point scale compared to a five-point scale, there is reasonable congruity between satisfaction scores on both surveys. The patterns of higher faculty satisfaction and lower undergraduate satisfaction hold true in both surveys (Figure 4). At the aggregate level, LibQUAL+™ can provide inexpensive tracking of user satisfaction.

Complement Existing Assessment Program

The University of Washington Libraries assessment program has been underway for more than a decade and uses a variety of methods and techniques to provide a three dimensional view of our user community, their library and information use patterns, needs, priorities and satisfaction. LibQUAL+™ has emerged as an inexpensive complement to our assessment program. Not only is it cost-effective, LibQUAL+™ asks service quality questions in a way that enables us to gauge the perceived importance of the service as well as our performance. Additionally, we can also compare our responses with those of other institutions.

Our local assessment efforts show a continued shift towards remote use of library resources as the availability of electronic resources and services grow. While the frequency of visits to the physical library has decreased, especially for faculty and graduate students, the library as a place for undergraduate students to do work remains important.[5]

FIGURE 4. UW Satisfaction Scores: 2002 LibQUAL+™ and 2001 Triennial Survey

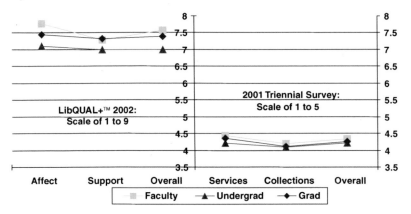

The large number of responses to our triennial survey, especially among faculty, enables us to perform analysis below the aggregate level such as by broad academic area, college or school. We have found substantial differences in some areas such as library use patterns and the value of print and electronic resources, and few differences in others such as satisfaction or library importance.[6] Since approximately 75% of our questions are the same for faculty and students, we can compare results between groups as well. Other surveys, such as those dealing with in-library use, provide additional information on why users visit the physical library and what they do while there.

We use such qualitative methods as focus groups and interviews to follow-up on survey results to better define issues from the user perspective. This information can be quite powerful as it comes directly from the user, but requires a different type of analysis that can be quite time-consuming.

A comparison of results from our last triennial survey and the LibQUAL+™ 2002 survey illustrates how LibQUAL+™ complements our local efforts. Our survey results showed a continued shift to remote use with faculty and students identifying desktop access to electronic resources as their overwhelming top priority. We also saw substantial increases in the importance of electronic journals to their work. Among a list of library services, student satisfaction with the Libraries Website was the highest and it was among the most used of any service. The LibQUAL+™ 2002 survey results for UW clearly identified the personal control dimension as critical for faculty and students with the highest minimum and desired expectation levels of any dimension for all groups (Figure 3). When we look at the individual questions with the highest desired level of service, they also tend to fall into the personal control dimension (Table 5).

The importance of the personal control dimension to all groups was a powerful message to library staff that providing remote access to resources and services without library mediation or intervention was the top priority of our faculty and students. A number of library activities ranging from Website usability to database interface reviews were initiated to improve our services in these areas.

Service affect results helped supply information on the elusive qualitative and human aspect of library service delivery. The UW Libraries had developed a comprehensive training and orientation program for new staff and student workers that emphasized service quality and user-centeredness. LibQUAL+™ gave us the opportunity to measure the outcomes of our service interactions.

While LibQUAL+™ complements our other survey efforts, it cannot replace our ability to locally tailor a survey, both in design and content, to our local environment, as well as draw a large response needed to perform sub-aggregate analysis by academic subject area. Our triennial surveys have a sufficiently large number of responses to allow us to an-

TABLE 5. LibQUAL+™ 2002–Five Questions with the Highest Desirable Rating by Group

Dimension	2002 Top 5 desirable by group with service adequacy gaps	UW Faculty		UW Grad		UW Undergrad	
		Des	Gap	Des	Gap	Des	Gap
Access	Convenient business hours	7.84		**8.34**	−.19	**8.21**	.78
Affect	Knowledgeable employees	**8.28**	.44	8.22		7.70	
Place	Comfortable and inviting location	6.94		7.37		**7.75**	.58
Control	Electronic resources available remotely	**8.44**	−.08	**8.55**	.18	**7.89**	.45
Control	Modern equipment	7.93		8.22		**7.89**	.79
Control	Library Website to locate info on my own	**8.30**	.28	**8.49**	.52	7.57	
Control	Easy-to-use access tools	**8.23**	.19	**8.36**	.54	7.56	
Control	Info easily accessible for independent use	**8.30**	.41	**8.30**	.60	7.59	
Control	Convenient access to library collections	7.98		8.23		**7.77**	.56

alyze results by academic subject area among faculty and graduate students. As a result, we can discern appreciable differences between subject areas, especially with faculty, and can plan our services and programs to take account of those differences.

Compare Results with Peer Institutions

Although the UW Libraries had an extensive record of survey data concerning the library and information needs and priorities of our users, their perception of library importance and satisfaction, we didn't have a sense of how this compared with other institutions. We hoped that using a standardized survey instrument along with other universities–especially peer ones–would allow us to better assess service quality in a context broader than just the University of Washington. This would enable us to identify and collaborate with peer institutions with high user satisfaction levels and large positive gap scores to establish a set of best practices.

Texas A&M and ARL produced a results notebook for the 2000 pilot survey that provided mean scores on the survey items by group at the aggregate level and for the specific library. Included were radar charts plotting mean scores by group for each institution, but not the data itself. Thus, it was difficult to compare a mean score at one institution with that of another either by dimension or question. Although we could compare University of Washington scores by group with that of the aggregate for the 12 institutions, the aggregate also included our own scores. Also, due to the relatively low number of institutions participating and the wide variation in response rates and numbers from each site, those numbers could be further skewed. However, there was sufficient information at the individual and aggregate level to note that our negative gaps on the "full text delivered electronically" and "complete journal runs" questions were lower than at most individual institutions and the aggregate means.

For 2001 survey results, a similar notebook was delivered to each participating institution. However, the LibQUAL+™ support team also provided Web accessible summary level data (usually mean scores) for each institution through a management center. Data was in HTML format and could be either printed or cut and pasted into local spreadsheets. Local institutional data could be compared to data from any one or set of institutions.

Distribution of 2002 survey results was handled differently due to the much larger number and broader range of participating institutions. In addition to the printed notebooks, electronic versions were made available to participants through a Web-based management center. A short set of institutional means was also provided in spreadsheet format. Score and gap norms[7] were also made available for comparisons. While it was useful to have the local institutional notebooks available, the PDF format also required more manual effort to put the data into spreadsheets for comparative analysis.

A comparison of UW results with those of other ARL libraries shows that mean perceived scores and gap scores were higher for UW faculty (Figure 5) and graduate students, while undergraduates generally had lower perceived scores and somewhat larger positive gap scores.

By manually entering LibQUAL+™ 2002 mean scores from selected universities, we can also analyze where UW fits among "peer" institutions, which we defined as those 18 libraries ranking among the top 40 in the ARL Index. As the UW Libraries ranks fourth in this "peer" group (12th in the ARL Index), we hoped to be in the upper quartile in satisfaction and positive gap scores. The UW ranks comparatively high in overall faculty and graduate student satisfaction (Figure 6). While undergraduate satisfaction and perceived service level scores are generally mid-range, service adequacy and superiority gaps rank nearer the top as can be seen for the personal control dimension (Figure 7). In general, we found the LibQUAL+™ data supported a favorable comparison of our service quality with our peer libraries.

FIGURE 5. LibQUAL+™ 2002–Faculty Scores by Dimension

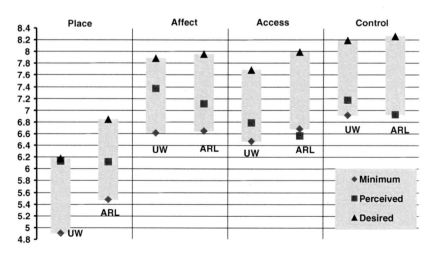

FIGURE 6. LibQUAL+™ 2000 Overall Faculty and Grad Student Satisfaction by ARL Ranking

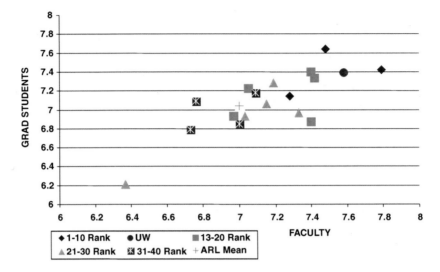

FIGURE 7. LibQUAL+™ 2002 Undergraduate Service Superiority Gap for Personal Control Dimension by ARL Ranking

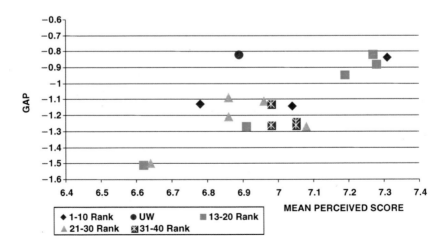

CONCLUSION

In general, our experience with LibQUAL+™ has been positive and instructive. The LibQUAL+™ project has demonstrated that a Web-based library survey can run efficiently and inexpensively, deliver results that are congruent with those achieved in large-scale more expensive surveys, and can provide comparative data on service quality over a range of institutions. While LibQUAL+™ will not substitute for local assessment efforts, it is a viable complementary tool that can be used to track user satisfaction and needs in a cost-effective manner. The ability of LibQUAL+™ to identify from the user perspective not only service deficiencies, but also service strengths, can be of immense value to libraries. Libraries need to understand what they do well as much as to discover what needs improvement.

NOTES

1. Steve Hiller and Jim Self, "A Decade of User Surveys: Utilizing and Assessing a Standard Assessment Tool to Measure Library Performance at the University of Virginia and the University of Washington," *Proceedings of the 4th Northumbria International Conference on Performance Measurement in Libraries and Information Services,* 2002, 253-262.

2. Steve Hiller, "Assessing User Needs, Satisfaction and Library Performance at the University of Washington Libraries," *Library Trends,* 41 (2001): 605-625.

3. Debbie McGhee, "The Student Survey on Educational Technology 2002: Methodology and Descriptives," *OEA Research Reports 03-04* (2003). Available at: <http://www.washington.edu/oea/0304.htm>.

4. Debbie McGhee, "The Student Survey on Educational Technology 2002: Methodology and Descriptives," *OEA Research Reports 03-04* (2003). Available at <http://www.washington.edu/oea/0304.htm>.

5. Steve Hiller, "The Impact of Information Technology and Online Library Resources on Research, Teaching, and Library Use at the University of Washington," *Performance Measurement and Metrics,* 3, no. 2 (2002a): 134-139.

6. Steve Hiller, "How Different are They? A Comparison by Academic Area of Library Use, Priorities, and Information Needs at the University of Washington," *Issues in Science and Technology Librarianship.* (Winter 2002). Available at: <http://www.istl.org/istl/02-winter/article1.html>.

7. See LibQUAL+™ survey score norms available online at <http://www.coe.tamu.edu/~bthompson/libq2002.htm>.

Mining LibQUAL+™ Data for Pointers to Service Quality at Wayne State University

Barton Lessin

SUMMARY. LibQUAL+™ data offers participating institutions a wealth of insight to existing and potential services and the perceptions of the institution's client-respondents. This paper explores the use of the LibQUAL+™ data at Wayne State University using three different methodologies. The first of these involved benchmarking with comparable urban, research institutions. A second approach termed Summary Group Analysis was helpful in that it allowed a clearer understanding of those services local LibQUAL+™ participants found most important, as well as how these individuals characterize the Libraries' success in accomplishing these services. The third approach focuses on the cross-tabulation of each LibQUAL+™ question by the fifteen disciplines included in the survey. This approach provided unexpected insight to local services and raised items about the national perceptions of those from selected disciplines. These three methodologies have proven helpful in communicating the value of LibQUAL+™ data and have provided those involved with service enhancement new tools to accomplish their work. *[Article copies available for a fee from The Haworth Document Delivery Service: 1-800-HAWORTH. E-mail address: <docdelivery@haworthpress.com> Website: <http://www.HaworthPress.com> © 2004 by The Haworth Press, Inc. All rights reserved.]*

Barton Lessin is Assistant Dean for Planning, Wayne State University Libraries, Wayne State University, Detroit, MI (E-mail: aa3327@wayne.edu).

[Haworth co-indexing entry note]: "Mining LibQUAL+™ Data for Pointers to Service Quality at Wayne State University." Lessin, Barton. Co-published simultaneously in *Journal of Library Administration* (The Haworth Information Press, an imprint of The Haworth Press, Inc.) Vol. 40, No. 3/4, 2004, pp. 139-155; and: *Libraries Act on Their LibQUAL+™ Findings: From Data to Action* (ed: Fred M. Heath, Martha Kyrillidou, and Consuella A. Askew) The Haworth Information Press, an imprint of The Haworth Press, Inc., 2004, pp. 139-155. Single or multiple copies of this article are available for a fee from The Haworth Document Delivery Service [1-800-HAWORTH, 9:00 a.m. - 5:00 p.m. (EST). E-mail address: docdelivery@haworthpress.com].

KEYWORDS. LibQUAL+™, benchmarking, peer comparison, library service quality, assessment, research institutions, urban institutions

INTRODUCTION

Red ink, regardless of whether it appears as an indication of deficit spending or negative service gaps as a part of the LibQUAL+™ survey process, is generally unwelcome. While red ink was a part of the LibQUAL+™ data results received by Wayne State University, these results effectively served to reinforce the need for an organizational change that was already underway. By emphasizing the negative service gaps identified by the respondents of the LibQUAL+™ survey, the Libraries' leadership team has gained a significant tool in its efforts to explain the importance of organizational and service changes in the very dynamic environment in which we work.

A number of different approaches were employed to interpret the data from the 2002 LibQUAL+™ survey results. These choices were predicated in no small part on the need to explain these data and make them useful for the Library System's operational teams and more understandable for members of the larger university community. Within the Library System, team meetings were utilized to describe the LibQUAL+™ process and the results for our institution. These team meetings featured an emphasis on LibQUAL+™ items that were of particular interest to a given team's operational focus. As an example, the Access Services Team heard more about item 8, 'timely document delivery/interlibrary loan,' than did the Resource Acquisitions and Metadata Services Team. This effort to tie LibQUAL+™ as closely as possible to the work of each team was done specifically to emphasize the role that every operational team has in establishing, maintaining, and enhancing client perceptions of quality directed toward the Wayne State University Library System. Through this process, each team was introduced to the gap theory of service quality[1] and how the Wayne State University Libraries' results compared with those from the aggregate and ARL participant libraries.

BENCHMARKING WITH URBAN, RESEARCH INSTITUTIONS

The service quality gaps proved to be of considerable interest for members of the operational teams. The discussion of our institution's negative service gaps was enhanced when data and tables were used to compare the Wayne State University LibQUAL+™ results with those from other peer universities. Provost Charles Bantz provided the Wayne State University deans with a listing of comparable urban research institutions. While not every institution named on Provost Bantz's list participated in LibQUAL+™ 2002, four referred to hereafter as A, B, C, and D, did participate and formed the basis of comparison with the Wayne State University LibQUAL+™ data.

Several differences in the LibQUAL+™ demographic information among the five institutions are worth noting. Wayne State University had the largest number of participants of the five institutions save one–institution B. This alone would not have made a significant impact had the distribution of participating population been reasonably consistent among the identified urban, research institutions. Wayne State had the smallest percentage of participating undergraduate students at 12.79% and the second highest percentage of participating faculty at 47.38% of its total population. These disproportionate percentages of undergrads and faculty in comparison with other status groups seem to have skewed the results of some items including those concerning the library as place. The Wayne State University demographic data also showed that our LibQUAL+™ population was the oldest of the five institutions with 43.28% of the population from the forty-five plus (45+) age group. Table 1 illustrates these comparative demographics.

The high percentage of faculty participating from Wayne State University was exceeded only by that from institution A, which was the only other university where LibQUAL+™ results pointed to numerous negative service quality gaps. It would be misleading to suggest that the large percentage of participating faculty from Wayne State University and institution A was the only reason that these two institutions experienced the results that they did. It does seem fair to suggest that the predominant faculty responses may well have contributed to larger negative gap scores, higher minimum expectations and desired scores than those from either of the two institutions that experienced greater numbers of positive gap scores with lower percentages of faculty participating. This should not be perceived as blaming the results on the faculty, but rather recognizing that the faculty may well have had more of an opportunity than students to compare library services among several institutions and may have simply reflected their experiences and familiarity with libraries and their services. This is exactly what we would want them to do when participating in LibQUAL+™.

TABLE 1. LibQUAL+™ Comparative Demographics

	Wayne State		A		B		C		D	
	Abs.	%	Abs.	%	Abs.	%	Abs.	%	Abs.	%
Age										
Less than 22	29	4.75	27	12.62	116	14.80	88	27.24	70	17.81
22-30	108	17.70	42	19.63	258	32.91	100	30.96	141	35.88
31-45	209	34.26	64	29.91	172	21.94	74	22.91	97	24.68
45+	264	43.28	81	37.85	238	30.36	61	18.89	85	21.63
Totals	610	100.00	214	100.00	784	100.00	323	100.00	393	100.00
Status										
Undergrad	78	12.79	46	21.50	164	20.92	114	35.29	115	29.26
Graduate	130	21.31	49	22.90	288	36.73	117	36.22	155	39.44
Faculty	289	47.38	116	54.21	183	23.34	83	25.70	113	28.75
Library Staff	57	9.34	0	0.00	75	9.57	0	0.00	6	1.53
Other Staff	56	9.18	3	1.40	74	9.44	9	2.79	4	1.02
Totals	610	100.00	214	100.00	784	100.00	323	100.00	393	100.00
Gender										
Female	314	51.48	112	52.34	393	50.13	185	57.28	215	54.71
Male	296	48.52	102	47.66	391	49.87	138	42.72	178	45.29
Totals	610	100.00	214	100.00	784	100.00	323	100.00	393	100.00

These comparisons proved more interesting than expected. The five libraries fell into two distinct groups that were marked by their dissimilarities with one another. Two of the libraries received client perception ratings resulting in negative service gaps for most if not virtually every LibQUAL+™ item. The third library did not experience the same high number of negative service quality gaps although each question category, except Affect of Service, was completely marked by negative service gaps. The two remaining libraries seemed to excel with virtually every question posed on the LibQUAL+™ survey. These latter libraries experienced very few negative service gaps; one received data with two negative service gaps, the other with none. This apparent dichotomy of perceived success is so obvious that Wayne State University team members asked about the service approaches emphasized at the two institutions (B and C) where those completing the survey rated library services so highly.

When the five institutions were used to compare minimum expectations for each LibQUAL+™ item, the results showed the highest minimum expectations were consistently registered from the participants at

Wayne State University. Table 2 shows that the highest minimum service level expectation was recorded at Wayne State University on twenty-one out of the twenty-five items (84%). Conversely, the highest perceived level of service was reported for 25 of 25 items (100%) at either institution B or C, where only a very limited number of the items had received the highest minimum rating among these five institutions.

Table 3 shows that the highest desired service level for each of the items was more widely distributed among the five libraries than the other characteristics considered here. In most cases (23 of 25 items, or

TABLE 2. Highest Minimum Expectations and Perceived Service Levels

Highest Minimum Expectation Among Five (5) Libraries Noted with ✕					
Highest Perceived Service Level Among Five (5) Libraries Noted with ☐					
Access to Information	Wayne State	A	B	C	D
3. Complete runs of journal titles	✕			☐	
8. Timely document delivery/ILL	✕		☐		
9. Interdisciplinary library needs met		✕	☐		
19. Convenient business hours	✕			☐	
22. Comprehensive print collections	✕		☐		
Affect of Service					
1. Willingness to help	✕			☐	
4. Employees who are . . . courteous	✕		☐	☐	
11. Dependability in handling . . . problems	✕			☐	
14. Giving users individual attention	✕			☐	
15. Employees who deal with users . . . caring	✕			☐	
17. Employees who have the knowledge . . .	✕			☐	
18. Readiness to respond to . . . questions	✕			☐	
20. Employees who instill confidence	✕			☐	
24. Employees who understand the needs . . .	✕			☐	
Library as Place					
2. Space that facilitates quiet study			☐✕		
10. A haven for quiet and reflection			☐✕		
13. A place for reflection and creativity	✕			☐	
21. A comfortable and inviting location	✕			☐	
23. A contemplative place			☐✕		
Personal Control					
5. Making electronic resources accessible	✕		☐		
6. Modern equipment . . . access information	✕		☐		
7. A library Website enabling . . .	✕		☐		
12. Easy-to-use access tools	✕			☐	
16. Making information easily accessible . . .	✕			☐	
25. Convenient access to library collections	✕			☐	

TABLE 3. Highest Desired Service Level

Highest Desired Service Level Among 5 Libraries Noted with ☒					
	Wayne State	A	B	C	D
Access to Information					
3. Complete runs of journal titles		☒			
8. Timely document delivery/ILL	☒	☒			
9. Interdisciplinary library needs met					☒
19. Convenient business hours				☒	
22. Comprehensive print collections		☒			
Affect of Service					
1. Willingness to help	☒				
4. Employees who are . . . courteous	☒				
11. Dependability in handling . . . problems	☒				
14. Giving users individual attention	☒				
15. Employees who deal with users . . . caring	☒				
17. Employees who have the knowledge . . .	☒				
18. Readiness to respond to . . . questions	☒				
20. Employees who instill confidence . . .		☒			
24. Employees who understand the needs		☒			☒
Library as Place					
2. Space that facilitates quiet study			☒		
10. A haven for quiet and reflection			☒		
13. A place for reflection and creativity					☒
21. A comfortable and inviting location					☒
23. A contemplative place					☒
Personal Control					
5. Making electronic resources accessible	☒				
6. Modern equipment . . . access information	☒				
7. A library Website enabling . . .	☒				
12. Easy-to-use access tools . . .	☒				
16. Making information easily accessible . . .	☒				
25. Convenient access to library collections		☒			

92%), the highest desired service level among these five was found at Wayne State University, institution A, or institution D. Again, of those in this small sample, these were the institutions that experienced numerous negative service gaps. In only three cases (12%), did the highest desired service level occur at either institution B or C. These two institutions received particularly strong client perceptions of their library services.

It was also determined in seventeen of twenty-five cases (68%) that the library reporting the highest minimum expectation for a question also reported the highest desired level of service for that same question. Table 4 also shows that the lowest minimum expectation of service and the highest perceived level of service occurred at the same institution in nineteen of the twenty-five cases (76%). With this particular benchmarking, all instances of the latter happened at institution C. Further comparisons may help to facilitate a more robust understanding as to why institutions B and C among this group of five urban, research institutions received more positive service gap scores than the other three benchmarked libraries. Size of collections, funding including endowments, staff size, and number of libraries should all be considered as factors worth exploring.

The comparison of LibQUAL+™ data using five urban, research institutions for benchmarking proved to be both interesting and useful. It provided insight into the apparent relationship between high expectations and high desired service levels, as well as lower expectations and higher perceptions of services. This kind of benchmarking has its limits and this process did not help to establish a set of priorities that would allow the Wayne State University Libraries' staff to understand what our patrons perceived as most important among the services that we offer. This had to be determined by a different exploration of the LibQUAL+™ data.

SUMMARY GAP ANALYSIS

The creation of a summary gap analysis chart with accompanying description of the derivation of the figures presented was well received by the Wayne State University library teams (see Chart 1). This illustration allowed team members to visually identify those services that our clients advised were most important, as well as those activities that were indicated as being handled most successfully based on the service gap. The summary gap analysis chart shows the importance on the horizontal scale and success in the form of the service gap on the vertical scale. Although the LibQUAL+™ scale goes from one (1) at the minimum to nine (9) at the maximum, this chart shows only the range between four (4) and 7.5 as each of the Wayne State University ratings for the LibQUAL+™ items fell into this abbreviated range. Importance here was calculated as the average of the minimum plus the desired for a

TABLE 4. Minimum Expectations and Highest Service Levels

Highest Minimum Expectation and Highest Desired Service at Same Site Noted with X					
Lowest Minimum Expectation and Highest Perceived Service at Same Site Noted with □					
	Wayne State	A	B	C	D
Access to Information					
3. Complete runs of journal titles				□	
8. Timely document delivery/ILL	X				
9. Interdisciplinary library needs met				□	
19. Convenient business hours	X				
22. Comprehensive print collections	X				
Affect of Service					
1. Willingness to help	X				
4. Employees who are . . . courteous	X			□	
11. Dependability in handling . . . problems	X				
14. Giving users individual attention	X			□	
15. Employees who deal with users . . . caring	X			□	
17. Employees who have the knowledge . . .	X			□	
18. Readiness to respond to . . . questions	X			□	
20. Employees who instill confidence . . .				□	
24. Employees who understand the needs				□	
Library as Place					
2. Space that facilitates quiet study			X	□	
10. A haven for quiet and reflection			X	□	
13. A place for reflection and creativity				□	
21. A comfortable and inviting location				□	
23. A contemplative place				□	
Personal Control					
5. Making electronic resources accessible	X			□	
6. Modern equipment . . . access information	X			□	
7. A library Website enabling . . .	X			□	
12. Easy-to-use access tools . . .	X			□	
16. Making information easily accessible . . .	X			□	
25. Convenient access to library collections					

given question. The vertical scale shows the aggregate of the Wayne State University responses for each of the items based on the perceived service rating minus the minimum expectation for service, or the "service adequacy gap." The advantage of the chart of this type is that it allows the reader to quickly identify services that are most important as being those farthest to the right side of the chart. They can just as

CHART 1. Summary Gap Analysis for the Aggregate Sample

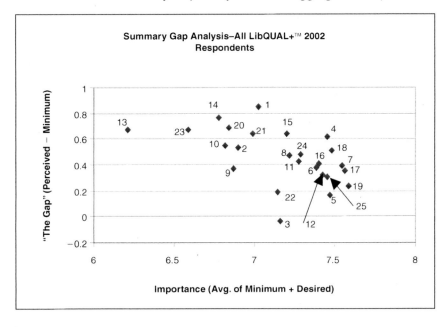

Summary Gap Analysis–All LibQUAL+™ 2002 Respondents

quickly recognize those services that are perceived by clients as being or not being well accomplished according to how high or low the service appears on the vertical scale of the chart.

For the team members, it was important to include notes that ranked the LibQUAL+™ items for each of the presentations where summary gap analysis was discussed. This ranking was arranged from highest to lowest and was based on the mean of the minimum expectation plus the desired service level. In the case of Wayne State University, the three most important items from the perspective of the client respondents were:

- Making electronic resources accessible from my home or office (item 5)
- Employees who have the knowledge to answer user questions (item 17)
- A library Website enabling me to locate information on my own (item 7).

It was possible to apply this same methodology to the aggregate LibQUAL+™ population to determine the items that the population as a whole determined were most important. In descending order from highest mean they include:

- Convenient business hours (item 19)
- Employees who have the knowledge to answer user questions (item 17)
- A library Website enabling me to locate information on my own (item 7).

This process showed that for the aggregate group, item 5 was ranked as the fifth most important service. The similarity of these two ranked lists was seen as encouraging by members of the operational teams. It was viewed as somewhat comforting to know that the interests of the local population are to some degree consistent with national trends.

The visual impact of the summary gap analysis could not be overstated. One need only to lead the team members from the top of the ranked listing to the chart, and point out the location of the "most important" service in its resting spot farthest to the right on the horizontal axis and far below the zero line on the vertical axis, for all to understand that work must be done for our libraries to meet and exceed the expectations of Wayne State University library clients. The comparison with the summary gap analysis for the aggregate group where the mean for each of the items other than number 3 (Complete runs of journal titles) appears over the zero line served as a wake-up call for action. Team members who attended these discussions were provided with additional data sheets that listed the items first by the question category (Access to Information, Affect of Service, Library as Place, and Personal Control) and then by the mean of the minimum plus the desired. As some categories are more important to some teams than to others, this data allowed team members to quickly find those items of greatest importance to the operations of a given team.

LibQUAL+™ ITEMS CROSS-TABULATED BY DISCIPLINE

An SPSS cross-tabulation of each of the LibQUAL+™ items by discipline provides a different perspective on service that can be helpful in understanding the needs of clients. Taking this process a step or two further resulted in some unexpected insights to local and national academic library services. Once the cross-tabulation was run, the percentages by discipline were stripped out and reassembled for each question resulting in a spreadsheet similar to the example in Table 5 that shows the results for item 1 (Willingness to help others). Approaching the data in this manner implies a potential problem that readers need to consider. The percentages for any given discipline could well represent a population too small to generalize in any meaningful way. On the other hand, looking at percentages makes comparison across disciplines possible, controlling for the number of participants when there are enough cases to generalize.With these caveats in mind, the data has proven of interest to better understand how those who represented the disciplines at one academic institution perceive of available library services.

In Table 5, the LibQUAL+™ scale was subdivided to show the lower end of the scale (1-5) and the upper end of the scale (6-9). One can argue that in order to reduce a negative service gap, an effort could be made to reduce the number and therefore the percentage of responses in the lower end of the scale. Table 5 emphasizes this approach by first summing the percentage for each discipline in the lower end of the scale and then averaging those results. This provides a group of responses that fall either above average (less desirable) for the lower end of the scale or below average (more desirable) for that part of the scale. Those that were above the average for the 1-5 range are noted in the shaded portion of the spreadsheet. A good place to begin to work on service enhancement might be with those disciplines identified as above the average for the lower end of the scale.

Perhaps the most interesting finding that resulted from this approach was the repetition of some disciplines in the above average section of the lower end of the scale. While variety in responses certainly occurred from item to item, several disciplines appeared more frequently than others. The composite Social Sciences/Psychology discipline appeared in the above average section of the lower part of the 1-9 scale for twenty-one (21) of the twenty-five (25) LibQUAL+™ items or 84% of the time. Other examples include:

- Other: 23 occurrences or 92% of LibQUAL+™ items
- Humanities: 20 occurrences or 80% of LibQUAL+™ items
- PFCA: 19 occurrences or 76% of LibQUAL+™ items
- Business: 16 occurrences or 64% of LibQUAL+™ items
- Communications: 15 occurrences or 60% of LibQUAL+™ items.

TABLE 5. LibQUAL+™ Question 1 Cross-Tabulated by Discipline

Q1	Willingness to help					Category:	Affect of Service			
Discipline	1	2	3	4	5	Sum 1-5	6	7	8	9
Gen Ed	0.00%	0.00%	0.00%	0.00%	0.00%	0.00%	25.00%	25.00%	25.00%	25.00%
Communication	0.00%	0.00%	11.80%	0.00%	0.00%	11.80%	23.50%	11.80%	41.20%	11.80%
Undecided	0.00%	0.00%	0.00%	0.00%	14.30%	14.30%	14.30%	28.60%	14.30%	28.60%
Education	1.30%	0.00%	5.30%	5.30%	6.60%	18.50%	19.70%	30.30%	14.50%	17.10%
Law	0.00%	0.00%	0.00%	6.30%	12.50%	18.80%	31.30%	12.50%	18.80%	18.80%
Health Sci	0.00%	2.70%	2.70%	4.50%	9.90%	19.80%	13.50%	25.20%	20.70%	20.70%
Science/Math	1.60%	0.00%	1.60%	4.70%	14.10%	22.00%	14.10%	23.40%	23.40%	17.20%
Engineering/CS	1.80%	0.00%	3.60%	9.10%	10.90%	25.40%	12.70%	27.30%	16.40%	18.20%
Other	1.10%	1.10%	8.00%	4.50%	13.60%	28.30%	18.20%	28.40%	11.40%	13.60%
Business	0.00%	11.80%	2.90%	8.80%	5.90%	29.40%	14.70%	20.60%	23.50%	11.80%
PFCA	10.00%	0.00%	0.00%	0.00%	20.00%	30.00%	10.00%	20.00%	30.00%	10.00%
Humanities	0.00%	1.90%	1.90%	13.00%	14.80%	31.60%	16.70%	26.00%	14.80%	11.10%
SS/Psych	0.00%	2.70%	4.10%	5.40%	20.30%	32.50%	21.60%	27.10%	10.80%	8.10%
					Average	21.72%				

The opposite of this situation is also of interest. Some disciplines represented by Wayne State University LibQUAL+™ participants were rated in such a manner that they appear infrequently above the average for the lower portion of the scale. It was in this grouping that Wayne State University LibQUAL+™ participants placed Education with only three occurrences (12%), Undecided, Health Sciences, and Science/Math with four occurrences each (16%), General Education with seven occurrences or 28%, and Engineering/Computer Science with eleven occurrences or 44%.

The fact that the responses for some disciplines fell above the average on the lower end of the LibQUAL+™ scale suggests that for those disciplines the respondents felt comparatively less positive about library services than was the case for other disciplines. This provides the operational teams at Wayne State University with data and information to consider in the context of strategic planning, including the setting of goals and objectives, a process that was ongoing as this article was written. In this context, it is important to recognize that some library services are not easily adapted to meet the needs of specific disciplines while others lend themselves to this kind of consideration. Circulation services, for example, tend frequently to be uniformly applied, particularly in those cases where services are centralized rather than distributed in departmental libraries. Contrast these with bibliographic instruction/information literacy services that are by necessity flexibly adjusted to meet the needs of the client. There is certainly a greater opportunity to provide individual or discipline-focused support with some services than with others. Having data that show which disciplines experienced higher than average results for the lower end of the LibQUAL+™ scale and knowing the LibQUAL+™ categories to which each of these items belongs is an advantage. These data can be used to help determine whether changes in service are needed. Existing services with additional attention can position a library to have positive impacts on service and therefore on the perceptions of service.

Table 6 shows a comparison of the results of the cross-tabulation of each LibQUAL+™ question by discipline for the participating national sample that included all respondents from four-year institutions. The use of these data helps to place the Wayne State University results into a broader perspective, and allows team leaders and team members alike opportunities to discuss the extent to which library services meet expectations and needs, locally and nationally for specific disciplines. It is intriguing to explore the possibilities that these data sets offer. Both the

TABLE 6. Frequency of Disciplines Above Average in the Lower Half of the Scale

National Population	No. Occur. Above Avg.	% Occur. Above Avg.	Wayne State University Population	No. Occur. Above Avg.	% Occur. Above Avg.
Architecture	24	96%	Other	23	92%
Gen Studies	23	92%	SS/Psych	21	84%
Law	22	88%	Humanities	19	76%
SS/Psych	20	80%	Business	17	68%
Tie: Science/Math	15	60%	Com/Journalism	16	60%
Humanities	15	60%	Law	12	48%
PFA	14	56%	Eng/CS	11	44%
Eng/CS	13	52%	General Ed	7	28%
Business	12	48%	Tie: Undecided	4	16%
Com/Journ.	10	40%	Health Sciences	4	16%
Undecided	9	36%	Science/Math	4	16%
Other	7	28%	Education	3	12%
Ag/Environ	1	4%			
Tie: Education	0	0%			
Health Sciences	0	0%			

WSU experience as well as that of the national sample, suggest that LibQUAL+™ respondents from the health sciences and education are more satisfied with the services they receive from their libraries than are the respondents from other disciplines included in the LibQUAL+™ survey. Perhaps we should be doing more to better understand why these clients held the perspectives they expressed.

In a like manner, it would be helpful to know much more about the perspectives of those from the combination Social Sciences/Psychology discipline as it appeared frequently above the average for the 1-5 range locally (84% of the cases) and nationally (80% of the 25 items). In fact, this discipline distinguished itself locally by being rated as that discipline most above average for the lower half of the scale in nine cases or for 36% of the LibQUAL+™ items. This combination discipline appeared so frequently above average for the lower half of the 1-9 scale it may suggest that the respondents who associate themselves with this discipline are more frequently dissatisfied with library services than most of the other disciplines on the survey. Whether this is perhaps owing to the interdisciplinary nature of psychology, or a different level of electronic access for behavioral psychology titles as opposed to neuro-psychology, or other factors that influenced the results is not clear from the

LibQUAL+™ data. The use of the national population helps to reinforce the findings from Wayne State University while minimizing the potential problem of too few individuals in the local population alluded to earlier. Even if there was an effort locally by the small sample to influence the results for this discipline, the national sample with its broad representation and similar results makes a strong case to suggest that the local results reflect as yet undetermined characteristics of the discipline, its literature, or interdisciplinary access.[2]

Business (17 occurrences and 68%) and Communications/Journalism (16 occurrences and 60%) were more frequently above average for the lower end of the scale at Wayne State University than for the national population. A next logical step in the examination of the data for these disciplines is to determine exactly which of the items was involved at the local and national level and to decide if there is any similarity between the two based on individual items or question categories that might help to provide a fuller understanding of the meaning of these numbers. There are other opportunities for comparison of the numbers from Table 6 as well as the data from each of the LibQUAL+™ items using the methodology illustrated in Table 5. Rather than attempt to determine the needs of the operational teams, this data has been made available to all members of the teams so that they can use the data to best meet team needs.

There are a number of factors that make approaching the data to emphasize the lower half of the LibQUAL+™ response scale relevant to enhancing library services:

- It focuses attention on service weaknesses regarding specific disciplines. This seems more appropriate than attempting to perform better only those services that our clients have already told us we are doing well.
- A discipline that appears with some consistency above average at the lower end of the scale both locally and nationally may signal service problems of a broad scope. The Social Sciences/Psychology discipline serves as an excellent example.
- The use of the national population and the comparison of results from that large group with the local population helps to minimize the impact that small numbers locally may have on the results.
- This approach provides yet another avenue for understanding the LibQUAL+™ results in a way that can assist libraries to improve service quality.

CONCLUSION

The Wayne State University Libraries staff is using the LibQUAL+™ results in a number of ways to facilitate its consideration of service quality. The three approaches included in this article each offer different advantages and disadvantages for the operational teams that are charged with the important work of enhancing client services and client perceptions of service. The comparison of the Wayne State University LibQUAL+™ results with those from other urban research libraries allows staff to contrast the results of individual items, question categories, or the entire 25-item list with similar results from other institutions. This treatment of the data helped to identify several positive service providers among a peer group chosen by the Provost. This approach did not help to determine what local clients think are the Libraries' most important services or how well any of its services are accomplished. These latter needs are better met with the summary gap analysis method that shows both importance and success based on the perspectives of those from our institution who completed the LibQUAL+™ survey.

The cross-tabulation of the LibQUAL+™ items by discipline provides yet another approach for examining this data. This method applied to both the Wayne State University LibQUAL+™ population, and the national four-year college and university LibQUAL+™ participating libraries, has been valuable in the way that it distinguishes among the perspectives of survey respondents who represent the variety of disciplines at our university. These methods, in combination with the data in the aggregate, ARL group libraries, and the Wayne State University LibQUAL+™ 2002 reports in addition to the comments offered by WSU survey respondents, provide valuable insight into client perspectives of our library services. This combination of approaches and data has enhanced the understanding of the LibQUAL+™ results for the Wayne State University staff and interested members of the university community, and has directly benefited the process of strategic planning while providing an opportunity for all to better understand the need for organizational and service changes.

ACKNOWLEDGMENTS

The author wishes to extend his appreciation to Joseph Zucca at the University of Pennsylvania Libraries for his assistance with the summary gap analysis for Wayne State University and to Martha Kyrillidou at the Association of Research Libraries for producing the SPSS cross-tabulation of LibQUAL+™ items by discipline for the sample population.

NOTES

1. Bruce Thompson, Colleen Cook, and Fred Heath, "The LibQUAL+™ gap measurement model: The bad, the ugly, and the good of gap measurement," Performance Measurement and Metrics 1, 3 (2000): 165-178.

2. Bruce Thompson, "Representativeness versus response rate: It ain't the response rate!" (paper presented at the Association of Research Libraries (ARL) Measuring Service Quality Symposium on the New Culture of Assessment: Measuring Service Quality, Washington, DC, October 21, 2000).

We Asked Them What They Thought, Now What Do We Do? The Use of LibQUAL+™ Data to Redesign Public Services at the University of Pittsburgh

Amy E. Knapp

SUMMARY. With the development of the LibQUAL+™ survey instrument, the University of Pittsburgh Library System libraries, particularly our public services division, were offered a tool by which we could begin to determine user satisfaction with library collections and services. Moreover, we now have a means to measure, on an annual basis, how successful new initiatives have been in addressing earlier perceived problems. This article focuses on how we used our institutional data to inform a process for redesigning our public service units, and to implement new, more user-designed services. *[Article copies available for a fee from The Haworth Document Delivery Service: 1-800-HAWORTH. E-mail address: <docdelivery@haworthpress.com> Website: <http://www.HaworthPress.com> © 2004 by The Haworth Press, Inc. All rights reserved.]*

Amy E. Knapp is Assistant University Librarian, University Library System, University of Pittsburgh, Pittsburgh, PA (E-mail: aknapp@pitt.edu).

[Haworth co-indexing entry note]: "We Asked Them What They Thought, Now What Do We Do? The Use of LibQUAL+™ Data to Redesign Public Services at the University of Pittsburgh." Knapp, Amy E. Co-published simultaneously in *Journal of Library Administration* (The Haworth Information Press, an imprint of The Haworth Press, Inc.) Vol. 40, No. 3/4, 2004, pp. 157-171; and: *Libraries Act on Their LibQUAL+™ Findings: From Data to Action* (ed: Fred M. Heath, Martha Kyrillidou, and Consuella A. Askew) The Haworth Information Press, an imprint of The Haworth Press, Inc., 2004, pp. 157-171. Single or multiple copies of this article are available for a fee from The Haworth Document Delivery Service [1-800-HAWORTH, 9:00 a.m. - 5:00 p.m. (EST). E-mail address: docdelivery@haworthpress.com].

http://www.haworthpress.com/web/JLA
© 2004 by The Haworth Press, Inc. All rights reserved.
Digital Object Identifier: 10.1300/J111v40n03_12

KEYWORDS. LibQUAL+™, public services redesign, user satisfaction, library service quality, academic libraries

INTRODUCTION

Libraries have long enjoyed popular perception as a public good, an indispensable part of scholarly and academic life. While individual schools and academic departments have had to justify expenditures and demonstrate the impact of enrollment, libraries have operated much as they have for decades. In an environment of rapid change, justification of expenditures and direct allocation of funding, however, is changing. Increasingly libraries are being asked to justify their existence to an extent never seen before. More and more libraries are being encouraged to determine the impact their resources and services are having on schools and programs, reallocate expenditures, implement new services and add significant numbers of new electronic resources, while maintaining those seen as indispensable by faculty and students. As Dugan argues "as never before, the federal government, state legislatures, students, parents, and the regional accreditation bodies, among others, demand that institutions of higher education demonstrate that, through applied accountability processes, they meet their stated educational missions and goals and that the evidence they provide is objectively and continuously gathered. . . ."[1] In order to address these new expectations and requirements, academic libraries are being forced to reexamine their methods for data collection and service evaluation in order to reallocate resources and demonstrate their impact on the institution. This article will discuss how we have used our LibQUAL+™ survey data to accomplish this.

WE'VE DONE A GOOD JOB AT COLLECTING WHAT IS EASY, NOW LET'S TRY TO GET SOMETHING USEFUL!

Even after years of collecting and reporting what people are doing in academic libraries, we have not made a great deal of progress on how satisfied users are with what we have provided in terms of public services. Traditionally, information on the extent and nature of material use has been captured and quantified. We have done an adequate job of collecting basic statistics that are easily collected and measured–number of circulations transactions, reference questions asked, ILL requests made and filled; number of titles added to the collection; number of people entering the building. What has been lacking, however, is how satisfied users have been with all these transactions. As Wells has argued, "the effectiveness of libraries has often been measured by the volume of library materials available to clients, the amount of use of services and resources, and the apparent or quantified satisfaction of clients. Very little research has taken into account the objectives of the clients."[2] In other words, we have traditionally captured statistics that are easy to capture, but not necessarily those that provide us with the information we need to evaluate and design services. Much more difficult to capture, but infinitely more useful for public services in particular, are data pertaining to general user satisfaction with the services we currently offer, and some information regarding what our users would like to see us offer in time. Even when some attempt was made to capture this information, it was often done informally, inconsistently, sporadically, and/or in a format that is not compatible with other data.

With the development of the LibQUAL+™ survey instrument by the Association of Research Libraries (ARL) and Texas A&M University Libraries, librarians–particularly in public services–were offered a tool by which they could begin to determine user satisfaction with library collections and services. Moreover, they could begin to measure on an annual basis how successful new initiatives had been in addressing earlier perceived problems. LibQUAL+™ has provided us with an affordable and reliable tool for measurement that enables us to begin to capture the impact our services are having on the members of the community we serve. As you will see later in this article, at the University of Pittsburgh Library System, we were able to institute very specific changes based on our LibQUAL+™ user data that had measurable impacts on our users' perception of our library system.

In this article the assumption is that the reader will be familiar with the LibQUAL+™ survey instrument, methodology, process for implementation, and data collection. This article will not review the fundamental techniques or details of the process, rather, the focus is on how we used our institutional data to inform a process for redesigning our public service units, and to implement new more user-designed services.

LibQUAL+™ AT THE UNIVERSITY OF PITTSBURGH LIBRARY SYSTEM

The University of Pittsburgh Library System libraries have participated in the LibQUAL+™ project since the initial pilot phase in 2000. We have been convinced since the earliest version of the survey that this process would provide us with invaluable data on our users' perceptions of our service and resources; information we were anxious to use to inform our process of continuous service and collection improvement. Over time, we have analyzed the collected data and attempted to identify areas that provided valuable information concerning not only what our patrons felt about our current services, but perhaps more importantly, about where they would like to see us going. We used the data collected not only to improve existing services but also to guide the implementation of new services and the significant restructuring of our public services administrative structure.

We began our process by reviewing all the data collected, in general and by specific user group and discipline. Naturally, there were a few simple issues we could address almost immediately. However, what we were really concerned with was looking at those areas over time where our users were telling us we had the most work to do in order to meet, and ultimately exceed, their expectations.

COMMITMENT TO CHANGE

As has been pointed out in the literature of LibQUAL+™, the process must begin with a commitment to trust the input of your users as a tool to implement real changes in public services.[3] This involves not only soliciting their opinions, but also making an internal commitment to address the issues, and concerns they raise. The by-product of this process is that it paves the way for innovative thinking by the public services librarians. As Phipps points out, "Service quality measurement is but one step in the process of transforming libraries so they can participate as full collaborators and leaders in the necessary and positive transformational changes in higher education. The library of the twenty-first century must be a new entity. Educating staff in the utilization of new measures will increase the required capacity for organizational learning that will support the creation of this new library."[4] Not only is it essential that the process begin with a commitment to change, but this commitment to change can have positive implications well beyond the life of the process.

DEALING WITH PERCEPTIONS

LibQUAL measures dimensions of perceived library quality; that is, each survey question is part of a broader category and scores within those categories are analyzed in order to derive more general information about library users' perceptions of service.[5]

One important concept that we struggled with early on was the notion that the data collected was based on user perceptions of library quality. It is easy when dealing with any user requested satisfaction data to become defensive and say, "they're wrong" or "they aren't aware of," or "we already do that." As librarians, we are privy to information regarding the implementation of services that is not available to patrons. Additionally, we are often forced to compromise and make service decisions that we know are not optimal. In any case, what you have to do as a unit or a library is to step back and objectively view the information your users have supplied. Even if you disagree with the information they have offered, which may be based on their perceptions of your library services, you can't say their perceptions are wrong. Perceptions are just that, perceptions. Your challenge in the library is to address these perceptions and come up with ways to increase user satisfaction. What we learned through this sometimes difficult process is that there are several different ways to accomplish this:

- Promote services and resources you already offer but which your users seem not to use or be aware of
- Place a greater emphasis on on-going customer service training for library staff
- Attempt to address significant collection and access issues with new services.

The remainder of the article will describe what we did, and what we learned from the process. Additionally, how we used subsequent LibQUAL+™ data to assess the impact of the changes we made will be addressed.

INTERPRETING THE DATA

When sharing the results internally, one of the first hurdles we as a library system had to address was how to approach the findings in a positive, proactive way, instead of defensively. What we discovered was that in some respects this was one of the greatest challenges we faced. We had to begin our presentation of the results by emphasizing that much of what we were dealing with was our users' perceptions. While recognizing that these data are incredibly valuable to us in terms of informing changes that would actually benefit our users, this type of information is not quantifiable as the type we are used to working with. The user satisfaction data we collected as part of the LibQUAL+™ survey was based entirely on our specific users' perceptions of our library system. While internally we might feel that we have adequate runs of journal titles, for example, that may not be our users' perception. It was important for us to communicate to our staff that you cannot argue with perceptions–whatever they are, they are. Our challenge was to take these perceptions and attempt to design methods and services to address them. As is probably the case at most institutions, we began the review of the data by looking at the best news and the worst news.

SURVEY COMMENTS

In many ways, the comments gathered from the open comments section of the survey form provided some of the most detailed information. Another, perhaps hidden, benefit of this comments section is that it provides users with the opportunity to expound on issues near and dear to them, and–let's be honest–to vent. Over the years we have found that while these comments are often too specific to be useful across a large system, they can often alert us to problems in specific locations or with specific functions. For example, one common issue from several different users was the lack of online book renewal. Online book renewal has been an available function in our OPAC for several years, but a common misperception was that it was not an available feature. We felt we could address this relatively easily now that we had been made aware of it. Building on what our users told us, we now know to be more diligent about pointing out this feature in informational materials, online help pages and in instruction sessions.

In another more indirect way, respondents utilized the comments section to connect with the person who sent out the survey invitation encouraging them to participate. Often users would take this more personal or direct approach to communicate some of their concerns. This was extremely helpful as it gave us the opportunity to "speak" directly to the respondent, and in many cases we were able to resolve an issue immediately.

Finally, what we often heard from users via the comments section was that they appreciated the fact that the library was actually expressing interest in what they thought! Several respondents acknowledged that while they may have initially been a bit reluctant to take the time to complete the questionnaire, they did appreciate that we were actively engaged in attempting to determine how they felt about our services and resources. In no small way did this provide our library system with general good will.

"INCOMPLETE RUNS OF JOURNAL TITLES AND MONOGRAPHS"

When one reviews the patron satisfaction data across institutions, one of the areas of greatest user dissatisfaction is that of complete runs of titles, both serials and monographs. While librarians from nearly every institution will agree that this is not an issue we are currently committed to address, it is obviously of great concern to our users. In particular, faculty and graduate students are concerned about this issue, and since our purpose in participating in the LibQUAL+™ survey is to take action to address patron concerns, we were committed to finding a way to address these concerns.

As was stated earlier, we were not going to go back and attempt to determine where all the gaps exist in our 15,000+ journal title collection. We did, however, feel compelled to examine where the most significant dissatisfaction existed. What we discovered was that the situation was a bit more complicated than just having the items. It was not that faculty and graduate students necessarily wanted complete runs of titles in the library, but, rather, they wanted access to all the issues of specific journals. This was a situation we could address. Our solution to address user dissatisfaction with "complete runs of journals" was a two-fold service solution. First, we began by aggressively seeking out back runs of journals that are available electronically that we could use to supplement our print collections. Over the course of the past year, we have purchased six backfile "packages" from publishers such as Elsevier. Additionally, we are moving our offsite storage collection to a facility equipped with a user reading room, that is closer to campus, and accessible by a campus shuttle. Finally, we instituted a document delivery service for faculty. This free service provides physical delivery of monographs to offices on campus, and electronic delivery of journal articles (including items in print and in storage) to the requestor's desktop. In part, we were able to secure institutional funding for this service because we were able to demonstrate that there was a significant need to enhance faculty access to materials. We were able to document this through our LibQUAL+™ data. Subsequently, we have been able to demonstrate marked improvements in our users', especially faculty, perceptions of access to complete runs of journal titles and monographs.

"LIBRARY AS PLACE"

As discussed, the area of most concern for our faculty and graduate students had been access to complete runs of journals and monographs. For our undergraduates, the dimension of service they were telling us that needed the most work was "library as place." Within this dimension of the LibQUAL+™ survey, they responded to questions concerning how satisfied they were with the library as a place for studying, working, making use of resources, and as a space for general use. They did not perceive the library to be a very friendly, welcoming or comfortable place for them. Although we felt we had done a wonderful job of creating what we thought a library should be, our undergraduates were telling us it really wasn't meeting their needs. We decided to address this issue in two ways.

The first way was fairly easy to implement. For years, one of the issues we struggled with in public services was that we were simultaneously attempting to be friendly and approachable, while also policing user behavior. In particular, we had a restrictive food and drink policy that was very unpopular with our undergraduate students. Not only was the policy unpopular, but it required in large part the public services staff to enforce this policy. Therefore, it was difficult for our public services staff to seem pleasant and approachable while acting as enforcers for this dreaded policy. Realizing the effect this was having on our undergraduates' perception of the library as a welcoming, comfortable place, we set out as a group to rethink the policy. We came up with a compromise that let them bring in drinks in covered containers and have food only in designated areas. This greatly eased the public services staff of their "policing" duties, and let them concentrate on being friendly and welcoming.

Our second service implementation was much more ambitious. Again responding to our students desires for a friendly, welcoming, food/drink tolerant environment, we partnered with food services on campus to open a coffee bar in the library. Not only did we enable users to purchase coffee, other drinks and light snacks, but we moved our popular browsing collection to this new area, and outfitted it with small couches and easy chairs! Needless to say, this area has become one of the most popular on campus, as is demonstrated by soaring assessments of the library as place in subsequent LibQUAL+™ surveys by our users.

RETHINKING PUBLIC SERVICES

Public services in the library system had experienced no significant administrative or functional change in several years. We had incorporated new technologies into our service points–reference, circulation, ILL–but had done little in the way of introducing new services. A group within public services was created to determine the future direction for public services in the library system. The Rethinking Public Services team was formed and charged with determining what our users thought of our current public services, what their needs are, and, based on this information, adapting our services to meet those needs. The group worked with Julia Blixrud of ARL who helped to develop a process for determining these needs and developing new services to meet them. One of the basic premises for the redesign project was to take a multi-system approach as a means of collecting as much information as possible in order to be certain that our direction was correct. We examined several national research studies, held open meetings with staff to gather their input, and then sat down with what is now several years of LibQUAL+™ data. This data helped us not only see where we had to go next, but helped us measure the impact of the services we had already implemented.

USING LibQUAL+™ TO IDENTIFY AREAS FOR IMPROVEMENT

After instituting many changes, including implementing new major services, as well as some other small and immediate service changes, for the Rethinking process we again reviewed our user satisfaction data. We then set about using the LibQUAL+™ findings to inform the focus group process we used within our reference redesign. The team took user input and began to develop methods for eliciting details as to what service improvements our users would like to see from us.

FOCUS GROUP QUESTION GENERATION

Working with our ARL consultant, Julia Blixrud, we began the focus group process. We wanted the focus groups to consist of users and non-users of our libraries. We asked librarians across the system to supply us with names of faculty and students who frequently used our libraries. These would make up our users' group. We identified random users from each group and contacted all potential participants via e-mail and ask them for their help. Our target was to have twelve groups of faculty, undergraduates, and graduate students from all disciplines served by the library system.

During this process, we were able to put our LibQUAL+™ findings to additional use. We developed a list of ten questions regarding the nature and frequency of use and user satisfaction with library resources and services. The ten questions were designed to build on areas within LibQUAL+™ where our users told us they had some real issues. The questions that we designed sought to provide us with additional, substantive, specific information on what aspects of our services our users were most dissatisfied with, what services worked for them, and most importantly, what we could do to improve their perceptions of our services and resources.

FOCUS GROUP FINDINGS

The focus group sessions proved invaluable as a means of providing very useful, detailed information regarding how our patrons were currently using, and in some cases, not using, library resources and services. The participants were enthusiastic about the process and eager to share their opinions with us. When we reviewed the focus group findings, one aspect that was most encouraging was that the data gathered validated what we had collected in the past several years as part of the LibQUAL+™ survey. A few of the most significant findings include:

- Many faculty and students, especially in the humanities, continue to rely on a mix of electronic and print resources.
- Users value the library as a place on campus where they can receive competent, immediate, in-person assistance.
- Another clear and strong finding is faculty believe their graduate students do not know how to conduct effective scholarly research utilizing library resources.

Next we took the findings and attempted to draft recommendations for redesigning our existing services, or implementing new services that met our identified user needs. We found that much of the work we had to do in the library system fell into a few specific areas: staff training, new services, library instruction and undergraduate initiatives.

INCREASED EMPHASIS ON STAFF TRAINING

What we heard over and over again from our users via LibQUAL+™ and verified by the focus group data was that they valued not just assistance, but competent, professional assistance. As Phipps points out,

New measures and a focus on customers are first steps in the right direction for inventing the future libraries that future customers will need . . . In this new customer-focused culture, every staff member cares about results. They partner with customers and seek to understand what is needed now and in the future. They know what future to prepare for and know when their work is progressing toward desired results. They know how to analyze their work processes for continuous improvement. All staff members make radical changes in how they organize and manage their work processes, and they learn the new skills and knowledge required for new services and products. And last, they are fully supported by an organization designed to tap their full potential and commitment and reward their efforts to succeed.[6]

This communicated to us the need to place a renewed emphasis on public service training. The literature has argued that for a training program to be successful it has to be mandatory, participatory and offered on a regularly scheduled basis. We have subsequently restructured our training group, focused on a variety of different types of customer service and professional competency training, and offered these sessions twice a week at a regularly scheduled time in order to accommodate all members of the public services team. One of the advantages of participating in LibQUAL+™ over time is that we can see if our users' satisfaction with the quality of the assistance provided increases.

IMPLEMENTING NEW SERVICES

Another finding that was most useful to us shed light on the nature of the student and faculty research process. What we discovered by talking with these groups was that regardless of where they ultimately found the information that they sought (e.g., in print in the library, online, via ILL) they began their research online. We felt we had to create a greater reference presence to meet our users where they are beginning their research–online and in real time. Although we have had a very popular e-mail reference option for a number of years, this fall we are launching a digital reference service, *Ask a Librarian Live!* We are planning to offer this chat service during peak hours when our users seem to be online and needing assistance. We will monitor the frequency and nature of this new service, and use this data and LibQUAL+™ to measure its success.

INCREASING LIBRARY INSTRUCTION

We were able to glean from the LibQUAL+™ data and the subsequent focus group process that faculty and students saw the need for increased library instruction, but described this need differently. The faculty told us very clearly that they were concerned that their undergraduates and graduate students were not prepared to conduct research in an increasingly online environment. They were interested in partnering with the library in order to ensure that these students understood the basics of both traditional research and conducting research in the rapidly evolving electronic environment. From graduate and undergraduate students, the findings revealed a sense that they know the library has tremendous amounts of information available, but they don't feel equipped to locate it, use it effectively, or evaluate what they find. With this information in mind, within public services we are looking for various ways we can reach out to specific groups with targeted instructional offerings. We are in the process of developing strategies to reach faculty and graduate students that for the most part build on our existing programs. However, for undergraduates, we have decided to be much more ambitious in developing new programs. Additionally, we accepted that the more aware our users are of our services and resources, the more likely it is that they will use them.

UNDERGRADUATE INITIATIVES

From the undergraduate data we have from LibQUAL+™ and the focus group sessions, we know that these students approach the research process a bit differently and have their own unique set of issues. They told us in LibQUAL+™ that they were unaware of resources the library offered and uncertain about how to use them effectively. In the follow-up focus group sessions they reiterated this, and then discussed the steps they follow when looking for information. Invariably, they told us when they have questions, they are much more likely to ask a friend or fellow student than a librarian. There were several reasons for this and just knowing that this is the case gave us an idea of how to possibly address this issue. Rather than struggling against this tendency of our users not to ask questions of the librarians, we decided to address it through the implementation of a new service that simply builds on a behavior that was already being displayed.

This fall we are working to implement what we are calling a Peer-to-Peer Library Consultants Program. Working with the office of student life and residence hall staff, we are working to develop a team of student consultants who would be trained to provide limited assistance to students where they're studying, in the library and in the residence halls. These consultants would be undergraduate students trained by librarians in how to get students started in locating resources, navigating the libraries' Web pages, and, most importantly, when to refer the student to in-person or online help.

As another attempt to provide our students with the access they want to our resources within our libraries, this fall we are also launching a wireless laptop project in the main undergraduate library. We heard from student users that increasingly the work they do in the library is group-based, and that our current computer configurations lend themselves to this process. Students wanted access to electronic library resources and word processing applications throughout the library buildings, and not just in arbitrarily (from their perspective) designated locations. To address these concerns, the main undergraduate library will soon offer laptops for students to use anywhere in the now wireless facility. The hope is that this will better enable group work, access to the Web from even deep in the stacks, while also increasing the number of devices available in general. As with the other implementations, we will monitor user satisfaction and use.

CONCLUSION

As has been demonstrated, as a library system we have found the data collected from users as part of the LibQUAL+™ process to be invaluable in beginning to plan and implement new services across our public services units. Not only has the data helped us to identify issues requiring some extensive reorganization, but also it has provided us with a tool to measure how successful we have been in instituting changes to address those gaps in services. Our involvement in this program has communicated to our users our commitment to involving them in our process of continuous service improvement. Another less tangible benefit has been that we have become more aware, as a system, of the need to utilize better methods for on-going data collection across units. Perhaps one of the most significant benefits we as a library system derived from the LibQUAL+™ process was the increased commitment to the ongoing solicitation of user input and an awareness of the role of users in guiding public service initiatives.

NOTES

1. Dugan, Robert E., Hernon, Peter. "Outcomes Assessment: Not Synonymous with Inputs and Outputs." *Journal of Academic Librarianship*. 28 (2002).

2. Wells, J. "The Influence of Library Usage on Undergraduate Academic Success." *Australian Academic & Research Libraries*, 26 no. 2 (1995): 121.

3. Wall, Tom. "LibQUAL+™ as a Transformative Experience." *Performance Measurement and Metric*, 3, no. 2 (2002): 43-47.

4. Phipps, Shelley. "Beyond Measuring Service Quality: Learning from the Voices of the Customers, the Staff, the Processes, and the Organization." *Library Trends*, 49 (2001): 635.

5. Parasuraman, A. Foreword to the special issue of *Performance Measurement and Metrics*, 3, no. 2 (2002): 37-39.

6. Phipps, Shelley. "Beyond Measuring Service Quality: Learning from the Voices of the Customers, the Staff, the Processes, and the Organization." *Library Trends*, 49 (2001): 636.

LibQUAL+™ Meets Strategic Planning at the University of Florida

Stephen R. Shorb
Lori Driscoll

SUMMARY. Effective strategic planning can help a library focus on a common sense of purpose and can steer the library in directions that respond to a changing environment. The University of Florida Libraries embarked on a series of strategic planning activities in June of 2001. The process of thinking strategically has produced a renewed interest in dependable information about users' perceptions of our service quality, and LibQUAL+™ emerged as one of the key contributors to this process. Our experience with LibQUAL+™ and with strategic planning has been gained simultaneously. We have found that it provides a structure to support further communication with our users. LibQUAL+™ will continue to shape our thinking as we move toward more strategic management methods that enable us to make informed decisions regarding our allocation of resources. *[Article copies available for a fee from The Haworth Document Delivery Service: 1-800-HAWORTH. E-mail address: <docdelivery@haworthpress.com> Website: <http://www. HaworthPress.com> © 2004 by The Haworth Press, Inc. All rights reserved.]*

Stephen R. Shorb (E-mail: sshorb@mail.uflib.ufl.edu) is Assistant Director, Support Services Division, and Lori Driscoll (E-mail: ldriscoll@mail.uflib.ufl.edu) is Chair, Access Services Department, both at George A. Smathers Libraries, University of Florida, Gainesville, FL.

[Haworth co-indexing entry note]: "LibQUAL+™ Meets Strategic Planning at the University of Florida." Shorb, Stephen R., and Lori Driscoll. Co-published simultaneously in *Journal of Library Administration* (The Haworth Information Press, an imprint of The Haworth Press, Inc.) Vol. 40, No. 3/4, 2004, pp. 173-180; and: *Libraries Act on Their LibQUAL+™ Findings: From Data to Action* (ed: Fred M. Heath, Martha Kyrillidou, and Consuella A. Askew) The Haworth Information Press, an imprint of The Haworth Press, Inc., 2004, pp. 173-180. Single or multiple copies of this article are available for a fee from The Haworth Document Delivery Service [1-800-HAWORTH, 9:00 a.m. - 5:00 p.m. (EST). E-mail address: docdelivery@haworthpress.com].

http://www.haworthpress.com/web/JLA
© 2004 by The Haworth Press, Inc. All rights reserved.
Digital Object Identifier: 10.1300/J111v40n03_13

KEYWORDS. LibQUAL+™, strategic planning, library service quality, SMART goals, customer satisfaction

INTRODUCTION

Strategic planning helps libraries do a better job in several ways. Effective planning helps focus energies, assures a common sense of purpose, and steers the library in directions that respond to a changing environment. The University of Florida Libraries embarked on a series of strategic planning activities in June of 2001. As the need for user input and objective performance measures became obvious, LibQUAL+™ emerged as one of the key contributors to the strategic process.

OVERVIEW OF OUR STRATEGIC PLANNING EXPERIENCE

The environment surrounding academic libraries has become increasingly unpredictable. Higher education in general is facing a funding crisis. The 2001-2002 academic year was a dramatic illustration of rapidly changing conditions requiring strategic, rather than tactical or operational responses. At UF, the 2001-2002 year included drastic budget cuts, small budget restorations, hiring freezes, an overhaul of the state university governance system, ballot initiatives attempting to reverse the overhaul, and a generous helping of vacillation, ambiguity, and rumor. We were faced with the familiar dilemma of doing more with less.

The UF Libraries have a long tradition of annual operations planning and long-range planning for foreseeable developments. Operating plans provide the means to express the current goals and objectives based on the budget allocation, and long-range plans are invaluable in gathering resources for large scale changes such as new buildings, new integrated library automation systems, new academic programs, and university-wide administrative systems. Paired with techniques such as SMART goals, these conventional planning methods are an effective way to manage and improve library services in a predictable environment.

During this year of turbulence and uncertainty, the UF Libraries started transitioning to a strategic planning process. Unlike the static conventional planning processes, strategic planning is an ongoing process that involves iterative learning and continuous improvement. The

Association of Research Libraries Office of Leadership and Management Services (ARL OLMS) was enlisted to help the libraries develop this process using the balanced scorecard approach. Our strategic methods are still under development, and we will probably need to make a few more circuits of the track. Diagrams 1 and 2 summarize the iterative process we plan to continue developing for our strategic processes.

HOW LibQUAL+™ FUELED OUR STRATEGIC PROCESS

Strategic planning through balanced scorecards created numerous objectives. We believe that the scorecards and underlying objectives were well-designed, at least to the extent that progress can be measured in quantifiable ways. Designing and implementing those measurements seemed to be a large task. LibQUAL+™ provided a convenient and standardized measurement system that addressed a surprisingly large number of our objectives. In addition to the time saved in developing our own surveys and other measures, LibQUAL+™ offered many additional benefits: good design, ease of implementation, pre-processed results, and a large number of peer participants to provide external comparisons.

DIAGRAM 1

**University of Florida Libraries
Strategic Planning Process**

Information Gathering (Internal and External)

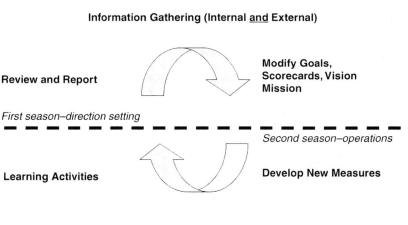

Review and Report

**Modify Goals,
Scorecards, Vision
Mission**

First season–direction setting

Second season–operations

Learning Activities

Develop New Measures

DIAGRAM 2

University of Florida Libraries
Strategic Planning Process

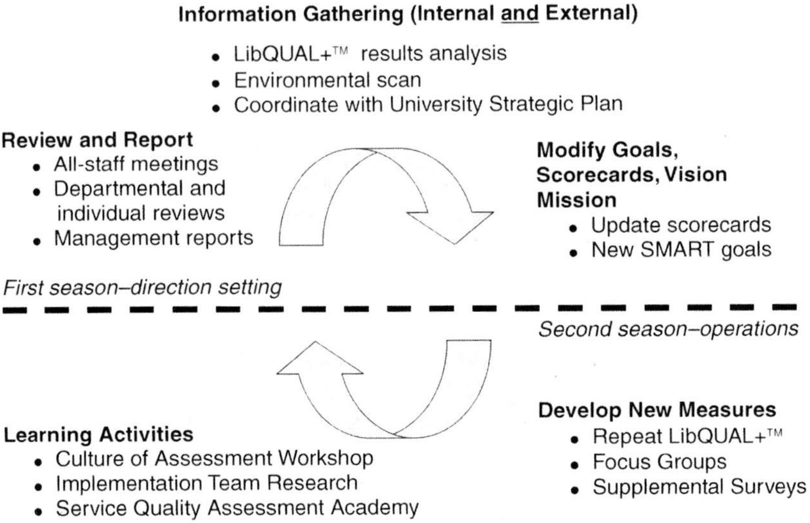

Information Gathering (Internal and External)

- LibQUAL+™ results analysis
- Environmental scan
- Coordinate with University Strategic Plan

Review and Report
- All-staff meetings
- Departmental and individual reviews
- Management reports

Modify Goals, Scorecards, Vision Mission
- Update scorecards
- New SMART goals

First season–direction setting

Second season–operations

Learning Activities
- Culture of Assessment Workshop
- Implementation Team Research
- Service Quality Assessment Academy

Develop New Measures
- Repeat LibQUAL+™
- Focus Groups
- Supplemental Surveys

We found that LibQUAL+™ could easily be adapted to our nascent strategic process and could be used for several purposes in both "seasons" of our cycle.

Information Gathering

Environmental scanning is an almost constant activity throughout the cycle, but especially before modifying the plan. The purpose of this information gathering is to identify key players and assess current conditions and future impacts in order to analyze strengths, weaknesses, opportunities, and threats (SWOT). The information gathered in this part of the process answers the question, "What's going on around us?" In meeting with our users, LibQUAL+™ results provided a way of focusing attention on the library and a way of finding "something to talk about" with our primary "customer" groups. We have used LibQUAL+™ as a discussion-starter with existing groups such as the faculty library committee and other groups not approached before such as the Graduate Student Senate.

Modify Goals, Scorecards, Mission, Vision

The SWOT analysis leads to the identification of best scenarios and courses of action. It allows us to answer the questions, "Where are we headed?" and "What should we be doing?" Accordingly, the strategy allows for flexibility, modification, and redirection. As Riggs has described, "The strategic plan should be viewed as a working document; it is never completed, and certainly has to undergo a rigorous updating/refinement on a regular basis."[1] LibQUAL+™ data will influence departmental and individual plans. Converting strategic directions into operating plans using the SMART goals technique will be easier if progress can be measured with LibQUAL+™ data. We will use the data to update our scorecards and to develop new SMART goals during the next planning cycle.

Develop New Measures

The most obvious question that this part of the cycle answers is, "How are we doing?" The LibQUAL+™ survey itself provided us a new measure for assessing library service quality and our progress toward associated objectives. Users thought the Libraries were deficient in complete runs of journal titles and comprehensive print collections. Many users expressed some unhappiness with convenient access to the collections, easy-to-use access tools that allow users to find things on their own, a library Website allowing users to locate information on their own, and making electronic resources available from offices or homes. It was apparent from the comments that many of the respondents were not aware of library services. We addressed this information need by publishing "Frequently Asked Questions" and highlighting those services in bibliographic instruction. For the next cycle, we will conduct follow-up surveys and focus groups to clarify what LibQUAL+™ showed us regarding access to information and personal control; measurable progress on our scorecards can be evaluated by changes in LibQUAL+™ results in subsequent years.

Learning Activities

Training supports the required organizational change necessary for strategic planning. LibQUAL+™ provided a learning experience for staff, not just in the administration of the survey instrument, but also in the activities related to the interpretation of data and the presentation of the results. In trying to make sense of the information presented by the comments participants provided, we grouped these comments into the four service quality quadrants: Affect of Service, Access to Information, Library as Place, and Personal Control. This analysis added qualitative reinforcement to the quantitative data collected by the LibQUAL+™ survey. In addition to these experiences, there was the spin-off effect of learning the science of survey research. Members of the Strategic Planning Implementation Team honed their skills in SPSS, Atlas.ti, and Nu*dist applications. In addition to application skills, team members also sought professional development opportunities to increase their knowledge about the research methodologies and development of the survey. One LibQUAL+™ coordinator attended the ARL Service Quality Evaluation Academy, another attended the LibQUAL+™ results session at ALA, and another enrolled in the ARL Online Lyceum Course: Measuring Library Service Quality. The ARL Culture of Assessment Workshop was offered to staff locally as another learning activity.[2]

Review and Report

Informed staff are better able to participate in the planning process. This part of the cycle answers the question, "What is going on around here?" Communicating the LibQUAL+™ data to all library staff included such methods as: a presentation at all-staff and departmental meetings, a Web page for the results, and articles in the library newsletters where the survey results were discussed in relation to strategic planning goals and objectives. A summary of the results of the survey and radar charts were also published in the University of Florida Faculty Library Newsletter (http://web.uflib.ufl.edu/ps/librarynews/LibNews0802/LibNews0802.pdf).

LibQUAL+™ RESULTS ASSIST IN IMPLEMENTING A STRATEGIC DIRECTION

Several of our priority objectives could be measured by LibQUAL+™: improved access to electronic information; improved customer service; increased visibility and interaction with users; improved knowledge of library services.

When we first reviewed the radar graphs of our LibQUAL+™ results, we noticed a "red zone" indicating a service gap for question 19, "Convenient Business Hours." This LibQUAL+™ question was directly related to an objective in our strategic plan. In order to offer superior service, we wanted to increase staffing to support additional open hours when users most needed them. But this objective was not ranked as one of our top priorities. Our LibQUAL+™ results indicated that users perceived a need for more, or different, business hours. The gap was most pronounced on the chart for graduate students. Again, this was directly related to our strategic thinking. The university's strategic plan calls for greater emphasis on graduate programs, so the library identified a need to support that direction with services better suited to the needs of graduate students. Not only was there a service gap, but the mean score of the desired level of service was high (8.41 on a scale of 1 to 9) in absolute terms. Graduate students' responses indicated a strong desire for improvement in this area. Now we knew that this should be a higher priority than we had previously ranked it. But what actions should be taken?

The SPSS files of all LibQUAL+™ responses provided an easy way to gain more insight into the problem. Using only a few basic features of SPSS, and with relatively little knowledge of statistics, we were able to analyze the responses and learn more about the sources of our service gap. Since branch libraries serving some academic disciplines have shorter hours (therefore are less convenient), we selected cases in which the perceived score was less than the minimum score, producing a service gap. These constituted about 27% of all responses for this item. These individual cases were then grouped by role–which shows student and faculty levels. The greatest number of cases with service gaps were Master's level and Ph.D. level graduate students. The percentage of dissatisfied users was also highest for those two groups (about 30% compared with about 20% for other categories). Given the large number of dissatisfied graduate students, we next divided that group by academic discipline. Lower perceived scores were shown to occur in disciplines served by smaller branch libraries. Higher average perceived scores were found in the disciplines served by longer-hour facilities.

We then turned to the survey comments from LibQUAL+™ respondents that related to hours of operation. The comments generally supported the quantitative data, indicating a preference for extending hours in branch libraries and other service areas (such as microforms and maps) that had both shorter operating hours and content that served the research interests of graduate students. The comments also helped identify specific times when additional hours might be helpful. This information can be used to develop a more specific survey or questions for a focus group.

The LibQUAL+™ data allowed library administration to consider problem areas and identify several courses of action in response. While we do not have the resources to extend the hours at all branch libraries, keeping user convenience a priority allows us to consider alternative services to help the libraries meet our graduate students' needs. Open meetings with staff resulted in suggestions for extended hours at the location that would reach the greatest number of students feasible with the current staffing. Comments from LibQUAL+™ indicated that many users were not aware of services already offered by the libraries, which indicated that we needed to improve the marketing of library services.

CONCLUSION

Our experience with LibQUAL+™ and with strategic planning has been gained simultaneously. The process of thinking strategically has produced a renewed interest in dependable information about user's perceptions of our service quality. LibQUAL+™ fills that need in part, and also provides a structure to support further communication with our users. In the future, LibQUAL+™ will continue to shape our thinking as we move toward more strategic management methods that enable us to make informed decisions regarding our allocation of resources.

We intend to use the 2003 LibQUAL+™ results to see if our educational efforts have been effective. We also hope to see progress on our priority objectives, which now include increased staffing for expanded hours and services. However, if the data indicate new service quality gaps, our strategic planning efforts allow us to quickly shift our focus to those areas of concern.

NOTES

1. Donald E. Riggs, "Editorial. Plan or Be Planned for: The Growing Significance of Strategic Planning," *College and Research Libraries, 58* (September 1997): 401.

2. *Creating a Culture of Assessment in Libraries* workshop was created by Amos Lakos, Amos and Shelley Phipps for the Association of Research Libraries, Washington, DC. For more information about the *Creating a Culture of Assessment* workshop visit, <http://www.arl.org/training/institutes/culture.html>.

Using LibQUAL+™ Data
in Strategic Planning:
Bowling Green State University

Lorraine J. Haricombe
Bonna J. Boettcher

SUMMARY. Like many other university libraries, Bowling Green State University (BGSU) faces the challenges of change due to reduced funding, competition from information vendors, and new emerging technologies that have fueled users' expectations. These factors have led to a review of the library's role and operations, which in turn has resulted in significant strategic planning to ensure the library's central role in higher education. Users' perceptions play a key role in defining the role and centrality of the library. Recognizing the value of user feedback in planning, BGSU Libraries participated in the LibQUAL+™ survey as a member library of the OhioLINK consortium in spring 2002. The LibQUAL+™ data, coupled with subsequent focus group interviews, provided valuable user feedback that will be helpful in developing plans to achieve our strategic goals. *[Article copies available for a fee from The Haworth Document Delivery Service: 1-800-HAWORTH. E-mail address: <docdelivery@haworthpress.com> Website: <http://www.HaworthPress.com> © 2004 by The Haworth Press, Inc. All rights reserved.]*

Lorraine J. Haricombe (E-mail: ljharic@bgnet.bgsu.edu) is Dean of University Libraries, and Bonna J. Boettcher (E-mail: bboettc@bgnet.bgsu.edu) is Chair, Department of Archival Collections and Branches/Head, Music Library & Sound Recordings Archives, both at the William T. Jerome Library, Bowling Green State University, Bowling Green, OH.

[Haworth co-indexing entry note]: "Using LibQUAL+™ Data in Strategic Planning: Bowling Green State University." Haricombe, Lorraine J., and Bonna J. Boettcher. Co-published simultaneously in *Journal of Library Administration* (The Haworth Information Press, an imprint of The Haworth Press, Inc.) Vol. 40, No. 3/4, 2004, pp. 181-195; and: *Libraries Act on Their LibQUAL+™ Findings: From Data to Action* (ed: Fred M. Heath, Martha Kyrillidou, and Consuella A. Askew) The Haworth Information Press, an imprint of The Haworth Press, Inc., 2004, pp. 181-195. Single or multiple copies of this article are available for a fee from The Haworth Document Delivery Service [1-800-HAWORTH, 9:00 a.m. - 5:00 p.m. (EST). E-mail address: docdelivery@haworthpress.com].

http://www.haworthpress.com/web/JLA
© 2004 by The Haworth Press, Inc. All rights reserved.
Digital Object Identifier: 10.1300/J111v40n03_14

181

KEYWORDS. LibQUAL+™, academic libraries, strategic planning, library service quality

INTRODUCTION

Demographics of the Campus. Bowling Green State University, located in semi-rural northwest Ohio, is a state-supported, regional institution and is primarily residential. Classified as Doctoral/Research–Intensive by the Carnegie Foundation, BGSU offers a wide range of bachelor's and master's degrees and selected doctoral programs. BGSU's Fall 2002 population included 15,703 undergraduate students, 3,070 graduate students, 802 full-time faculty members, and 203 part-time faculty members.[1] Many BGSU undergraduate students are first-generation college students. BGSU does not support professional schools such as medical, law, or engineering.

Climate of Assessment at BGSU. A university-wide assessment committee was established in 1996, and the institution has made substantial progress toward developing a culture of assessment since then. The library has had a representative on the university committee since it was established, and prior to the LibQUAL+™ initiative had managed several effective, but isolated, assessment projects, primarily in the area of user instruction. LibQUAL+™ presented an opportunity to measure the quality and effectiveness of our services library-wide, while also providing a way to begin listening to our users differently than we had in the past.

OhioLINK. BGSU is a founding member of the OhioLINK consortium. Our membership has allowed us to provide resources and services to our users far beyond what is possible on our own. We have statewide access to a far greater number of electronic resources, such as databases and journals, as well as a wider range of print materials than we could afford on our own. In addition, the effects and demands of OhioLINK influence many of our processes, decisions, priorities, and budget allocations. By participating in LibQUAL+™ as a consortium, OhioLINK was able to tailor five "local" questions on the survey instrument to measure users' expectations and perceptions of specific OhioLINK resources and services. The responses to these questions, along with comments from focus groups and an undergraduate survey, have given us invaluable insight into our users' opinions of the benefits and drawbacks of our consortium membership.

WORK WITH RESULTS

Initial Review of Results. With BGSU, OhioLINK, and national aggregate results analysis notebooks in hand, our local LibQUAL+™ task force members began an initial review of the results. The norms tables were useful to a point. We learned that, for the most part, our results were firmly in the middle. We were not at the top, but we also were not at the bottom when comparing ourselves to the other institutions in the group. Considering our circumstances, we decided that was good. We were able to quickly identify areas relative to where we fell out of the mid-range of the norms. After brief discussion, we left the norms tables. While we understand the value of comparing BGSU to other institutions and the need to be aware of and employ best practices, our greater concern was learning what our users had to say about our library. We reasoned that our universities are not carbon copies of each other, and therefore, neither should be our libraries.

Along with our local task force's data analyses, we shared additional information with the entire library staff. Staff members were invited to test the survey instrument before it was available to the public, and updates have been a standing agenda item for monthly all-staff meetings. We also used our electronic reserves system to post the resulting notebooks, comments, and norms-analyses to enable all staff to have easy access to the information.

Microsoft Access; SPSS Analysis. Recognizing that the comments received (189 of 523 respondents chose to add comments) should be viewed as an amplification of the quantitative data, we decided to use Microsoft Access to develop a rough means of analyzing the content of the comments. The comments file, originally sent in Excel, was transferred to Access. After some initial analysis, we decided that comments could be grouped into eight categories: building, collections, hours, ILL, OhioLINK, online forms/remote access, services, and "other." These categories were set up as yes/no check boxes and each comment was analyzed according to its content (some comments covered several categories). This allowed us to easily create sets of comments pertaining to each category, in addition to allowing us to compare the comments to the relevant quantitative data.

After the quantitative raw data files were released, we began analysis using SPSS software. Although we ran a number of reports, charts, and graphs, those that proved most helpful for our purposes were Hi-Lo graphs, which were sorted by user group and discipline. Initially we planned to focus on specific disciplines whose scores were low. We learned, however, that those disciplines also had low response rates. Some of the discipline groupings (social sciences, fine arts) were too broad to determine which users in specific discipline areas were pleased with or dissatisfied with our services and collections. Rather than spending an inordinate amount of time manipulating quantitative data, we decided that it was time to talk with our users.

UNDERGRADUATE SURVEY

University Libraries holds "Research Project Clinics" (RPCs) for several weeks during the middle of semesters. Undergraduate students with a specific research assignment may meet with a librarian for an hour for assistance in locating materials and understanding how to use the library. Our undergraduate response rate to the LibQUAL+™ survey was low and we knew we were too far into the semester to try to persuade undergraduates to attend focus groups. Yet, we wanted to get some information from the undergraduate students. The librarian coordinating the RPCs suggested that we prepare a one-page survey to give to students at the end of their appointments. Surveys also were made available at several public service desks for any undergraduate student to complete. (See Appendix A.)

What Was Learned from Survey. One hundred and fourteen undergraduate students participated in the RPCs. In all 137 undergraduates completed the survey: 50 (36.5%) were seniors, 27 (19.7%) were juniors, 18 (13.1%) were sophomores, and 40 (29.2%) were first-year students. We used the LibQUAL+™ discipline breakdown; participants in our local survey represented all disciplines except Engineering/Computer Science, with the majority (more than 53%) of respondents from Business, Communication, and Education.

More than 72% of users completing the survey were "mostly satisfied" or "very satisfied" with materials found in the research databases. Slightly over 53% were mostly or very satisfied with the book collection, while more than 31% were only partially satisfied or not satisfied. Just over half of the respondents were mostly or very satisfied with off-campus access to library resources, while slightly under 15% were only partially satisfied or not satisfied. Again, just over half of the respondents were mostly or very satisfied with the process for requesting materials from remote storage, just over 10% were partially or not satisfied, and 39% did not answer the question. Just under 60% of the respondents were mostly or very satisfied with spaces provided for study, while fewer than 9% were partially or not satisfied.

Although more than 41% of the respondents prefer to ask a permanent staff member for assistance, more than 33% state that they have no preference for permanent staff over student staff. Those who prefer to ask permanent staff members for assistance do so because the staff members are perceived to have better training and a more thorough knowledge about finding information. Those who have no preference indicate that accurate information and a friendly demeanor are most important to them.

When asked what one thing they would like to change about the libraries, their answers ran the gamut. No one thing stood out, except hours (they want more). Also LC Classification (they find it confusing) and variety of materials (more needed) received more responses than other categories. The number of staff members available to assist patrons and the responsiveness of those staff members represented something students did not want to see changed. The atmosphere and study spaces also received numerous responses.

WORK WITH MASTER OF ORGANIZATIONAL DEVELOPMENT (MOD) STUDENTS

BGSU's College of Business Administration includes master's programs in Organizational Development among its graduate degree offerings. Students enrolled in these programs are required to complete internships. In continuing efforts to establish partnerships with other areas on campus and to utilize local expertise, the University Libraries hired four students from the MOD program to assist with various planning initiatives, including planning and conducting focus groups as part of our LibQUAL+™ efforts.[2]

Hiring and Planning for Focus Groups. All internship referrals are handled by the assistant director of the MOD program. After discussing the organization's needs, the assistant director recommended students for interviews. During the interviews, we described the LibQUAL+™ goal and summarized our local results. We indicated what we hoped to learn from focus groups and asked the students to comment on how their experience and expertise would help move our work forward. Students were clearly well prepared for their interviews and conveyed an excitement that has been contagious.

Focus Groups. The LibQUAL+™ task force identified four major areas to cover in the focus groups: satisfaction with the materials provided by the library; satisfaction with library services; how patrons learn about library services; the user/study spaces provided in the library. Working with one of the interns, we developed one major question for each of the areas with additional "probing" questions. We were careful to insure that the focus group questions could be mapped to the quantitative data from the LibQUAL+™ survey. (See Appendix C.)

Developing the questions served to highlight the preparation and expertise of the MOD intern. She questioned closely the purpose of devoting time to each of the areas and made sure she knew what we hoped to learn by including that area in the focus group questions. Nothing was accepted at face value: we needed to state a specific purpose for asking each question.

The intern also worked with the format of each session. We prepared a brief overview of the LibQUAL+™ survey and why we were talking to our users; we distributed brief demographic questionnaires to the participants; we gave them a general outline of the questions we planned to ask. (See Appendix B for the demographic questionnaire.)

From mid-November through early December 2002, we were able to conduct three focus groups. The first drew on BGSU's Library Advisory Council and included faculty members from several disciplines. The second was assembled with the assistance of the Graduate Student Senate and included only graduate students. Our intern, an international student herself, worked with BGSU's World Student Association to assemble the third group, which included several graduate students and one undergraduate. Additional focus group sessions will be conducted during Spring 2003.

Areas of concern from the LibQUAL+™ survey were primarily from the Access to Collections and Personal Control dimensions. From the graduate student focus groups, we learned that in general, BGSU's collections do support their coursework, and their concerns are with support provided for research and thesis/dissertation work. However, participants did identify specific areas of the collection that they thought were weak. We also learned that some graduate-student concerns included the materials selection process; they would like greater involvement in their departmental processes for recommending purchases. Other suggestions included physical facilities, such as the location of photocopiers and individual study spaces. Both groups suggested purchasing some kind of baskets for students to use in carrying materials around the library.

Not surprisingly, faculty members were concerned about journal holdings, especially in the sciences and social sciences fields. Human interactions were rated highly. It became clear that faculty members did not understand the variety of methods used to obtain the materials they needed. There was real confusion between OhioLINK borrowing, Interlibrary Loan, materials retrieved from the Depository, and purchases of new materials.

During the summer of 2002, we made concerted efforts to bring up the ILLiad Interlibrary Loan system and to address problems with our proxy server for remote access. E-mail notices for this service were activated during the fall 2002 semester. These efforts were reflected in responses to questions about personal control during the focus groups, especially from the graduate students. Graduate students clearly have embraced ILLiad. It was also found that problems with remote access centered more on technical problems with connections than on proxy-server authentication.

From comments submitted with the survey, we learned that we are not marketing our services effectively. This was reinforced in comments from the focus groups. Even though e-mail notices were available and had been advertised via the library's Web page, in inserts sent with print notices, inserts placed in books, and flyers at circulation points, several participants indicated that we should add e-mail notices. Services that we thought were prominently displayed or easy to find on the Website had been completely missed by users. Participants were divided on the best means of advertising services, indicating to us that we must employ a variety of methods.

CONCLUSION:
PROPOSED USES OF LibQUAL+™ DATA
TO ACHIEVE STRATEGIC OUTCOMES

Library Modification

In 2002, the University Libraries engaged in major initiatives in the areas of facilities planning and fundraising to address long overdue spatial and environmental concerns for our unique and special collections. These initiatives followed a feasibility study of the building that was completed in October 2001. The report highlighted various problems including HVAC, plumbing, electric lighting, cramped storage, lack of a fire suppression system and leakages. In 2002, a building committee was formed to explore the possibility for renovation and expansion of the library building to accommodate and showcase our unique and special collections. To complement this effort (and to coincide with the upcoming 100th anniversary of BGSU), we also launched a centennial campaign to raise awareness and funds for secure storage of our special collections. The primary charge of the building committee is to work with the university's capital planning office to identify space to secure and showcase our unique and special collections, and also to review vacated space for facilities that will meet our users' needs. To this end, we have found the LibQUAL+™ results helpful in providing user feedback as we continue discussions in spatially reorganizing the library.

For example, our graduate students have requested a graduate study space, while undergraduates have expressed the need for quiet individual study spaces. Some users have asked for a coffee shop in the library, a larger computer laboratory, and small group study facilities. Spatial reorganization also opens up possibilities for collaboration with other academic support units to consider relocating to the library to provide a "one-stop shop" for our users. Simply put, our goal is to transform the traditional library into an academic center that will provide users with all the support services readily available in one place.

Communication and Marketing

One of our strategic directions is to improve communication with the BGSU community to market our products and services. Routinely, librarians find that many users are not aware of available products and services. The LibQUAL+™ data confirmed the anecdotal evidence that patrons lacked sufficient knowledge about library services and resources. Who is to blame–the ignorant user or the passive librarian? The answer to this question probably lies somewhere in between, validating the use of LibQUAL+™ data to plan for a stronger investment in communication with patrons about library services to better inform them and manage their expectations. Ultimately, patrons create, shape, and define the character of the demand for all products and services.

Despite our efforts to inform library users, many still remain ignorant of the various library products and services. We regularly announce new library services in the campus media, and we have created an on-line library newsletter to inform the university community of library initiatives, products and services once a semester. In the absence of an outreach librarian, we encourage all staff members to actively market the library's resources as an integral part of their jobs. To this end, library instructors and bibliographers are taking steps to ensure that faculty and students are regularly informed of resources in their specific subject areas, but we need to do more. Our LibQUAL+™ data have been helpful in identifying users' preferences for learning about library products and services. For example, undergraduate students prefer e-mail notices, but would also like to see announcements in the student newspaper, in the residence halls and in the high traffic areas such as the student union. Our graduate students were most vocal about their needs and request a special Website for graduate students on the library's home page, announcements in their newsletter and more direct involvement in suggesting materials for the library's collection. The focus on communication and marketing will require a change in staff roles to become less "place-bound" while assuming more creative ways to sell the library's resources to users and non-users alike.

Creating a User-Centered Focus

Inasmuch as we attempt to satisfy our users' needs, LibQUAL+™ data provide significant user feedback, but it is by no means the only tool for this purpose. Analysis of LibQUAL+™ data has prompted us to explore and delve deeper into the users' responses to clarify the issues they raised and to glean from them directions for improvements. Focus group interviews have also been very helpful in generating qualitative data to help us listen and respond to our users. We also plan to use cards for user feedback at the time of a transaction or when exiting the library. While other data gathering methods exist (e.g., ask a librarian, complaints, suggestion box), the LibQUAL+™ survey provided a systematic approach and rich data set, which have led to a high level of open discussion among staff to address our users' concerns. Results of LibQUAL+™ user feedback and focus group interviews are available through electronic reserves for easy access by all library staff. Additionally, we provide updates at the monthly all-staff meetings to keep everybody informed of the issues or pending actions to address user concerns. It is our goal to cultivate and maintain a user-centered culture, through continuous assessment of our library's programs and services.

Managing Access to Information

Uniformly, the LibQUAL+™ data showed users wanted more personal control in accessing library resources remotely. At the time of the spring 2001 LibQUAL+™ survey, BGSU Libraries had initiated some pilot projects in electronic services, namely: electronic reference ("chat reference"), electronic reserves, and unmediated interlibrary loan services (ILLiad). The LibQUAL+™ data reinforced the need to move quickly in the direction of unmediated services that would allow users more personal control in using the library remotely. Another significant improvement was authenticating users to provide remote access to electronic databases. Remote access, coupled with OhioLINK's switch to EBSCO databases in fall 2002, provided our users more access to increased electronic information. It is our goal to participate in LibQUAL+™ 2003 to compare user feedback, especially in the area of access and personal control.

The implementation of remote access coupled with all the electronic services described earlier also supports the University's strategic direction to reach niche markets through distance education programs.

Challenges

Articulating, developing, and implementing a user-service focus remains a challenge, one that will receive significant attention in our strategic directions. LibQUAL+™ is one data-gathering tool that has proven very helpful in establishing directions for gathering further information. Though response rates were low, we have been able to use focus group interviews to help segment the data by user group. While we do communicate user feedback to all staff members, we have not yet developed an action plan to reflect a systematic response to address our users' needs. An additional challenge is the lack of statistical analysis skills among our staff and our dependency on other campus agencies to assist with effective data analysis. Finally, we have much work to do in convincing the university administrators of the value of user feedback and obtaining the resources to make transformational changes to address their needs.

Despite these challenges we have established a renewed sensitivity to user perceptions and a culture of assessment in all library areas. We have also initiated data-gathering methods that have been helpful in cultivating user relations. It is our goal to participate in future LibQUAL+™ surveys, to maintain a culture of assessment and user-centeredness.

NOTES

1. Bowling Green State University. Office of Institutional Research. *BGSU Fact Book, 2002-2003.* Available at http://www.bgsu.edu/offices/ir/factbook/coverpage.htm. Accessed 18 December 2002.

2. For more information about Bowling Green State University College of Business Administration's Master of Organizational Development program, visit: http://www. cba.bgsu.edu/mod/html/home.html.

APPENDIX A. Undergraduate Survey

Fall 2002 Undergraduate Survey

Thank you for agreeing to complete our undergraduate survey.

Your Year of Study	*Please check one*		
□ First-year	□ Sophomore	□ Junior	□ Senior

A. Your Major Area/Discipline   **Please check one**

□ Architecture
□ Business
□ Communication/Journalism
□ Education
□ Engineering/Computer Science
□ Health Sciences
□ Humanities
□ Law
□ Performing & Fine Arts
□ Science/Math
□ Social Sciences/Psychology
□ Undecided
□ Other

You Most Often Use	*Please check one*
□ Jerome Library	□ Science Library

Please indicate your agreement with the following statements on a scale from 1-5.

1. The library or the library's research databases have most of the magazine and journal articles I need for my assignments.

1	2	3	4	5
Not satisfied	Partially satisfied	Satisfied	Mostly satisfied	Very satisfied

APPENDIX A (continued)

2. The library has most of the books I need for my assignments.

1	2	3	4	5
Not satisfied	Partially satisfied	Satisfied	Mostly satisfied	Very satisfied

3. I am able to access the databases and electronic journals from off-campus.

1	2	3	4	5
Not satisfied	Partially satisfied	Satisfied	Mostly satisfied	Very satisfied

4. I am satisfied with the process for requesting and retrieving materials from the Northwest Regional Book Depository.

1	2	3	4	5
Not satisfied	Partially satisfied	Satisfied	Mostly satisfied	Very satisfied

5. I am satisfied with the space for study and use of library materials in the Libraries.

1	2	3	4	5
Not satisfied	Partially satisfied	Satisfied	Mostly satisfied	Very satisfied

The best way for the Libraries to inform me about new library services and materials would be to   *Please check one.*

 ☐ Send me an e-mail
 ☐ Put an ad in the BGNews
 ☐ Make an announcement in one of my classes
 ☐ Put up flyers or table tents around campus
 ☐ Send out a paper newsletter
 ☐ Other (tell us how: _____)

Would you prefer to seek assistance in the libraries from student workers or permanent staff? Why?

What one thing would you most like to change about the Libraries?

What one thing would you most like to stay the same about the Libraries?

Thank you! Please place the completed survey in one of the many boxes located around the Libraries or return to Jerome Library, Information Services Dept., Room 152.

APPENDIX B. Focus Group Demographic Questionnaire

LibQUAL+™ GSS Group Session

Information shared will be treated as confidential, and shall be used for LibQUAL+™ purposes only.

Are you a graduate assistant:	☐ Yes	☐ No
If yes, *Please Check one*		
☐ Research Assistant	☐ Teaching Assistant	☐ Other _____

Department:
_____

I am a: Master's student _____ **Doctoral student** _____ **Other** _____

Number of years at BGSU:
_____

You Most Often Use: ☐ Jerome Library   ☐ Science Library

Please indicate your satisfaction level of the current information and services provided by the BGSU Library.

	Not Satisfied	Partially Satisfied	Satisfied	Mostly Satisfied	Very Satisfied
Books					
Research Databases					
Requesting & Retrieving materials from Northwest Regional Depository					
Library Study Space					
Electronic Database and E-Journals					
Off-Campus service access					
Overall Library services					

Thank you for the time and effort to help us serve you better!

APPENDIX C. Focus Group Questions

GSS FOCUS GROUP QUESTIONS
This session should roughly take about 50 minutes

I. How satisfied are you with the access to information provided by the library? Specifically indicate your satisfaction around the range of information access, quality of the same and the timely delivery? *15 mins*

   A. Do you find the materials required for the following–(i) Course work (ii) Thesis?
   B. What kind of material do you need that the library isn't already providing?
   C. How can the library make the "Northwest Regional Book Depository" most convenient for you?
   D. As a research/ teaching assistant, do you find material at the library?
   E. Any other comments.

II. In your opinion, does the Library provide effective service? *15 mins*

   A. How knowledgeable are the employees in providing information and handling users' service problem?
   B. As a graduate student, how do you learn about the services and especially new services provided by the library? Please specify the medium.
   C. What is the best way to reach you to provide information about current or new library services?
   D. In your opinion, how could the library enhance or improve its services?
   E. As a graduate student, do you seek a permanent library staff member instead of student staff?
   F. Any other comments.

III. As a user, comment about your satisfaction with the provided Library space? *8 mins*

   A. What places in the library do you use most often?
   B. Would you rather work in the library or take the library material to your office/home and work from there? Why?
   C. What is your 'ideal' library space?
   D. What else could the library do to make it a better place to be at?
   E. Any other comments.

IV. Are you 'in control' with the library services, such that you feel that you could work independently? *12 mins*

   A. How well can you access the library electronic services from office and off-campus?
   B. What are the general problems that you encounter when you access the library electronic services?
   C. In your opinion, is it easy to access and navigate the library Website?

D. What are some of the features that would make access to the library most convenient?

E. Any other comments.

Protocol:

A. Participants will fill the Survey forms and Harsha will collect them.–5 mins

B. Bonna will present information to the participants.–10 mins

C. Meanwhile, Harsha and recorder will list the department of participants.

D. Focus group session- 15 + 15 + 8 + 12 = 50 mins

E. Wrap-up and Adjourn

TOTAL TIME = About 1 hour 5 mins.

LibQUAL+™ 2002 at Vanderbilt University: What Do the Results Mean and Where Do We Go from Here?

Flo Wilson

SUMMARY. The Jean and Alexander Heard Library at Vanderbilt University was one of 164 libraries that participated in the spring 2002 LibQUAL+™ survey. Nine hundred and thirty-four individuals (27.2% response rate) responded to over 25 survey items measuring four dimensions of library service quality. Our analysis of the resulting data has allowed the Library to identify more clearly areas of service needing improvement to better meet our users' expectations. Additionally, we are able to consider our scores in comparison with other peer institutions. Library management will continue to analyze the results and consider additional service improvements. Meanwhile, two immediate actions are underway–the establishment of a 24-hour library facility on a trial basis and the development of a service improvement program across the Vanderbilt University library system. *[Article copies available for a fee from The Haworth Document Delivery Service: 1-800-HAWORTH. E-mail address: <docdelivery@haworthpress.com> Website: <http://www.HaworthPress.com> © 2004 by The Haworth Press, Inc. All rights reserved.]*

Flo Wilson is Deputy University Librarian, Vanderbilt University, Nashville, TN (E-mail: flo.wilson@vanderbilt.edu).

[Haworth co-indexing entry note]: "LibQUAL+™ 2002 at Vanderbilt University: What Do the Results Mean and Where Do We Go from Here?" Wilson, Flo. Co-published simultaneously in *Journal of Library Administration* (The Haworth Information Press, an imprint of The Haworth Press, Inc.) Vol. 40, No. 3/4, 2004, pp. 197-240; and: *Libraries Act on Their LibQUAL+™ Findings: From Data to Action* (ed: Fred M. Heath, Martha Kyrillidou, and Consuella A. Askew) The Haworth Information Press, an imprint of The Haworth Press, Inc., 2004, pp. 197-240. Single or multiple copies of this article are available for a fee from The Haworth Document Delivery Service [1-800-HAWORTH, 9:00 a.m. - 5:00 p.m. (EST). E-mail address: docdelivery@haworthpress.com].

http://www.haworthpress.com/web/JLA
© 2004 by The Haworth Press, Inc. All rights reserved.
Digital Object Identifier: 10.1300/J111v40n03_15

KEYWORDS. LibQUAL+™, library service quality, peer comparisons

INTRODUCTION

The Jean and Alexander Heard Library conducted the LibQUAL+™ survey in Spring 2002 along with 163 libraries across the nation. LibQUAL+™ is a part of the Association of Research Libraries' (ARL) New Measures Initiative, which seeks to explore innovative ways for libraries to describe their contributions to their institutions. The LibQUAL+™ project is a joint venture between ARL and the Texas A&M University Libraries. The LibQUAL+™ survey attempts to identify user perceptions of library service quality.[1]

The data gathered from this study is invaluable and will benefit the Library and our University community as we explore ways to improve our services and to ensure that we establish appropriate priorities in our ongoing activities. Not only are we learning how well we measure up to the expectations of our faculty and students, but we are also learning how we compare with other institutions in terms of user expectations and perceptions.

ABOUT THE SURVEY

In April 2002, we administered the LibQUAL+™ survey to a sampling of undergraduates and graduate students, as well as to all non-medical faculty at Vanderbilt. The sample groups consisted of 923 faculty, 1,017 graduate students and 1,499 undergraduates; the latter two were randomly selected by the Registrar's Office. In all, 934 usable responses were received–281 from faculty, 296 from graduate students, and 357 from undergraduates. The overall response rate was 27.2%. Responses were gathered over a three-week period, and the data were collected at a server located at Texas A&M. Roughly during this same time period, another 163 libraries sought the same feedback from their user communities.

The survey questionnaire asked for brief demographic information–sex, age group, library user group, and discipline. At the core of the survey was a set of 25 items relating to four different dimensions of library service quality: *Affect of Service, Access to Information, Library as*

Place and *Personal Control.* For each question, the respondents were asked to indicate their minimum acceptable service level, their desired service level, and their perception of the actual service provided by the library using a numerical scale of 1 to 9. Items posed about the frequency of library use and overall satisfaction were included and also rated on a scale from 1 to 9. A comments box was provided so that respondents could add any additional comments they might like.

The primary analysis of the data collected provides the mean scores for the minimum, desired and perceived levels of expectations for each core item. Mean scores for these items have also been generated for each of the demographic groupings. For analysis purposes, the 25 items are grouped into the four service dimensions and mean scores are generated for these dimensions as well. Of particular interest to our library in reviewing the results are the gap scores, which reflect the magnitude of the difference between the minimum level of expectation and the perceived level of service, and the difference between the desired level of service and the perceived level. Looking at all three of these measures together provides a much better understanding of how well the library is performing relative to user expectations and desires. For ease of reading, graphical representation of the data can be found in the Appendix at the end of the article.

INDIVIDUAL QUESTION RESULTS

In order to provide a graphical view of the perceptions for each of the 25 core items, the data have been plotted on a chart (see Figure 1. Survey Results by Question) that shows the minimum expectation (low point), desired service level (high point), and the perceived level of service (horizontal mark). Specific items on which we might focus for performance improvement are those for which the perceived service level is close to the minimum. These would include 'complete runs of journals' (item #3), 'convenient business hours' (item #19), 'comfortable inviting location' (item #21), and 'easy access to collections' (item #25).

The several items that are part of the *Affect of Service* dimension show almost all the perceived levels closer to desired than to minimum. This appears to be an area of service in which the library has some strength. However, we might benefit from considering improvements for 'dependability in handling users' service problems' (#11) and 'employees who have the knowledge to answer user questions' (#17), since they show the largest gaps from desired levels.

DIMENSIONS' RESULTS

The 25 core items are grouped into the four dimensions of library service and means were derived for the minimum, desired, and perceived service levels for each. The *Access to Information* dimension focuses on the collection breadth and scope, interlibrary loan services for materials not held, and hours of operation. *Affect of Service* includes all of the customer-service aspects of dealing with library users, and it comments on the success of library staff in dealing with the public. *Library as Place* seeks to identify users' perceptions of many of the traditional environmental qualities of libraries–quiet, comfortable, inviting, contemplative. *Personal Control* consists of the items related to the users' ability to find information easily, independently, and remotely.

In order to provide a graphical view of these dimensions, the data have been plotted on a chart that shows the minimum expectation (low point), desired service level (high point), and perceived service level (horizontal mark) (see Figure 2. Dimension Summary). The desired service level can be thought of as an indicator of the importance of that type of service to the users. The *Personal Control* dimension, with the highest desired score, clearly identifies users' desires to function independently–both without assistance and without requiring physical presence in the library. Minimum expectations in the *Library as Place* dimension are significantly lower than the other dimensions, and this may be the result of accepting the limitations of the main library at Vanderbilt as well as lesser interest in this factor. The existence of many different libraries offering very different environments makes the results difficult to interpret. The expectation ranges for *Affect of Service* and *Access to Information* are very similar, but the Library's performance in providing positive customer service, *affect*, is clearly more successful, i.e., closer to desired, than our ability to meet users' access and collection needs.

In the dimension summary, the *Personal Control* dimension seemed to be an important one. Looking at the six component items, we can see that each has a high desired service level, and the gap between that and the perceived level may suggest we explore ways in which we can make high-impact service improvements.

OVERALL SATISFACTION

As a validity check and to gather expressions of more general satisfaction with the Library, respondents were asked to respond to three items on a scale of 1 to 9. The mean scores on these three items for all Vanderbilt respondents fall in the range of 6.85 to 7.34 (see Figure 3. General Satisfaction Indicators). It is useful to put this in some perspective by comparing this range to the aggregate mean scores for all participating ARL libraries; our scores for these items are slightly higher. Yet, we are just slightly below the midpoint of all of the participating libraries–indicating there is clearly room for improvement.

FREQUENCY OF USE

Survey respondents were asked about the frequency with which they used the library–on-site and electronically (see Figure 4. Frequency of Library Use of All User Groups). While the responses may be skewed somewhat *toward* library use, only 1% of the respondents reported never using the library on-site and slightly more (5%) respond that they never use the library's electronic services. Fifty-eight percent of the respondents indicated that they use the libraries in person on a frequent basis, daily or weekly; 68% frequently use the library electronically. In general, library users at Vanderbilt use the library more frequently than the aggregate of respondents at other ARL institutions. By way of comparison, 53% of users at all of the participating ARL libraries report daily or weekly use on-site, and 63% of users at ARL libraries report this level of usage electronically.

When looking at the three primary user groups, differences in usage patterns become apparent. Only 52% (on-site) and 51% (electronically) of undergraduates use the library daily or weekly. Graduate students are the heaviest users of the libraries on-site–70% daily or weekly, and faculty are the group that shows the highest percentage (80%) of electronic usage daily or weekly.

LIBRARY USER COMMENTS

Comments were collected at the end of the survey form and the qualitative information gleaned from these comments constitutes some of the most specific and valuable data gathered from the survey. Of the 934 surveys completed, 380 respondents chose to add comments. These 380 people offered 650 discrete observations; 428 of the comments were critical and 232 were positive. We attempted to categorize the comments according to the dimension grouping used in the results of the survey *Access to Information, Affect of Service, Library as Place* and *Personal Control.* Of the 428 negative comments, 129 related to the library building (i.e., the *Library as Place* category) and their responses focused on the aging and confusing main library. In the *Access to Information* category, which covers hours and collection scope, 162 comments had negative connotations. On the other hand, the library appears to meet our users' expectations in the *Affect of Service* area, with 97 of the 232 positive comments referring to this dimension. Additional information provided along with the full text of the comments included the user category and discipline of the respondent–permitting us to glean significant constructive criticism from this information.

SELECTED OBSERVATIONS
BY DISCIPLINE, USER GROUP, AND ROLE

Our deliverables for the survey included the actual data file of the responses in SPSS format, permitting us to do some additional data manipulation. Further analysis of the 25 core items by discipline (as reported) and 'role' (freshman, sophomore, junior, senior, assistant professor, associate professor, professor) enabled identification of some of the differences among the various user groups in their perceptions of the library and its services. A caveat about the disciplinary breakdown generated from the surveys is in order. All selections of discipline were self-reported by the respondent as being the "best choice" that described their position in the university. It is tempting to match up disciplines with one of our divisional libraries, but this pattern is not reliable. For example, a number of respondents selected "Health Sciences" as their discipline although we did not survey medical or nursing school faculty and students. As well, some of the undergraduate students identified their discipline as "Law." It seems likely that these respondents are pre-med and pre-law students, and so it's likely that the primary libraries they use are not the Law and Biomedical libraries.

The data for these measures are presented by the following radar charts, a circular diagram with axes around the circle representing the categories within these demographic breakdowns, and three points on each axis representing the reported desired, perceived, and minimum service levels. Two radar charts are provided for each of the items discussed–one by discipline, one by role. This presentation helps to identify particularly problematic areas by group; the most in need of attention are those in which the solid line, perceived service, crosses below the line for minimum expectations. The following are several examples of items in which this additional analysis is informative.

Complete Runs of Journal Titles (Figures 5a-b). Respondents from the Humanities and Education disciplines report that their perceptions of service in this area are below their minimum expectations. The Performing and Fine Arts and Health Sciences are just barely meeting the users' minimum expectations of complete runs of journal titles. The discipline having a perceived service level close to desired is Business. Students in each of these disciplines are, for the most part, satisfied with the library's collection of journal titles. It is at the faculty level that journal runs are perceived to be lower than minimum expectations, the negative gap being most severe for assistant professors and full professors. It should be noted that the analysis of the aggregate data for the Association of Research Libraries (ARL) reflects that this particular negative adequacy gap for 'complete runs of journal titles' is common across institutions of varying collection size.

Convenient Business Hours (Figures 5c-d). The Library's business hours clearly are not meeting library users' expectations. The disciplines in which expectations appear to have been satisfied are Business, Science/Math, and Engineering/Computer Science. Perceptions of adequacy are borderline for Law, Education, Social Sciences/Psychology, Health Sciences, and Humanities. The mean scores for the Performing and Fine Arts indicate users' dissatisfaction with the Library's hours, with the perceived level of service dropping substantially below the minimum expectation. Looking at the library's business hours by user group and role, substantial dissatisfaction exists for sophomores, juniors, and seniors. For Assistant Professors, the perception of service just matches the minimum expectation. Other user groups seem more satisfied with hours.

Comprehensive Print Collections (Figures 5e-f). Library users in the Humanities are the one group that feels the library's print collections do not meet minimum expectations. More positive views of the print collections are found in Business, Communications/Journalism, and Science/Math. Students (freshmen through doctoral) report that the library's print collections exceed their minimum expectations. Faculty (more so at the assistant professor level than associate and full) mean scores indicate that the library's print collections are not meeting their minimum expectations.

Giving Users Individual Attention (Figures 5g-h). In the discipline areas of Science/Math, Engineering/CS, and Business, library users score their perceptions of library service for this item as almost meeting their desired expectations. Assistant professors and lecturers perceive that the library's service level exceeds their desired level, in part because their expectations are lower than those of other groups. Generally, undergraduate students do not perceive this same level of service.

Employees Who Instill Confidence in Users (Figures 5i-j). The users scored the library very well on this item. In many of the demographic breakdowns, the perceived service levels are closer to the desired than to the minimum level of expectation. The exceptions to this were sophomores and respondents in the disciplines of Communication/Journalism and Education.

Space That Facilitates Quiet Study (Figures 5k-l). In general, the Library receives positive marks for providing quiet study areas. The noticeable exceptions by discipline are Law and Humanities. By role, there are substantial differences in desired and minimum levels of service with students having higher expectations than faculty. The perceived level of service, though, is higher for undergraduates and lower for graduate students. It is also low for associate professors, relative to expectations.

Place for Reflection and Creativity (Figures 5m-n). This function of the libraries has the lowest minimum expectation and desired mean scores of any of the other 25 items. We might suppose that this is not a primary concern of users with respect to their library perceptions. Within their expectations, the library does reasonably well, with the exception of Humanities, Performing and Fine Arts, and Law. Sophomores, juniors, and associate professors see the library as a "place for reflection and creativity" as approaching their minimum level of expectations.

Comfortable and Inviting Location (Figures 5o-p). Of all the *Library as Place* items, users deem this item as having the highest desired level of service. In this same area, the Library appears to fall significantly short of expectations. The perceived level of service is substantially below minimum expectations for those in the Humanities, and it falls below or at the minimum for Law and the Social Sciences/Psychology disciplines. By role, the Library does not meet the minimum expectations for sophomores, juniors, and seniors. However, it does meet the minimum level of expectation for associate professors, professors, and lecturers. The Library received better scores from users in the Science areas, Education, Performing and Fine Arts, and Business (the last three being libraries that have been renovated recently). In general, graduate students, assistant professors, and freshmen seem satisfied with the library as a comfortable and inviting location.

Electronic Resources Accessible from Home or Office (Figures 5q-r). This item generated the highest level of desired service. The perceived level of service was reported just at or slightly above the minimum expectation for users by role and discipline. Demographic groups that indicated that these areas need improvement are Education, doctoral students and faculty. This is an area in which the Library has invested heavily, so the meaning of the results is not clear as yet. Open-ended comments collected by the survey reflect the desire to have *everything* available electronically in full text, and further investigation is needed.

Convenient Access to Library Collections (Figures 5s-t). This is another item for which users indicated high desired level of expectation. In general, the Library's perceived scores are lower than might have been expected. Particular demographic areas in which performance is perceived as needing improvement are Humanities, Health Sciences, Social Sciences/Psychology, Education, and all faculty categories. It may reflect the existence of a number of different disciplinary libraries, or having many materials in off-site storage. This is another question that requires further follow-up to better and fully understand the results.

IDENTIFICATION OF OPPORTUNITY AREAS

The wealth of information to be gained from the survey results complicates the identification of areas of clearest opportunity for improvement. Such identification is made more difficult by the inability to determine more precisely what respondents might have thought in answering particular items. One way of examining areas of greatest potential for service improvement is to look at those items that scored highest on the desired service level and had the largest gap between the perceived and desired levels of service (see Figure 6. Service Satisfaction Elements, for rankings by these two factors). If we choose those items having a mean desired service level of 8 or higher and a service adequacy gap between perceived and desired of more than 1.0 for any of the three user groups, we can identify the items that appear most important for consideration across all respondents.

COMPARISONS WITH OTHER SURVEY PARTICIPANTS

One of the goals of the LibQUAL+™ survey is to provide a mechanism by which libraries can learn how they compare with other libraries in meeting users' expectations, to enable the identification and sharing of best practices. Each participating library has access to the aggregate data for "consortial" or library groups in which they are members and for individual participating libraries. In the earlier discussion about the overall satisfaction indicators, it was noted that the Vanderbilt library's mean scores on the three general satisfaction items were slightly higher than the mean score for respondents at all of the participating 46 ARL libraries. In Figure 7 (Library Comparisons–Overall Satisfaction) the scores on the three satisfaction items for Vanderbilt, all ARL respondents, and ten other peer libraries are depicted. Once again, Vanderbilt's scores are above the overall ARL mean, and they are above seven of the other ten libraries on the first question, six out of ten on the second, and six out of ten on the third. Institutions with high mean scores for the general satisfaction items with whom Vanderbilt may wish to do further analysis are libraries 3, 10 and 11.

Perceived Level of Service. Figure 8 shows the mean scores for Vanderbilt compared to the overall ARL respondents' mean score for each of the 25 items. Here, too, Vanderbilt appears to be slightly higher than the ARL group on all items except Convenient Business Hours (#19), A Place for Reflection and Creativity (#13), Comfortable Inviting Location (#21), a Contemplative Environment (#23), and Convenient Access to Library Collections (#25). Additional analysis on these individual items in comparison with the other peer institutions should highlight those libraries we might approach for further information regarding the practices, procedures, and policies that contribute to their users' favorable perceptions.

Another way of comparing our results with those of other groups is through the survey norms provided by LibQUAL+™.[2] Since the mean scores cluster closely together, the use of norm comparisons provides a better understanding of our relative performance as compared with other libraries. If we look at the distribution of scores for an aggregate (average) measure of all 25 items from all respondents in ARL libraries, Vanderbilt's mean score of 6.92 places our 'average' respondent at the 47th percentile of all respondents, which is slightly below the median. Looking at faculty, graduate student, and undergraduate student scores, the mean score of the 25 items for these groups falls in the 39th, 53rd, and 42nd percentiles respectively. Rather than looking at the means alone, our comparison with these norms shows that there is more room for improvement.

Institutional score norms are also provided and with these norms we can compare our mean score against the means of each of the 167 participating libraries. Looking at the institutional norms, Vanderbilt places at the 46th percentile of institutions, which is still below the median. For the four dimensions, our percentile ranking is the 45th percentile on *Access to Information*, 51st on *Affect of Service*, 32nd on *Library as Place*, and 58th on *Personal Control*. Looking at the service adequacy gap score (perceived level of expectation minus the minimum level of expectation), Vanderbilt ranks at the 80th percentile. This gap indicates that the minimum expectations of the Vanderbilt community seem to be lower than average, even when the perceived is higher than average, and the desired is about the same. For the *Service Superiority* gap, Vanderbilt ranks at the 55th percentile.

LIBRARY REVIEW AND ACTION ITEMS

As the data became available to the library directors and other library administrators, the Library Management Council (LMC) reviewed the results, discussed the possible meanings and interpretations, and formulated a set of possible future action items. Some important observations from this review are:

- While the Vanderbilt Library's mean scores are better than the ARL average and better than many of our primary peers, our position remains near the middle and offers substantial room for improvement.
- The highest mean scores for desired level of service are in the *Personal Control* category, indicating that issues of quality of electronic access have become very important to our patrons.
- Faculty responses to the *Personal Control* items indicate that they want us to continue to build our digital collections, but that they may experience some difficulty using digital services.
- Faculty desire more extensive collections in both print and digital form.
- Our highest perceived scores were in the *Affect of Service* dimension, indicating that our users are highly pleased with the quality of service we provide, though there are some negative statements in

the free-text comments that point out specific service issues we need to address.

- Undergraduates, in particular, are highly dissatisfied with our hours of operation.
- The results from a number of the survey items were unclear, because from the responses it was not obvious how respondents interpreted the item. The most significant example is the 'Convenient access to library collections' question. Our relatively problematic scores here could reflect the decentralized nature of the library system and thus the difficulty of having to go to multiple libraries to use the collections. Or, it could be a reaction to the off-site storage of a large part of the collection that is not readily and immediately accessible. There may be other interpretations as well. Another item with unclear results is the 'making electronic resources accessible from home or office.' The electronic resources we have are, for the most part, readily accessible, so the dissatisfaction may result from difficulties in accessing them remotely, a lack of awareness that remote access is available, or use of lower-end technology at the remote site, which may make such access seem difficult or unsatisfactory.
- The results from a number of items suggest that users may be unaware of what is available by way of services and collections; therefore, improved communication in a variety of forms is in order.
- The state of the main library building generated many disparaging comments from respondents, which were reflected by the responses to the 'comfortable and inviting location' item. The mean scores suggest, by role and by discipline, that the Library is marginally meeting minimum expectations for some and for many is perceived as below expectations.

Where Vanderbilt's mean desired service levels coincide quite closely with those of ARL libraries as a group and often with other peer individual libraries, the minimum expectations appear to be consistently lower.

Action Items. In following-up the various observations of the survey results in fall 2002, the LMC decided to proceed with two action items: (a) develop and submit a proposal for a 24-hour library facility–a trial has begun in the Science and Engineering Library for the spring semester, funded by several university offices; (b) develop and implement a quality of service improvement program across the Library system–the University Librarian has committed to the development of a program, encouraging and requiring library-wide participation. A task force composed of three library directors was tasked with the development of a program proposal.

FUTURE EFFORTS

The LMC will pass along some of the other observations that require follow-up to appropriate library-wide committees–the Web Task Force, the Information Services Advisory Group, the Collection Development Advisory Group, and the Staff Development Coordinating Committee. These committees will then implement changes and/or report back to the LMC. The following are actions that have been identified for the future:

- Focus groups or follow-up surveys to clarify issues that need further investigation.
- More analysis of the data, particularly with respect to norm comparisons, once they become available for individual items.
- Follow-up with peers with substantially higher scores in particular areas to identify information on 'best practices.'
- At some point, the Library may want to establish quantitative goals for improvement in perceived service quality as a measure of our progress on our assessment and improvement efforts.

CONCLUSION

Use of the LibQUAL+™ survey at Vanderbilt Library in 2002 has been very helpful for the Library and beneficial for the University community as the Library proceeds to explore improvements in services. We have gathered a great deal of data and completed some analysis of it. We have identified target areas for improvement and have begun development of programs to address them. We hope to work with several other participant peer libraries to investigate areas where we might benefit from understanding the underlying reasons for their 'better' results. Follow-up areas have been identified, and we have begun to consider how we can explore these further. The Vanderbilt Library fully supports the continued availability of such cooperative assessment efforts, and we anticipate participating in them in the future.

NOTES

1. Colleen C. Cook, *A Mixed Methods Approach to the Identification and Measurement of Academic Library Service Quality Constructs: LibQUAL+™*. Doctoral dissertation, Texas A&M University, 2001; Colleen Cook and Fred Heath, "The Association of Research Libraries LibQUAL+™ Project: An Update" *ARL Newsletter: A Bimonthly Report on Research Library Issues and Actions from ARL, CNI and SPARC*, 211 (August 2000): 12-14; _____ "Users' Perceptions of Library Service Quality: A LibQUAL+™ Qualitative Interview Study" *Library Trends* 49, no. 4 (2001): 548-584; Colleen Cook, Fred Heath, Martha Kyrillidou, and Duane Webster, "The Forging of Consensus: A Methodological Approach to Service Quality Assessment in Research Libraries–The LibQUAL+™ Experience." In Joan Stein, Martha Kyrillidou and Denise Davis (Eds.), *Proceedings of the 4th Northumbria International Conference on Performance Measurement in Libraries and Information Services* (Washington, DC: Association of Research Libraries, 2002): 93-104; Colleen Cook, Fred Heath and Bruce Thompson, "Users' Hierarchical Perspectives on Library Service Quality: A LibQUAL+™ Study" *College and Research Libraries* 62 (2001): 147-153; _____ "Score Norms for Improving Library Service Quality: A LibQUAL+™ Study." *portal: Libraries and the Academy* 2, no. 1 (January 2002): 13-26; Colleen Cook and Bruce Thompson, "Scaling for the LibQUAL+™ Instrument: A Comparison of Desired, Perceived and Minimum Expectation Responses versus Perceived Only." In Joan Stein, Martha Kyrillidou and Denise Davis (Eds.), *Proceedings of the 4th Northumbria International Conference on Performance Measurement in Libraries and Information Services:* (Washington, DC: Association of Research Libraries, 2002): 211-214; Colleen Cook, Fred Heath, Bruce Thompson, and R. L. Thompson, "The Search for New Measures: The ARL LibQUAL+™ Study–A Preliminary Report." *portal: Libraries and the Academy*, 1 (2001): 103-112; Colleen Cook, Fred Heath, R. L. Thompson, and Bruce Thompson, "Score Reliability in Web- or Internet-Based Surveys: Unnumbered Graphic Rating Scales versus Likert-Type Scales." *Educational and Psychological Measurement* 61 (2001): 697-706; Colleen Cook and Bruce Thompson, "Higher-Order Factor Analytic Perspectives on Users' Perceptions of Library Service Quality" *Library Information Science Research* 22 (2000): 393-404; _____ "Reliability and Validity of SERVQUAL Scores Used to Evaluate Perceptions of Library Service Quality" *Journal of Academic Librarianship* 26, 248-258; _____ "Psychometric Properties of Scores from the Web-Based LibQUAL+™ Study of Perceptions of Library Service Quality." *Library Trends* 49, no. 4 (2001): 585-604; Fred Heath, Colleen Cook, Martha Kyrillidou, and Bruce Thompson, "ARL Index and Other Validity Correlates of LibQUAL+™ Scores" *portal: Libraries and the Academy* 2, no. 1 (January 2002): 27-42; Bruce Thompson, "Representativeness versus Response Rate: It Ain't the Response Rate!" Paper presented at the Association of Research Libraries (ARL) Measuring Service Quality Symposium on the New Culture of Assessment: Measuring Service Quality, Washington DC (October 2000); Bruce Thompson, Colleen Cook, and Fred Heath, "The LibQUAL+™ Gap Measurement Model: The Bad, the Ugly and the Good of Gap Measurement." *Performance Measurement and Metrics* 1 (2000): 165-178; _____ "How Many Dimensions Does It Take to Measure Users' Perceptions of Libraries? A LibQUAL+™ Study" *portal: Libraries and the Academy* 1 (2001):

129-138; Bruce Thompson, Colleen Cook, and R. L. Thompson, "Reliability and Structure of LibQUAL+™ Scores" *portal: Libraries and the Academy* 2, no. 1: 3-12. An updated bibliography is also available at: <http://www.libqual.org/Publications/index. cfm>.

   2. Colleen Cook and Bruce Thompson. "Score Norms for Improving Library Service Quality: A LibQUAL+™ Study." *portal: Libraries and the Academy* 2, no. 1 (January 2002):13-26. See: <http://www.coe.tamu.edu/~bthompson/libq2002.htm>.

APPENDIX

FIGURE 1. Survey Results by Question

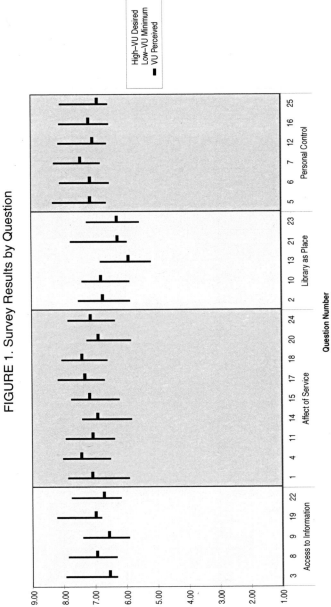

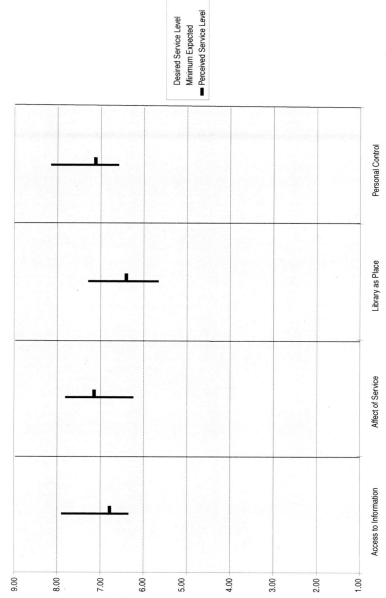

FIGURE 2. Dimension Summary

Desired Service Level
Minimum Expected
■ Perceived Service Level

213

APPENDIX (continued)

FIGURE 3. General Satisfaction Indicators

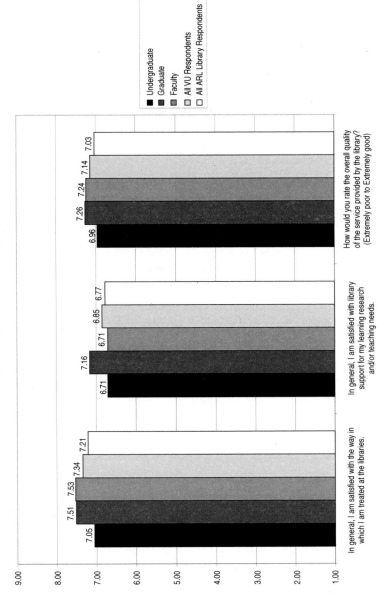

Legend:
- ■ Undergraduate
- ■ Graduate
- ■ Faculty
- □ All VU Respondents
- □ All ARL Library Respondents

In general, I am satisfied with the way in which I am treated at the libraries.
- Undergraduate: 7.05
- Graduate: 7.51
- Faculty: 7.53
- All VU Respondents: 7.34
- All ARL Library Respondents: 7.21

In general, I am satisfied with library support for my learning research and/or teaching needs.
- Undergraduate: 6.71
- Graduate: 7.16
- Faculty: 6.71
- All VU Respondents: 6.85
- All ARL Library Respondents: 6.77

How would you rate the overall quality of the service provided by the library? (Extremely poor to Extremely good)
- Undergraduate: 6.96
- Graduate: 7.26
- Faculty: 7.24
- All VU Respondents: 7.14
- All ARL Library Respondents: 7.03

FIGURE 4. Frequency of Library Use for All User Groups

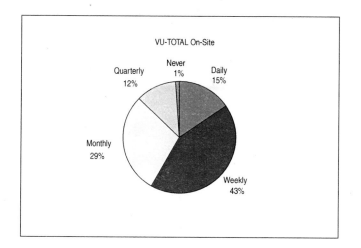

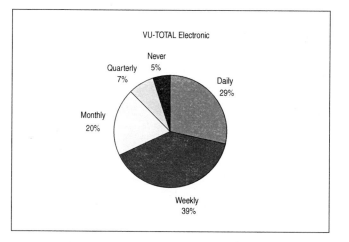

APPENDIX (continued)

FIGURE 5a. Complete Runs of Journal Titles by Discipline

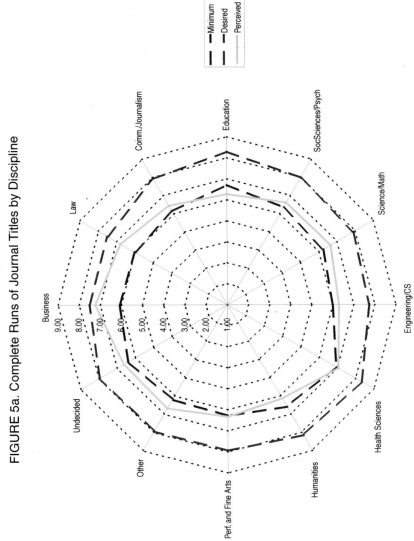

FIGURE 5b. Complete Runs of Journal Titles by Role

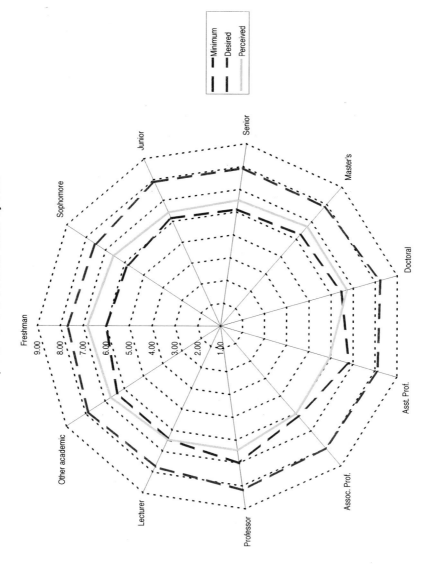

217

APPENDIX (continued)

FIGURE 5c. Convenient Business Hours by Discipline

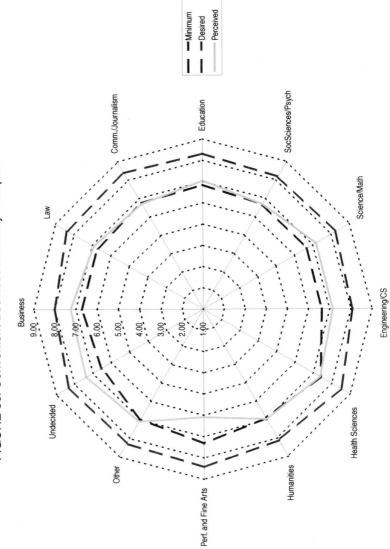

218

FIGURE 5d. Convenient Business Hours by Role

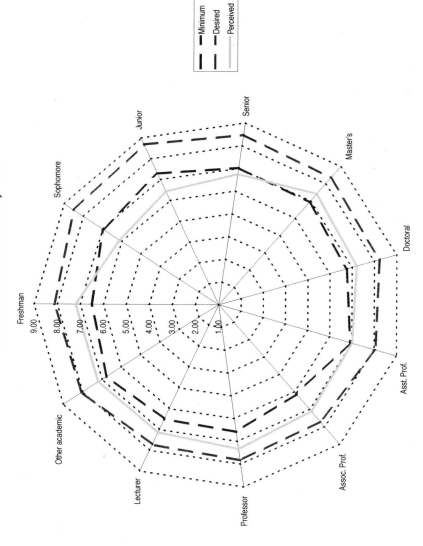

Minimum
Desired
Perceived

219

APPENDIX (continued)

FIGURE 5e. Comprehensive Print Collections by Discipline

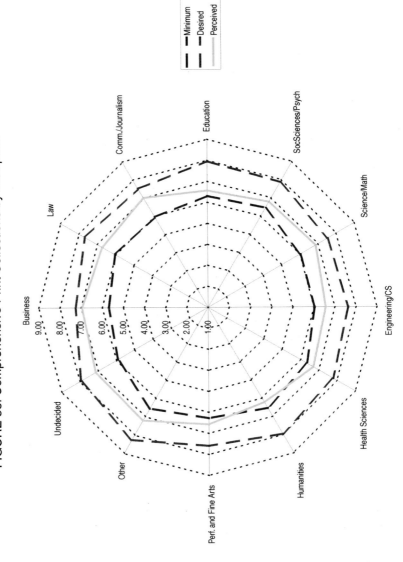

FIGURE 5f. Comprehensive Print Collections by Role

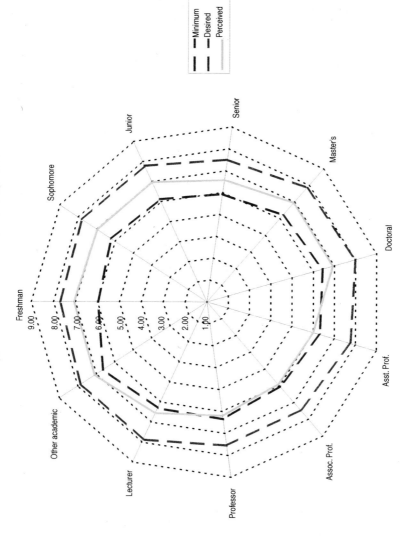

Minimum
Desired
Perceived

APPENDIX (continued)

FIGURE 5g. Giving Users Individual Attention by Discipline

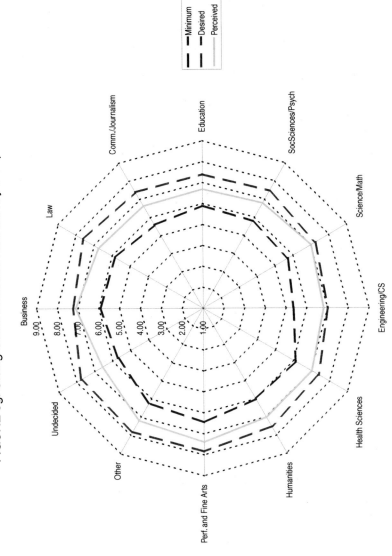

FIGURE 5h. Giving Users Individual Attention by Role

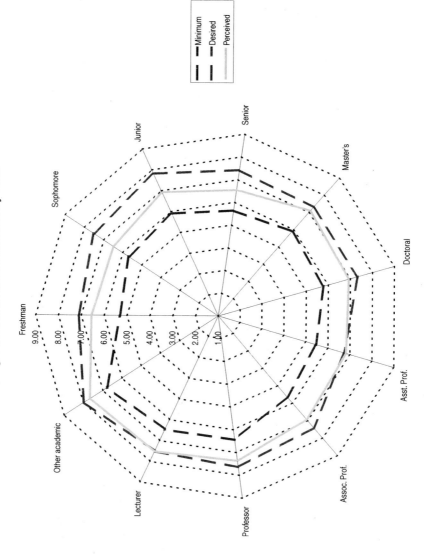

Minimum
Desired
Perceived

223

APPENDIX (continued)

FIGURE 5i. Employees Who Instill Confidence in Users by Discipline

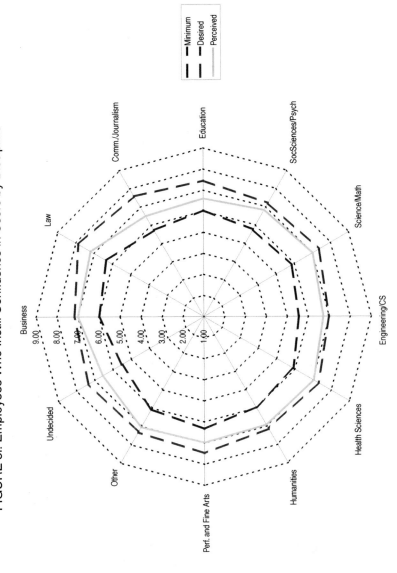

FIGURE 5j. Employees Who Instill Confidence in Users by Role

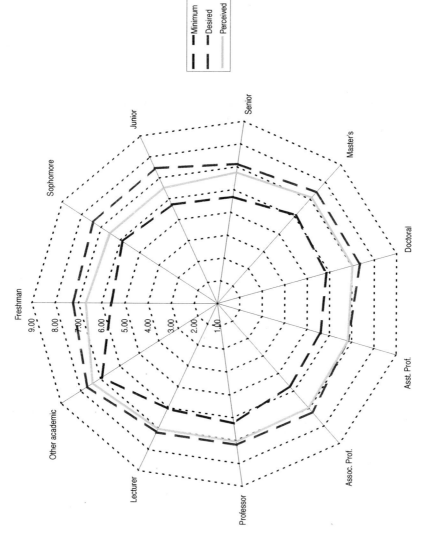

APPENDIX (continued)

FIGURE 5k. Space That Facilitates Quiet Study by Discipline

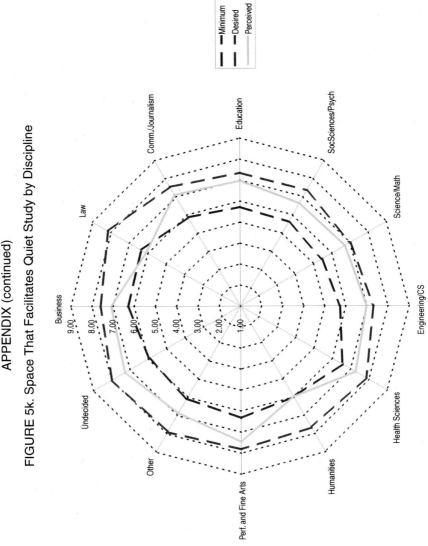

226

FIGURE 5I. Space That Facilitates Quiet Study by Role

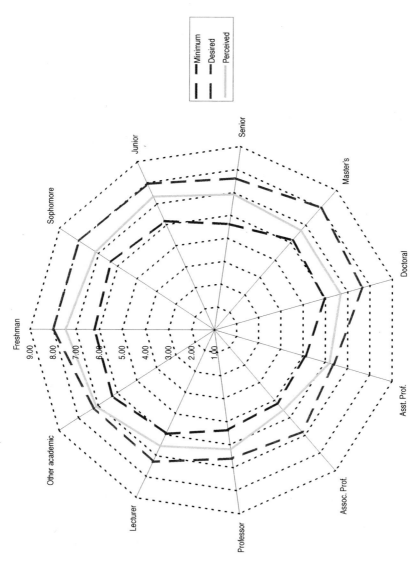

Legend:
- Minimum
- Desired
- Perceived

227

APPENDIX (continued)

FIGURE 5m. A Place for Reflection and Creativity by Discipline

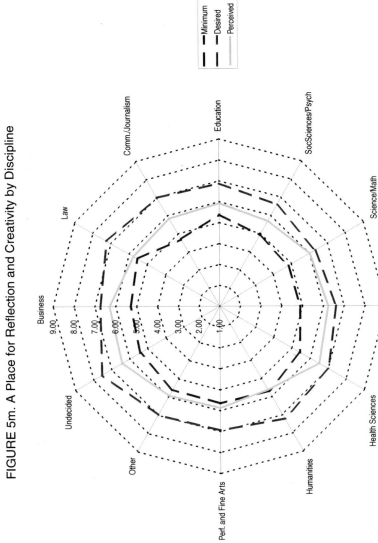

FIGURE 5n. A Place for Reflection and Creativity by Role

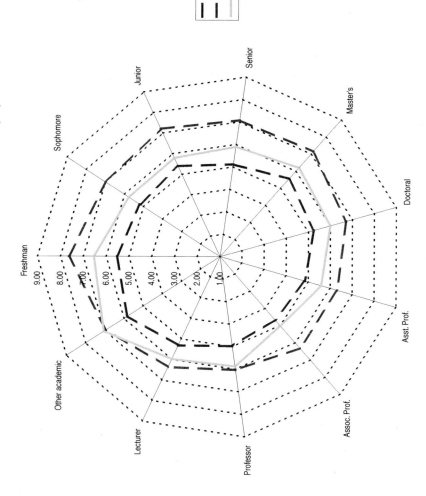

APPENDIX (continued)

FIGURE 5o. A Comfortable and Inviting Location by Discipline

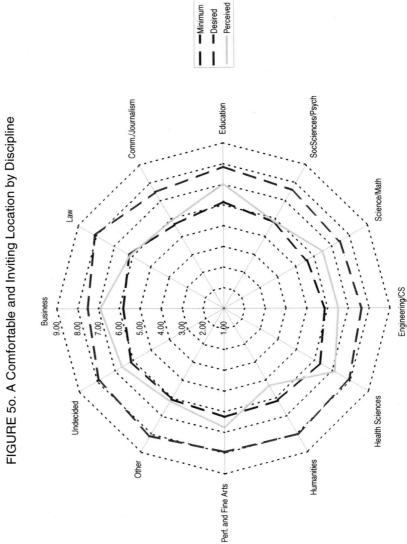

FIGURE 5p. A Comfortable and Inviting Location by Role

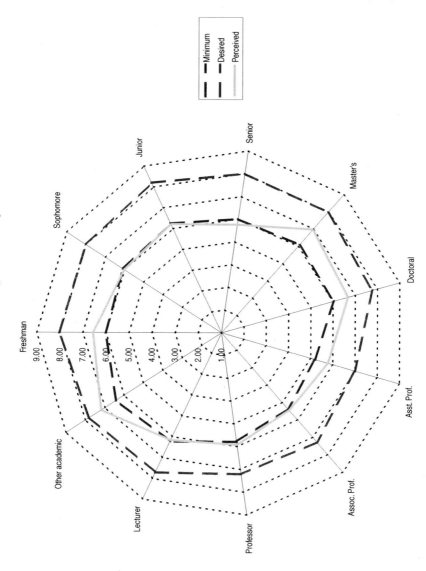

APPENDIX (continued)

FIGURE 5q. Making Electronic Resources Accessible from Home or Office by Discipline

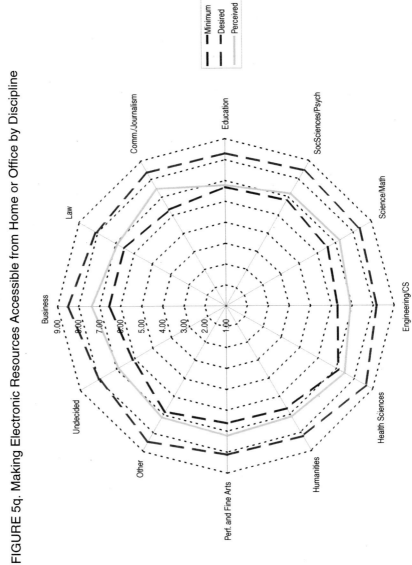

FIGURE 5r. Making Electronic Resources Accessible from Home or Office by Role

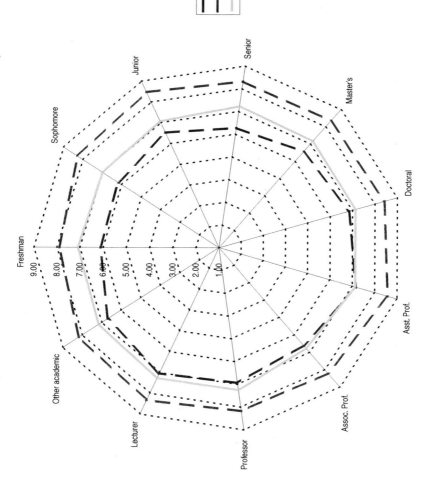

233

APPENDIX (continued)

FIGURE 5s. Convenient Access to Library Collections by Discipline

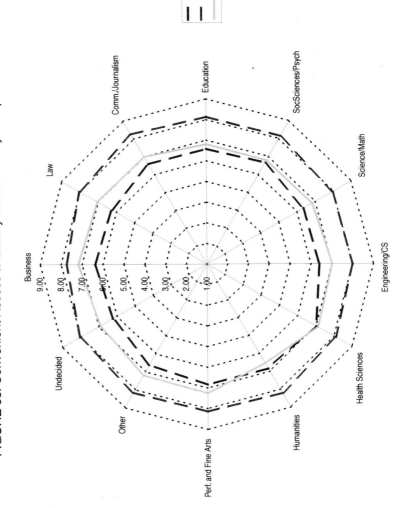

FIGURE 5t. Convenient Access to Library Collections by Role

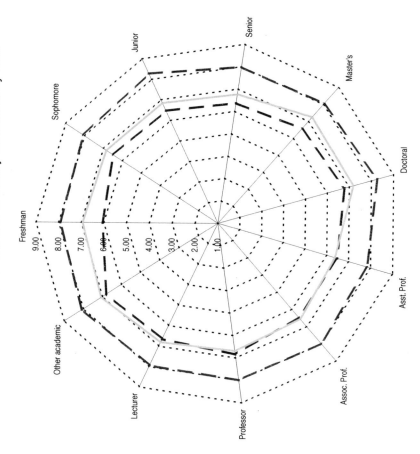

APPENDIX (continued)

FIGURE 6. Service Satisfaction Elements

UNDERGRADUATES
SORTED BY DESIRED

		VU Minimum	VU Desired	VU Perceived
19	Convenient business hours	6.96	8.45	6.57
5	Electronic resources accessible from home or office	6.25	8.24	7.09
7	Website enables me to locate information on my own	6.52	8.22	7.54
17	Employees with knowledge to answer questions	6.65	8.19	7.25
6	Modern equipment that lets me easily access information	6.35	8.18	7.11
4	Employees consistently courteous	6.39	8.11	7.24
12	Easy-to-use access tools to find things on my own	6.43	8.10	6.88
18	Readiness to respond to questions	6.51	8.10	7.21
25	Convenient access to library collections	6.33	8.06	6.83
21	Comfortable inviting location	6.09	8.05	6.13
16	Making information accessible for independent use	6.22	8.02	7.09
10	Haven for quiet and solitude	6.32	7.94	7.24
15	Employees deal with users in a caring fashion	6.21	7.91	7.00
2	Space that facilitates quiet study	6.11	7.90	7.21
1	Willingness to help users	5.66	7.87	6.61
11	Dependability in handling service problems	6.16	7.85	6.83
24	Employees understand needs	6.21	7.85	7.01
3	Complete runs of journal titles	5.91	7.69	6.64
22	Comprehensive print collections	5.96	7.67	6.98
8	Timely DD/ILL	5.91	7.62	6.81
23	Contemplative environment	5.75	7.62	6.41
14	Giving individual attention	5.62	7.48	6.61
20	Employees instill confidence	5.66	7.29	6.58
9	Interdisciplinary needs met	5.69	7.25	6.49
13	Place for reflection and creativity	5.28	7.22	5.96

SORTED BY LARGEST GAP BETWEEN PERCEIVED AND DESIRED

		Gap
21	Comfortable inviting location	1.92
19	Convenient business hours	1.88
1	Willingness to help users	1.26
13	Place for reflection and creativity	1.26
25	Convenient access to library collections	1.23
12	Easy-to-use access tools to find things on my own	1.22
23	Contemplative environment	1.21
5	Electronic resources accessible from home or office	1.15
6	Modern equipment that lets me easily access information	1.07
3	Complete runs of journal titles	1.05
11	Dependability in handling service problems	1.02
17	Employees with knowledge to answer questions	0.94
16	Making information accessible for independent use	0.93
15	Employees deal with users in a caring fashion	0.91
18	Readiness to respond to questions	0.89
14	Giving individual attention	0.87
4	Employees consistently courteous	0.87
24	Employees understand needs	0.84
8	Timely DD/ILL	0.81
9	Interdisciplinary needs met	0.76
20	Employees instill confidence	0.71
10	Haven for quiet and solitude	0.70
2	Space that facilitates quiet study	0.69
22	Comprehensive print collections	0.69
7	Website enables me to locate information on my own	0.68

GRADUATE STUDENTS
SORTED BY DESIRED

		VU Minimum	VU Desired	VU Perceived
5	Electronic resources accessible from home or office	6.76	8.40	7.16
7	Website enables me to locate information on my own	6.99	8.35	7.60
19	Convenient business hours	6.81	8.28	7.28
17	Employees with knowledge to answer questions	6.73	8.26	7.38
12	Easy-to-use access tools to find things on my own	6.66	8.21	7.26
25	Convenient access to library collections	6.70	8.20	7.21
6	Modern equipment that lets me easily access information	6.69	8.18	7.26
16	Making information accessible for independent use	6.68	8.18	7.37
18	Readiness to respond to questions	6.60	8.13	7.53
3	Complete runs of journal titles	6.39	8.12	6.75
8	Timely DD/ILL	6.53	8.10	7.00
11	Dependability in handling service problems	6.44	8.03	7.23
22	Comprehensive print collections	6.34	7.97	6.98
24	Employees understand needs	6.39	7.95	7.19
4	Employees consistently courteous	6.32	7.90	7.45
1	Willingness to help users	5.93	7.87	7.28
21	Comfortable inviting location	6.06	7.85	6.78
2	Space that facilitates quiet study	6.03	7.79	6.69
15	Employees deal with users in a caring fashion	6.12	7.66	7.25
9	Interdisciplinary needs met	6.18	7.65	6.95
10	Haven for quiet and solitude	5.98	7.56	6.81
23	Contemplative environment	5.69	7.37	6.55
20	Employees instill confidence	5.89	7.35	7.09
14	Giving individual attention	5.81	7.32	7.00
13	Place for reflection and creativity	5.35	6.87	6.07

SORTED BY LARGEST GAP BETWEEN PERCEIVED AND DESIRED

		Gap
3	Complete runs of journal titles	1.37
5	Electronic resources accessible from home or office	1.24
2	Space that facilitates quiet study	1.10
8	Timely DD/ILL	1.10
21	Comfortable inviting location	1.07
19	Convenient business hours	1.00
22	Comprehensive print collections	0.99
25	Convenient access to library collections	0.99
12	Easy-to-use access tools to find things on my own	0.95
6	Modern equipment that lets me easily access information	0.92
17	Employees with knowledge to answer questions	0.88
23	Contemplative environment	0.82
16	Making information accessible for independent use	0.81
13	Place for reflection and creativity	0.80
11	Dependability in handling service problems	0.80
24	Employees understand needs	0.76
7	Website enables me to locate information on my own	0.75
10	Haven for quiet and solitude	0.75
9	Interdisciplinary needs met	0.70
18	Readiness to respond to questions	0.60
1	Willingness to help users	0.59
4	Employees consistently courteous	0.45
15	Employees deal with users in a caring fashion	0.41
14	Giving individual attention	0.32
20	Employees instill confidence	0.26

APPENDIX (continued)

FIGURE 6 (continued)

FACULTY

SORTED BY DESIRED

		VU Minimum	VU Desired	VU Perceived
5	Electronic resources accessible from home or office	6.91	8.30	7.13
7	Website enables me to locate information on my own	6.91	8.23	7.09
16	Making information accessible for independent use	6.75	8.12	7.06
12	Easy-to-use access tools to find things on my own	6.73	8.07	7.00
17	Employees with knowledge to answer questions	6.70	8.07	7.34
4	Employees consistently courteous	6.83	8.06	7.66
3	Complete runs of journal titles	6.65	8.05	6.26
25	Convenient access to library collections	6.65	7.96	6.63
11	Dependability in handling service problems	6.57	7.93	7.18
18	Readiness to respond to questions	6.69	7.92	7.50
1	Willingness to help users	6.21	7.88	7.46
8	Timely DD/ILL	6.48	7.86	7.02
6	Modern equipment that lets me easily access information	6.52	7.85	6.99
19	Convenient business hours	6.55	7.85	7.18
24	Employees understand needs	6.49	7.77	7.22
15	Employees deal with users in a caring fashion	6.32	7.65	7.32
22	Comprehensive print collections	6.27	7.60	6.13
14	Giving individual attention	6.10	7.41	7.22
9	Interdisciplinary needs met	5.89	7.30	6.33
21	Comfortable inviting location	5.63	7.25	5.84
20	Employees instill confidence	6.02	7.12	7.03
2	Space that facilitates quiet study	5.33	6.63	6.12
23	Contemplative environment	5.14	6.53	5.76
10	Haven for quiet and solitude	5.14	6.40	6.13
13	Place for reflection and creativity	4.89	6.14	5.66

SORTED BY LARGEST GAP BETWEEN PERCEIVED AND DESIRED

		Gap
3	Complete runs of journal titles	1.79
22	Comprehensive print collections	1.47
21	Comfortable inviting location	1.41
25	Convenient access to library collections	1.33
5	Electronic resources accessible from home or office	1.17
7	Website enables me to locate information on my own	1.14
12	Easy-to-use access tools to find things on my own	1.07
16	Making information accessible for independent use	1.06
9	Interdisciplinary needs met	0.97
6	Modern equipment that lets me easily access information	0.86
8	Timely DD/ILL	0.84
23	Contemplative environment	0.77
11	Dependability in handling service problems	0.75
17	Employees with knowledge to answer questions	0.73
19	Convenient business hours	0.67
24	Employees understand needs	0.55
2	Space that facilitates quiet study	0.51
13	Place for reflection and creativity	0.48
1	Willingness to help users	0.42
18	Readiness to respond to questions	0.42
4	Employees consistently courteous	0.40
15	Employees deal with users in a caring fashion	0.33
10	Haven for quiet and solitude	0.27
14	Giving individual attention	0.19
20	Employees instill confidence	0.09

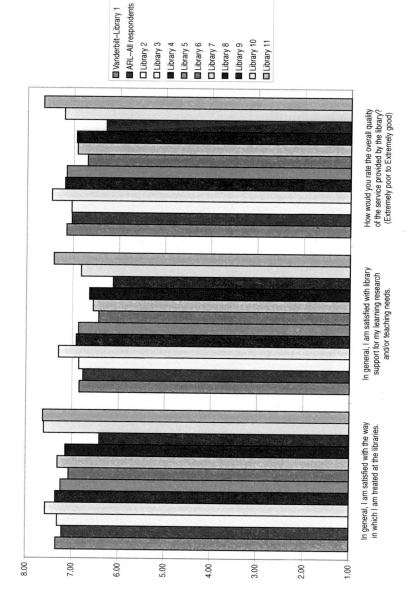

FIGURE 7. Library Comparisons—Overall Satisfaction

APPENDIX (continued)

FIGURE 8. Perceived Level of Service–VU and ARL

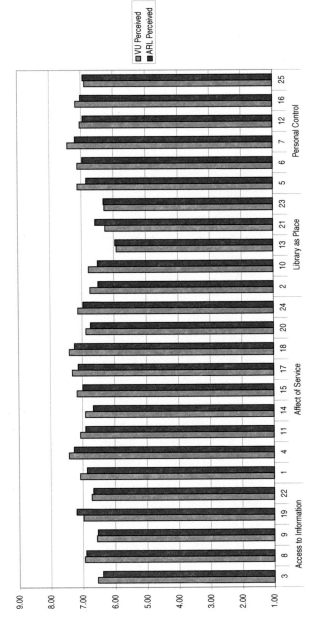

240

Index

AAHSL participation. *See* Association of Academic Health Sciences Libraries (AAHSL) participation

AAMC (Association of American Medical Colleges), 50-51

Academic medical center implications, 83-98
  analyses (score data), 84-98
    of focus groups, 97
    hospital staff impact on, 94-97
    overviews of, 92
    of participant groups, 84-87,92-94
    processes for, 87-92
  Association of Academic Health Sciences Libraries (AAHSL) participation and, 93-98
  future perspectives of, 97-98
  historical perspectives of, 84-86
  overviews of, 83-84

Access analyses, 22-23,29,117-118, 190,212,232-235

Action item reviews, 207-209

Analyses (score data). *See also under individual topics*
  Association of Academic Health Sciences Libraries (AAHSL)-specific questions, 55-56
  benchmarking and, 140-145
  of business hours, 218-219
  of category labels and coded comments, 114-115
  of collections, 216-217,220-221
  of comments, 114-115,201-202
  comparative, 68,79-80,104-109, 134-136,206-207,239
  discipline cross-tabulations, 148-154

of environments, 117-118
of expectation levels, 146-148
of focus groups, 97,109,166-167
of four dimensions, 28,34,36,38, 106-108,200-201,213
of graduate groups, 185-187
hospital staff impact on, 94-97
of information access, 22-23,29, 117-118,190,212,232-235
institutional characteristic-score relationships, 3-8
lessons learned from, 125-137
of library as place, 23,25,164-165, 212,225-231
of library use frequency, 62-63
of OhioLINK-specific questions, 22,31,35,37,39
of participant groups, 22,32-39, 44-48,52-53,61-64,84-87,92, 115-116,125-127,141-142, 182-187,202-205
of peer groups, 27-32
of personal control, 22,26,30,212
processes for, 87-92,124,182-184
recommendations for, 41-42
reviews of, 160-166
of satisfaction levels, 33,53-54,64-65, 131-133,142-145,163-164, 201,214,236-238
score interpretations and, 197-240
of service levels, 240
of service quality, 54-55,117-118, 212
summary gap, 64-67,107-109, 128-131,145-148,236-238
of undergraduate groups, 184-185
urban research institution comparisons, 140-145

© 2004 by The Haworth Press, Inc. All rights reserved.

The Future of Information Services, edited by Virginia Steel, MA, and C. Brigid Welch, MLS (Vol. 20, No. 3/4, 1995). *"The leadership discussions will be useful for library managers as will the discussions of how library structures and services might work in the next century." (Australian Special Libraries)*

The Dynamic Library Organizations in a Changing Environment, edited by Joan Giesecke, MLS, DPA (Vol. 20, No. 2, 1995). *"Provides a significant look at potential changes in the library world and presents its readers with possible ways to address the negative results of such changes. . . . Covers the key issues facing today's libraries . . . Two thumbs up!" (Marketing Library Resources)*

Access, Ownership, and Resource Sharing, edited by Sul H. Lee (Vol. 20, No. 1, 1995). *The contributing authors present a useful and informative look at the current status of information provision and some of the challenges the subject presents.*

Libraries as User-Centered Organizations: Imperatives for Organizational Change, edited by Meredith A. Butler (Vol. 19, No. 3/4, 1994). *"Presents a very timely and well-organized discussion of major trends and influences causing organizational changes." (Science Books & Films)*

Declining Acquisitions Budgets: Allocation, Collection Development and Impact Communication, edited by Sul H. Lee (Vol. 19, No. 2, 1994). *"Expert and provocative. . . . Presents many ways of looking at library budget deterioration and responses to it . . . There is much food for thought here." (Library Resources & Technical Services)*

The Role and Future of Special Collections in Research Libraries: British and American Perspectives, edited by Sul H. Lee (Vol. 19, No. 1, 1993). *"A provocative but informative read for library users, academic administrators, and private sponsors." (International Journal of Information and Library Research)*

Catalysts for Change: Managing Libraries in the 1990s, edited by Gisela M. von Dran, DPA, MLS, and Jennifer Cargill, MSLS, MSEd (Vol. 18, No. 3/4, 1994). *"A useful collection of articles which focuses on the need for librarians to employ enlightened management practices in order to adapt to and thrive in the rapidly changing information environment." (Australian Library Review)*

Integrating Total Quality Management in a Library Setting, edited by Susan Jurow, MLS, and Susan B. Barnard, MLS (Vol. 18, No. 1/2, 1993). *"Especially valuable are the librarian experiences that directly relate to real concerns about TQM. Recommended for all professional reading collections." (Library Journal)*

Leadership in Academic Libraries: Proceedings of the W. Porter Kellam Conference, The University of Georgia, May 7, 1991, edited by William Gray Potter (Vol. 17, No. 4, 1993). *"Will be of interest to those concerned with the history of American academic libraries." (Australian Library Review)*

Collection Assessment and Acquisitions Budgets, edited by Sul H. Lee (Vol. 17, No. 2, 1993). *Contains timely information about the assessment of academic library collections and the relationship of collection assessment to acquisition budgets.*

Developing Library Staff for the 21st Century, edited by Maureen Sullivan (Vol. 17, No. 1, 1992). *"I found myself enthralled with this highly readable publication. It is one of those rare compilations that manages to successfully integrate current general management operational thinking in the context of academic library management." (Bimonthly Review of Law Books)*

Vendor Evaluation and Acquisition Budgets, edited by Sul H. Lee (Vol. 16, No. 3, 1992). *"The title doesn't do justice to the true scope of this excellent collection of papers delivered at the sixth annual conference on library acquisitions sponsored by the University of Oklahoma Libraries." (Kent K. Hendrickson, BS, MALS, Dean of Libraries, University of Nebraska-Lincoln) Find insightful discussions on the impact of rising costs on library budgets and management in this groundbreaking book.*

The Management of Library and Information Studies Education, edited by Herman L. Totten, PhD, MLS (Vol. 16, No. 1/2, 1992). *"Offers something of interest to everyone connected with LIS education–the undergraduate contemplating a master's degree, the doctoral student struggling with courses and career choices, the new faculty member aghast at conflicting responsibilities, the experienced but stressed LIS professor, and directors of LIS Schools." (Education Libraries)*

Library Management in the Information Technology Environment: Issues, Policies, and Practice for Administrators, edited by Brice G. Hobrock, PhD, MLS (Vol. 15, No. 3/4, 1992). *"A road map to identify some of the alternative routes to the electronic library." (Stephen Rollins, Associate Dean for Library Services, General Library, University of New Mexico)*

Managing Technical Services in the 90's, edited by Drew Racine (Vol. 15, No. 1/2, 1991). *"Presents an eclectic overview of the challenges currently facing all library technical services efforts. . . . Recommended to library administrators and interested practitioners." (Library Journal)*

Budgets for Acquisitions: Strategies for Serials, Monographs, and Electronic Formats, edited by Sul H. Lee (Vol. 14, No. 3, 1991). *"Much more than a series of handy tips for the careful shopper. This [book] is a most useful one–well-informed, thought-provoking, and authoritative." (Australian Library Review)*

Creative Planning for Library Administration: Leadership for the Future, edited by Kent Hendrickson, MALS (Vol. 14, No. 2, 1991). *"Provides some essential information on the planning process, and the mix of opinions and methodologies, as well as examples relevant to every library manager, resulting in a very readable foray into a topic too long avoided by many of us." (Canadian Library Journal)*

Strategic Planning in Higher Education: Implementing New Roles for the Academic Library, edited by James F. Williams, II, MLS (Vol. 13, No. 3/4, 1991). *"A welcome addition to the sparse literature on strategic planning in university libraries. Academic librarians considering strategic planning for their libraries will learn a great deal from this work." (Canadian Library Journal)*

Personnel Administration in an Automated Environment, edited by Philip E. Leinbach, MLS (Vol. 13, No. 1/2, 1990). *"An interesting and worthwhile volume, recommended to university library administrators and to others interested in thought-provoking discussion of the personnel implications of automation." (Canadian Library Journal)*

Library Development: A Future Imperative, edited by Dwight F. Burlingame, PhD (Vol. 12, No. 4, 1990). *"This volume provides an excellent overview of fundraising with special application to libraries. . . . A useful book that is highly recommended for all libraries." (Library Journal)*

Library Material Costs and Access to Information, edited by Sul H. Lee (Vol. 12, No. 3, 1991). *"A cohesive treatment of the issue. Although the book's contributors possess a research library perspective, the data and the ideas presented are of interest and benefit to the entire profession, especially academic librarians." (Library Resources and Technical Services)*

Training Issues and Strategies in Libraries, edited by Paul M. Gherman, MALS, and Frances O. Painter, MLS, MBA (Vol. 12, No. 2, 1990). *"There are . . . useful chapters, all by different authors, each with a preliminary summary of the content–a device that saves much time in deciding whether to read the whole chapter or merely skim through it. Many of the chapters are essentially practical without too much emphasis on theory. This book is a good investment." (Library Association Record)*

Library Education and Employer Expectations, edited by E. Dale Cluff, PhD, MLS (Vol. 11, No. 3/4, 1990). *"Useful to library-school students and faculty interested in employment problems and employer perspectives. Librarians concerned with recruitment practices will also be interested." (Information Technology and Libraries)*

Managing Public Libraries in the 21st Century, edited by Pat Woodrum, MLS (Vol. 11, No. 1/2, 1989). *"A broad-based collection of topics that explores the management problems and possibilities public libraries will be facing in the 21st century." (Robert Swisher, PhD, Director, School of Library and Information Studies, University of Oklahoma)*

Human Resources Management in Libraries, edited by Gisela M. Webb, MLS, MPA (Vol. 10, No. 4, 1989). *"Thought provoking and enjoyable reading. . . . Provides valuable insights for the effective information manager." (Special Libraries)*

Creativity, Innovation, and Entrepreneurship in Libraries, edited by Donald E. Riggs, EdD, MLS (Vol. 10, No. 2/3, 1989). *"The volume is well worth reading as a whole. . . . There is very little repetition, and it should stimulate thought." (Australian Library Review)*

The Impact of Rising Costs of Serials and Monographs on Library Services and Programs, edited by Sul H. Lee (Vol. 10, No. 1, 1989). *". . . Sul Lee hit a winner here." (Serials Review)*

Computing, Electronic Publishing, and Information Technology: Their Impact on Academic Libraries, edited by Robin N. Downes (Vol. 9, No. 4, 1989). *"For a relatively short and easily digestible discussion of these issues, this book can be recommended, not only to those in academic libraries, but also to those in similar types of library or information unit, and to academics and educators in the field." (Journal of Documentation)*

Library Management and Technical Services: The Changing Role of Technical Services in Library Organizations, edited by Jennifer Cargill, MSLS, MSEd (Vol. 9, No. 1, 1988). *"As a practical and instructive guide to issues such as automation, personnel matters, education, management techniques and liaison with other services, senior library managers with a sincere interest in evaluating the role of their technical services should find this a timely publication." (Library Association Record)*

Management Issues in the Networking Environment, edited by Edward R. Johnson, PhD (Vol. 8, No. 3/4, 1989). *"Particularly useful for librarians/information specialists contemplating establishing a local network." (Australian Library Review)*

Acquisitions, Budgets, and Material Costs: Issues and Approaches, edited by Sul H. Lee (Supp. #2, 1988). *"The advice of these library practitioners is sensible and their insights illuminating for librarians in academic libraries." (American Reference Books Annual)*

Pricing and Costs of Monographs and Serials: National and International Issues, edited by Sul H. Lee (Supp. #1, 1987). *"Eminently readable. There is a good balance of chapters on serials and monographs and the perspective of suppliers, publishers, and library practitioners are presented. A book well worth reading." (Australasian College Libraries)*

Legal Issues for Library and Information Managers, edited by William Z. Nasri, JD, PhD (Vol. 7, No. 4, 1987). *"Useful to any librarian looking for protection or wondering where responsibilities end and liabilities begin. Recommended." (Academic Library Book Review)*

Archives and Library Administration: Divergent Traditions and Common Concerns, edited by Lawrence J. McCrank, PhD, MLS (Vol. 7, No. 2/3, 1986). *"A forward-looking view of archives and libraries. . . . Recommend[ed] to students, teachers, and practitioners alike of archival and library science. It is readable, thought-provoking, and provides a summary of the major areas of divergence and convergence." (Association of Canadian Map Libraries and Archives)*

Excellence in Library Management, edited by Charlotte Georgi, MLS, and Robert Bellanti, MLS, MBA (Vol. 6, No. 3, 1985). *"Most beneficial for library administrators . . . for anyone interested in either library/information science or management." (Special Libraries)*

Marketing and the Library, edited by Gary T. Ford (Vol. 4, No. 4, 1984). *Discover the latest methods for more effective information dissemination and learn to develop successful programs for specific target areas.*

Finance Planning for Libraries, edited by Murray S. Martin (Vol. 3, No. 3/4, 1983). *Stresses the need for libraries to weed out expenditures which do not contribute to their basic role–the collection and organization of information–when planning where and when to spend money.*

Planning for Library Services: A Guide to Utilizing Planning Methods for Library Management, edited by Charles R. McClure, PhD (Vol. 2, No. 3/4, 1982). *"Should be read by anyone who is involved in planning processes of libraries–certainly by every administrator of a library or system." (American Reference Books Annual)*

BOOK ORDER FORM!

Order a copy of this book with this form or online at:
http://www.haworthpress.com/store/product.asp?sku=5341

Libraries Act on Their LibQUAL+™ Findings
From Data to Action

____ in softbound at $29.95 (ISBN: 0-7890-2602-3)
____ in hardbound at $49.95 (ISBN: 0-7890-2601-5)

COST OF BOOKS ____

POSTAGE & HANDLING ____
US: $4.00 for first book & $1.50
for each additional book.
Outside US: $5.00 for first book
& $2.00 for each additional book.

SUBTOTAL ____

In Canada: add 7% GST. ____

STATE TAX ____
CA, IL, IN, MN, NJ, NY, OH & SD residents
please add appropriate local sales tax.

FINAL TOTAL ____
If paying in Canadian funds, convert
using the current exchange rate.
UNESCO coupons welcome.

❑ BILL ME LATER:
Bill-me option is good on US/Canada/
Mexico orders only; not good to jobbers,
wholesalers, or subscription agencies.

❑ Signature ____

❑ Payment Enclosed: $ ____

❑ PLEASE CHARGE TO MY CREDIT CARD:

❑ Visa ❑ MasterCard ❑ AmEx ❑ Discover
❑ Diner's Club ❑ Eurocard ❑ JCB

Account # ____

Exp Date ____

Signature ____
(Prices in US dollars and subject to change without notice.)

PLEASE PRINT ALL INFORMATION OR ATTACH YOUR BUSINESS CARD

Name

Address

City   State/Province   Zip/Postal Code

Country

Tel   Fax

E-Mail

May we use your e-mail address for confirmations and other types of information? ❑ Yes ❑ No We appreciate receiving
your e-mail address. Haworth would like to e-mail special discount offers to you, as a preferred customer.
We will never share, rent, or exchange your e-mail address. We regard such actions as an invasion of your privacy.

Order From Your **Local Bookstore** or Directly From
The Haworth Press, Inc. 10 Alice Street, Binghamton, New York 13904-1580 • USA
Call Our toll-free number (1-800-429-6784) / Outside US/Canada: (607) 722-5857
Fax: 1-800-895-0582 / Outside US/Canada: (607) 771-0012
E-mail your order to us: orders@haworthpress.com

For orders outside US and Canada, you may wish to order through your local
sales representative, distributor, or bookseller.
For information, see http://haworthpress.com/distributors

(Discounts are available for individual orders in US and Canada only, not booksellers/distributors.)

Please photocopy this form for your personal use.
www.HaworthPress.com

BOF04